Instrumental Music Teaching: *Perspectives and Challenges*

Edited by Nick Beach
and Gary Spruce

Published by
Trinity College London Press Ltd
trinitycollege.com
Registered in England
Company no. 09726123

Copyright © 2024 Trinity College London Press Ltd
First impression, May 2024

Unauthorised photocopying is illegal
No part of this publication may be copied or reproduced in any
form or by any means without the prior permission of the publisher.

Cover artwork: Mike Reid
Illustrations: James Treweek
Index compiled by Melanie Gee

Printed in England by Caligraving Ltd

Contents

Editors & Contributors 4
Foreword: Gary McPherson 8
Introduction 9

Part One: History, Background and Contexts

1. The Historical Context of Instrumental Teaching – Erin Johnson-Williams 15
2. The Changing Landscapes of Contemporary Instrumental Music Teaching: Policy and Practice – Randall Everett Allsup and George Nicholson 29
3. Instrumental Music Teaching: Contemporary Research Perspectives – Andrea Creech 45

Part Two: Music Learning, Development and Progress

4. What Does it Mean to be Musical? Musical Ability and Learning in Instrumental Education – Alison Daubney 71
5. Development and Instrumental Learning – Kim Burwell 89
6. Sustaining Interest and Motivation: Agency and Self-regulation – Nick Beach 101

Part Three: Practices and Pedagogies

7. Creativities in Instrumental Teaching and Learning: Unlocking Musical Imaginations – Jennie Henley 115
8. Inclusive Approaches to Instrumental Teaching and Learning: A Social Justice Perspective – Gary Spruce 131
9. Assessment, Values, Beliefs: Working Towards a 'Conscientised' Approach to Assessment in Instrumental Music Teaching – Francesca Christmas 151
10. Instrumental Teaching as Part of a General Musical Education – Adam Whittaker and Martin Fautley 165

Part Four: The Future of Instrumental Teaching and Learning

11. Music and Technology: Approaches, Challenges and Potential in Instrumental Music Teaching – Andrew King 181
12. The Musician Teacher – Julie Ballantyne 197

Index 213

Editors & Contributors

Editors

Nick Beach is a music education consultant and violinist. He was previously Academic Director at Trinity College London where he was instrumental in the development of new approaches to assessment in music and the arts, including Trinity's Arts Award and Rock & Pop qualifications. He worked as a full-time peripatetic (itinerant) violin teacher for many years and was closely associated with the development of whole class approaches to instrumental teaching. Most recently he has renovated a watermill in Cornwall where he and his wife are developing and promoting opportunities for live music-making and learning.

Gary Spruce is a visiting lecturer in music education at Birmingham City University and an academic consultant for Trinity College London. Previously he was a secondary school music teacher and music subject leader for The Open University's initial teacher training course. From 2007–2012 he was co-editor of the British Journal of Music Education. He has written and published widely on music education particularly around the areas of secondary music education, teacher professional development and the relationship between music education and social justice. He is a practising musician with a particular interest in theatre music.

Contributors

Randall Everett Allsup is Professor of Music and Music Education at Teachers College Columbia University in the City of New York. Randall earned degrees in music performance and music education from Northwestern University and Columbia University. He is an awardee of a Fulbright grant that brought him to the Sibelius Academy, Helsinki, Finland to teach and conduct research. He has taught courses at Xiamen University, China, and Toyo University, Tokyo, Japan. He is the proud recipient of the Outstanding Teaching Award at Teachers College. Randall is book series editor of *Counterpoints in Music and Education* at Indiana University Press.

Julie Ballantyne is at the University of Queensland, Australia. She is known for her work in the areas of music teacher identities, social justice, music teacher education, and the social and psychological impacts of musical engagement. An Associate Professor in Music Education, she has won commendations and fellowships for her teaching, and also holds leadership positions with organisations such as the International Society for Music Education. Currently Editor for the journal *Research Studies in Music Education*, Julie has published her own work in key journals and books. She enjoys teaching pre-service and in-service teachers at the Bachelor and Masters Level, as well as supervising several PhD students.

Kim Burwell is the convener of music performance pedagogy in the School of the Arts and Media, University of New South Wales. An enthusiastic piano teacher, her interests include professional development for instrumental and vocal teachers, and postgraduate supervision in areas related to musical performance. Much of her research, including *Studio-based instrumental learning* (2012, 2016), is focused on the dynamics of studio lesson behaviour, with particular reference to teacher-student interactions in the context of musical apprenticeship. Her undergraduate courses combine workshop experience with scholarship to support the evolving practices of studio teachers.

Francesca Christmas is Director of Music at Trinity College London, overseeing the development of Trinity's international music assessment portfolio. Her research activity explores the influences of assessment on music teaching and learning, with a particular focus on the social justice implications of examining in instrumental music education. Francesca has published book chapters and papers in leading music education journals on the subjects of teacher development, critical pedagogy in music education, and assessment in instrumental teaching. She has a background in secondary teacher education and in instrumental teaching, and has worked professionally as a session vocalist.

Andrea Creech is Professor of Music Pedagogy and Associate Dean at the Schulich School of Music, McGill University. She has published widely on topics concerned with lifelong learning and musical development, including as co-author of *Contexts for Music Learning and Participation: developing and sustaining musical possible selves*, and as co-editor of the *Routledge International Handbook of Music Psychology in Education and the Community*. Formerly, following a career as a professional violist, Andrea held positions as Canada Research Chair in Music in Community (Laval University) and Reader in Education (Institute of Education, UCL).

Alison Daubney is a freelance researcher and teacher with a specific interest in creative arts curriculum and assessment. She has taught music and trained teachers across all ages and stages of education from pre-school to postgraduate. Alison works nationally and internationally with education, arts and cultural organisations, universities, schools and music services, undertaking research and evaluation, developing training and leading workshops. Alison is an Honorary Senior Lecturer in Education at the University of Sussex. She is the current co-editor of the *British Journal of Music Education* and author of numerous books including *Play: A Psychological Toolkit for Optimal Music Performance* (2020) and *Teaching Primary Music* (2017).

Martin Fautley is a Professor of Education at Birmingham City University in the UK. After many years as a classroom music teacher, he then undertook full-time doctoral research in the education and music faculties at Cambridge University, investigating teaching, learning, and assessment of classroom music making. He has authored ten books, including *Assessment in Music Education*, published by Oxford University Press, and has written and published over sixty journal articles, book chapters, and academic research papers on various aspects of music teaching and learning. He is co-editor of the *British Journal of Music Education*.

Jennie Henley is Director of Programmes and Professor in Music Education at the Royal Northern College of Music, Manchester, UK where she is responsible for junior, undergraduate and postgraduate programmes of study. Jennie has taught music in various contexts. Her experience spans instrumental teaching, ensemble direction, class teaching, and she continues to teach at the RNCM. She has worked in teacher education and professional development since 2008, working with a wide range of class and instrumental teachers. Covering diverse contexts, Jennie's research is concerned with the relationship between pedagogy and inclusion.

Erin Johnson-Williams is a Lecturer in Music Education and Social Justice at the University of Southampton, where she is also Director of the Centre for Music Education and Social Justice. Her research focuses on the imperial legacies of music education, decolonizing the nineteenth century, trauma studies, gender and maternity, and biopolitics. Erin is co-editor of *Intersectional Encounters in the Nineteenth-Century Archive* (2022), and the forthcoming volumes *Hymns and Constructions of Race: Mobility, Agency, De/Coloniality* (2023) and *The Oxford Handbook of Music Colonialism* (2024).

Andrew King is the Head of the School of the Arts at the University of Hull (UK) and holds a personal chair in music and technology. A Principal Fellow of the Higher Education Academy he has led major research projects funded by the AHRC, the Arts Council, and the Paul Hamlyn Foundation (via PRSF and Sound & Music). He was editor of the *Routledge Companion to Music, Technology, and Education* and *Music, Technology, and Education: Critical perspectives*, and Editor in Chief for *The Journal of Music, Technology, and Education* since 2009.

George Nicholson is the Assistant Professor of Music Education at the University of New Mexico. He received his Bachelor's degree from the University of Miami, FL, and his Master's degree from the University of Georgia. Dr. Nicholson had the privilege of teaching orchestra in Cobb County, GA at the middle school and high school level to wonderful, passionate, and thoughtful students. In 2020, George completed his doctoral degree in music education at Teachers College at Columbia University. His research interests focus on the connection of theory to practice, particularly in the domains of policy, equity, creativity, and string pedagogy.

Adam Whittaker is Head of Pedagogy and Lecturer in Music at Royal Birmingham Conservatoire, and is an internationally recognised scholar in musicology and music education. He has researched in the fields of music education and musicology, and has taught music in a range of settings. His recent research has explored key issues in British music education, including inequalities within pedagogical structures in English schools, and the state of instrumental teaching in the UK. He is currently working on a number of projects exploring access to music education and A-level music provision in the UK. His work has been published in the *British Journal of Music Education*, research reports for Arts Council England and has been featured on BBC *Music Matters* alongside appearances in many major national newspapers.

Foreword

I have always felt that through music we become more fully human. Nowhere is this seen more clearly than when individuals learn to play a musical instrument, but whilst we might celebrate the rich variety of opinions and techniques for introducing and teaching our youth to play and perform music, it is also the case that much of how we do this hasn't changed for centuries. In recent decades however, we have seen much more interrogation of issues surrounding an effective music education and what this might mean and imply. Often this is based upon research into various aspects of how novices through to experts develop competence and especially their motivation to pursue music as an important part of their lives. One of the most important changes in thinking, is a major refocus from views that knowledge is a flow of information from teacher to student, to a more contemporary acknowledgement that what matters most are learners, and the types of practices and beliefs that might shape their view of their own music learning.

And so, it is with the greatest pleasure that I read the chapters that comprise *Instrumental Music Teaching: Perspectives and Challenges*. Not only do all 13 chapters interrogate and disrupt past assumptions but they do so in a way that provides directions for the future about issues that might drive and contextualise our thinking. The editors of this volume – Gary Spruce and Nick Beach – are to be congratulated for carefully selecting authors who are experts in each of the topics covered in their volume. Not only does it 'speak' to readers across the world but it does so by disrupting many commonly held assumptions about effective music performance teaching, and drawing readers in so that they themselves can decide how best to update and redefine their own teaching practices.

I feel confident that this publication will drive change and thinking well into the future and be seen as an important publication that all intending and professional teachers of music performance should examine and use as one of their most important sources of inspiration.

Professor Gary E. McPherson

Introduction

Instrumental Music Teaching: Perspectives and Challenges

Instrumental[1] teaching is a major part of music education in almost all cultures and traditions. For many people a musical education is understood as being synonymous with learning to play a musical instrument, and for some young people learning to play a musical instrument is the principal focus of their music education. The scale of musical instrument learning is immense, and huge numbers of teachers have dedicated their lives to helping young musicians to fulfill their potential. A desire to better meet the musical needs of their students has led some of the most significant thinkers in music education to develop tools, methods, systems, etc., to help meet this aim. The work of Kodaly, Orff, Dalcroze and Suzuki have huge followings amongst teachers, including instrumental and vocal teachers, who endeavour to support the best musical outcomes for their students through learning about and following these approaches.

However, the place of music in young people's lives has changed dramatically over the last 100 years, and it has become an increasingly important part of their individual and collective identities. Advances in digital and communications technology have transformed their relationship with music. The diversity and richness of the world's music is available at the touch of a button and is an ever-present soundtrack to their lives. There are previously unimagined opportunities for young people to learn, create and share music. The dramatic expansion of online learning has put learning a musical instrument within reach for many more young people.

It is arguable that music education has not always recognised and responded to changes in the ways that young people engage with music. Nor has it necessarily reflected the diversity of music making in the world or recognised the much greater agency many young people have over their musical lives. The teaching of musical instruments in western classical contexts has typically been underpinned by what might loosely be termed a master/apprentice model. This approach has produced generations of expert musicians, and individual teachers have constantly striven to improve outcomes for their students through creative and innovative developments within this paradigm of teaching and learning.

---

1   On the basis that the voice is an instrument we have elected to save space by not referring to 'instrumental and vocal' in the main text. Where the words instrument and instrumental are used these generally refer to both instrumental and vocal teaching and learning.

However, the master/apprentice model (particularly within western classical contexts) projects a particular set of assumptions about what it is to be a musician and a music teacher, what it is to teach and learn music and what we mean by musical knowledge. These assumptions and relationships have remained largely unquestioned and uninterrogated, resulting in some of the practices and delivery mechanisms in the teaching of musical instruments remaining largely unchanged and unchallenged since the 19th century. This has served to favour a particular set of musical practices and values (primarily those associated with western art music) to the detriment of other musical traditions and those who practise within them. This has resulted in the creation of musical hierarchies and, where these have been exported to non-western contexts, a form of musical imperialism has resulted; grade examinations are a particularly acute example of the mechanisms by which such musical imperialism can take place.

One of the purposes of this book is to interrogate and disrupt the assumptions inherent in both the master/apprentice model and other approaches by drawing on recent thinking and research in music education in order to ask some fundamental questions about instrumental learning, e.g. what should a music education be and what should it attempt to achieve? It asks how research challenges our assumptions about what we do as music teachers and aims to help us think about our approaches to, and assumptions about music and music education in new ways. In addressing such questions, the book aims to help bridge what is sometimes a gap between music education research, thinking and scholarship and instrumental teaching practice.

The book is in four parts:

Part One: History, Background and Contexts looks at the historical background to instrumental teaching and recent changes to the context of instrumental teaching both in terms of policy and practice. It also explores recent research trends in instrumental teaching.

Part Two: Music Learning, Development and Progress explores the concepts of musical ability, progress and development in relation to instrumental teaching. The chapters ask us to consider what an understanding of these can contribute to our understanding of how children and young people learn musical instruments and how instrumental teachers can help sustain their interest and motivation in that learning.

Part Three: Practices and Pedagogies considers the 'how' of instrumental teaching. It looks at how creative approaches to instrumental teaching can nurture creative and musical responses in children and young people. The place of instrumental teaching and the wider curriculum and what we can learn from different musical and pedagogical traditions are also explored, along with the place of assessment and feedback in supporting instrumental learning.

Part Four: The Future of Instrumental Teaching and Learning addresses a range of questions about instrumental teaching and learning in the 21st century, both in terms of the impact of digital technologies and the changing role of the teacher themselves.

We have invited chapter contributions from a range of the most eminent and experienced music educators including both those who work purely in a research context and those who have ongoing day to day experience of teaching musical instruments. Each chapter therefore has an individual voice, but each also has an introduction in which we aim to summarise how the chapter meets the overall aims of the book. Whilst there is much to be gained by a through reading of this book, readers are encouraged also to re-read chapters and give particular attention to areas of interest.

Within each chapter the reader will find a number of activities which they are invited to undertake. These activities have been designed as 'research into practice', helping the teacher to think about the implications of the chapter for their own practice and how they might be catalysts for change. The activities present the opportunity to engage with the chapter content at a deeper level and we do recommend them to the reader.

Finally, the aim of this book is to disrupt some of the common understandings about instrumental teaching, to provoke debate, and to bring together instrumental teachers and music education academics. The reader will find much that reinforces what they already do, some things that they might think about further, and other things they strongly disagree with. The authors' hope is that the book generates some debate about instrumental teaching that results in a better understanding of why we do what we do, as well as some drivers for change.

Nick Beach & Gary Spruce (Editors)

Part One:
History, Background and Contexts

Chapter 1 Commentary

As instrumental teachers, we sometimes take for granted the way things are. Much about the day-to-day business of teaching a musical instrument might seem to be timeless and to have existed for as long as children and young people have wanted to learn to play musical instruments. The individual or small group weekly lesson, the progression from simple tunes to works of the great composers of western classical music, the graded exam progress check, etc. But do we ever stop to ask how and why these paradigms of instrumental music teaching developed? Did they come about as a result of a selection process which favoured successful approaches, or were there other factors at play? Does the fact that many of the structures within which instrumental teaching is organised have seemingly remained the same for many years indicate that they are the right ones or the only ones – or have they merely become systematised, the result of habit or of cultural norms and pressures?

In the opening chapter of this book, Erin Johnson-Williams examines the historical roots of many of the most commonly held assumptions about how musical instruments are best taught and learnt. With a particular focus on the development of graded music examinations, she describes how the musical values of western classical music have come to be seen as self-evidently superior and have exerted a dominant influence on the pedagogies of instrumental teaching. This dominance has been achieved through the side-lining of alternative approaches – e.g. brass bands pedagogies, peer learning, class learning, self-taught, etc. – from both historical and contemporary narratives.

Questions that are perhaps prompted by this chapter are: Did the dominance of the individual lesson emerge because it was the most appropriate for the learning of western classical music, and did the perceived status of that genre lead to an associated high value placed on individual learning? Has the requirement to learn the classical canon resulted in an elitist hierarchy which is self-fulfilling – the fact that it is deemed that learning to play classical music is something that can only be done in individual lessons means that it is expensive and only available to the financial elite?

Perhaps an understanding of the history behind the origins of western classical instrumental music teaching might help us with answers to these questions and offer some ways forward.

1 The Historical Context of Instrumental Teaching

Erin Johnson-Williams

Introduction

This chapter traces the development of music instrumental education, particularly in western cultures, since the nineteenth century. I provide an analysis and description of how particular pedagogical approaches, underpinned by epistemological and ontological assumptions rooted in western art music, have achieved pre-eminence, such that they are rarely questioned or problematised. I also consider the impact such models have had on the way music is learned around the world, particularly considering the role of graded examinations.

Recent growing debates about decolonising western imperial and settler colonial history have significant and meaningful implications for how we understand the traditions of classical instrumental teaching today. Indeed, the ingrained standardisation of music teaching in western cultures – and, specifically for this chapter, in British colonial and postcolonial contexts – has been profoundly influenced by economic, social and ideological assumptions about what constitutes 'good' musical practice. Many of these epistemological and ontological values stem from the development of standardised music teaching systems (such as graded exams) in the nineteenth century.

In this chapter I argue that if we challenge ourselves to view this history through a contextual lens, we can come to recognise that the history of instrumental teaching reflects many of the Victorian values that gained pre-eminence at the expense of less elite musical traditions. After discussing the concept of 'normalised standardisation' (the process whereby a constructed system of grades and musical standards is so deeply entrenched that it becomes seen as inevitable and accepted, without awareness of the history of its cultural constructions), I will give a brief account of the emergence of standardised instrumental teaching in Victorian Britain, offering three contrasting case studies of how these practices were part of an imperial project. By providing a contextual backdrop for the epistemologies (the types or modes of knowledge) and the ontologies (the ideas about the very nature of existence of this knowledge) of 'musical standards' as a hierarchical system, I suggest that we may be better placed to understand the standardisation and professionalisation of music teaching today as being historically conditioned. If we can do this, we may also be freed from defining our musical practices in relation to antiquated ideas about standardisation, in order to more flexibly approach music teaching in the future.

Normalised Standardisation

Despite the imperial and capitalist origins of standardised music education, many practising musicians today are unaware that large examining institutions such as the Associated Board of the Royal Schools of Music (ABRSM) and Trinity College London (TCL) became successful within a culture of western imperialism. Both exam boards, from the late nineteenth century, sent out examiners from London to assess musical candidates across the colonies, a practice that still continues. Yet, as a growing group of scholars and musicians have recently acknowledged, the experience of preparing for and taking a graded examination in the postcolonial world can often be tied to highly complex issues of financial prestige, postcolonial guilt, and gendered and racial inequalities, which can be challenging to disentangle from the intimidating aspects of the classical repertoire itself.

These hierarchies have been well documented in a recent book by sociologist Anna Bull (2020), who argues that the very historical possibility of graded musical standards stems from Victorian attitudes to class and race. In practice, hierarchical learning cultures may become additionally problematic if music students view graded exams as the official means of gaining access to classical music, when this is certainly not the only way of successfully becoming a classical musician: in many other European countries and in the United States of America, for example, graded exam systems have not taken off (Banfield, 2007). Thus, in order to understand the cultural legacies of instrumental teaching traditions, it is worth asking exactly how the 'normalised standardisation' of British instrumental assessment occurred.

Activity 1.1

Are graded exams an important feature of the country or setting in which you teach? If so, what do you think is the impact of graded exams on instrumental teaching? Note down your thoughts, revisiting them at the end of the chapter to see if they have changed in any way.

If graded exams are not an important feature of your country or setting, by what other means (if any) is progression in instrumental learning measured and certificated, and what impact do you think these criteria have on instrumental teaching and learning? Have any alternative criteria become normalised in the way described above?

The first question to ask is: was the evolution of British instrumental teaching practices inevitable? And, relatedly: is the so-called 'western canon' the only type of music that was being taught in the past? Within Britain alone there were, indeed, many forms of nineteenth-century instrumental and vocal teaching practices – such as brass bands (e.g. Herbert, 2000) and mass choral movements (McGuire, 2009) – that have now been virtually 'erased' from histories of mainstream music teaching due to the fact that the historical success of these traditions might complicate a more straightforward narrative about the growth and popularity of the 'great tradition'. Furthermore, it is worth considering that the incorporation of more vernacular repertoires into standardised teaching and assessment practices today might not only appeal to a wider range of students, but could also facilitate a more nuanced understanding of the history of the musical traditions that were contemporaneous to the classical repertoires that we already know so well. For example: what kinds of music did Handel really hear on the London streets; in the country villages that he passed through; in the churches? Or, when considering that someone like Elgar was actually an outsider to the elite conservatoires, how did he position his own compositions in relation to 'working class' musical traditions? What did these less-canonic repertoires sound like, and how did that influence what eventually came to be known as 'canonical' compositions?

The second relevant question concerns how the standardisation of repertoire influenced, in turn, the normalising of teaching and assessment practices. For if a society believes itself to have a great repertoire of aesthetically important music, then it follows that the teaching and performing of that repertoire must likewise be held to high (and easily measurable) standards. And yet, the very process of canonising both the repertoire and the performing traditions of classical music excludes other traditions. Thus, with the rise of the 'great canon' we see the first official division in European society between 'classical' and 'popular' traditions, with all of the problematic connotations that this binary brings. Therefore, one worrying result of the 'normalised standardisation' of classical music teaching is that pedagogy, repertoire, class, and race ultimately become linked together in practice, and the normalisation of exclusionary practices (such as the fact that most orchestra members, conductors, and classical audiences tend to belong to the same demographic) are justified by subconscious implications that only those who can master the canon can truly understand the 'greatness' of the music. Further, there is also the issue of gender within the classical music world: the majority of widely-recognised composers are male, and those in positions of power in the performance world – conductors, examiners, staging directors, institutional managers, and conservatoire directors – are also overwhelmingly male. This is despite the fact that, according to sociological research about Britain today, more female than male students are encouraged to take music lessons as children (Scharff, 2015).

> **Activity 1.2**
>
> Thinking about your own setting, are there any Indigenous musical traditions or styles that you feel are ignored or sidelined in formal music education, i.e. the music education that takes place in schools, conservatoires and music colleges?
>
> Choose one of these musical styles and traditions and try and find out how instrumental teaching and learning takes place within it. Is there anything about these pedagogies that might be relevant to all instrumental teachers in whatever tradition they are working?

A potentially significant problem with the expectations around musical accreditation today, of course, is that only an elite sector of the world's population has the appropriate role models and resources to access classical training, and, as explored by Geoffrey Baker (2014), if students come from deprived backgrounds, then utopian ideals about classical music as a means of transcending one's upbringing can create a myriad of social challenges. It is thus worth recognising that the canonisation of repertoire and the standardisation of instrumental teaching were two sides of the same coin. They both emerged as part of a uniquely nineteenth-century drive to categorise and commercialise the arts (even when the aesthetic claims of Romantic nineteenth-century music were that the 'great repertoire' was, by its very nature, resistant to categorisation and commercialisation). It is therefore useful to debunk the myth of the 'inevitability' of standardised classical music teaching by looking at its historical evolution.

Historical Background

Prior to the nineteenth century the master-apprentice model was the most common way that students in Europe learned music professionally. The standardised expectations of the 'grades' now expected by many university music departments, conservatoires and exam boards would have seemed like a bizarre concept. Yet it was largely political and strategic social shifts, many linked to the rise of nationalism, that inspired the change towards large, official institutions becoming the goal for an increasing number of music students. In 1795, the French Revolution was the springboard for the opening of the Paris Conservatoire, and its foundation was gradually followed by the rise of national conservatoires in most major cities across Europe. In Britain, the Royal Academy of Music was founded in 1822, although it was not widely successful until the end of the nineteenth century, around the time it joined forces with the new Royal College of Music (founded in 1882 as part of Prince Albert's desire to make South Kensington a centre for imperial artistic excellence) to form the ABRSM in 1899. Trinity College of Music was founded in 1872, followed by the Guildhall School of Music (1880). Trinity was the first institution to offer graded examinations across Britain and the colonial world, followed quickly by the ABRSM.

Surveying these dates, it is worth noting that standardised instrumental teaching is a relatively recent development in the history of western classical music. Graded exams, in particular, were only a dominant force from the 1880s and 1890s onwards, and created the new concept of assessment as having a financial value (the examination fee) and a physical reward (the examination certificate). The achieving of a 'grade' was all the more prestigious if bestowed by an examining body that was associated with an established London conservatoire. Yet the institutionalised hierarchies of standardised music teaching (i.e. graded exams and conservatoire entry requirements) were at odds with the pedagogical methods of indigenous and popular forms of music-making, both then and now.

The early graded exams, indeed, were met with a fair amount of suspicion in the nineteenth century itself. In 1889, for example, an article in the *Musical Times* expressed concern that Britain was the 'most examined nation on earth', and many music critics were worried that over-examination would compromise natural musicality, and/or that the cost of examinations would prohibit many students from gaining access to the system. Nevertheless, the growth of standardised exams, while controversial, was remarkably swift: 1,143 child candidates were examined in Britain during the first inspection cycle of the ABRSM in 1889, and by the 1890s, thousands more were being assessed across the colonies (Wright, 2013). Trinity had already established around 200 examination centres across Britain in 1879, and by 1891 overseas centres were opening in South Africa, India, Ceylon and Australia (Banfield, 2007; and Rutland, 1972).

One of the results of the growing institutional success of the nineteenth-century conservatoires and their exam boards was the increased distancing of formal, 'elite' musical education from working-class musical practices, despite the fact that several of the conservatoires offered generous scholarships for lower-income students. Nevertheless, the growing prestige associated with elite music institutions effectively 'othered' more grassroots forms of musical practice that were widespread at the same time; for example, music hall songs, brass bands, and working-class singing movements such as tonic sol-fa choirs with their alternative pedagogical approaches (McGuire, 2009). Today, the story of these less canonical forms of music teaching has traditionally been erased from histories of music teaching in Britain, despite the fact that they reached a larger portion of the population than the conservatoires did. It is thus incumbent upon educators today to acknowledge that many of the structures in place around how instrumental music teaching now operates have gradually gathered these associations as they became normalised in a capitalist, imperial economy. When this history is not acknowledged, teachers and students alike risk the unconscious internalisation of certain problematic concepts, such as financial privilege, whiteness and gender going in tandem with accessing classical music. Yet if the musical material of the classical canon, on its own terms, is not inherently elitist but has instead accumulated these associations through cultural circumstances, then it may be possible for classical music teachers to work with their students to transcend these potentially elitist connotations. This awareness will give agency to music teachers and students in shaping how the western canon might be taught and examined in the future.

Activity 1.3
Would you say that there is a standardised teaching approach in your own setting/country? If so, what are its main characteristics? Does it reflect a master-apprentice model? To what extent do you feel that this approach has grown from within or is externally imposed?

Imperial Histories

The growth of graded music exams in the colonial world is deeply and intrinsically tied to imperialistic expansion. Music historians have been largely uncritical of this rather uncomfortable aspect of the history of graded exams, such as Wright (2013) in his institutional account of the ABRSM, where he frames the Board's international expansion across the British empire in a relatively positive light. Musicologist Roe-Min Kok, on the other hand, has approached this same history against the grain, by illustrating how the act of taking a graded exam in postcolonial Malaysia can be a traumatic childhood experience indicative of racist and sexist hierarchies. The exam, in Kok's formulation, becomes a ritual that exposes how British cultural authority has been embedded into postcolonial music teaching in a way that deeply complicates the negotiation of her own identity (a Malaysian, female child) in relation to gaining accreditation in western classical music from a figure of immeasurable authority (a white-British, male examiner). She recalls that, motivated by different reasons, all of the participants in the postcolonial examination system (which included the ABRSM examiners who travelled from London to examine in Malaysia, her parents, her piano teacher, and herself) 'participated willingly if unwittingly in an ideological process that ultimately reinforced the colonizers' cultural subjugation of the colonized' (Kok, 2007: 98).

Such identities are particularly complex to navigate if the examinee and/or their teacher is from a postcolonial background and the British examiner is white. The case studies below provide three brief snapshots of the complex imperial history of British graded exams, suggesting that the authority and presence of these systems around the world was neither straightforward nor inevitable.

Case Study 1: India

In India, Trinity examinations have dominated the graded exam marketplace since they were first established there in the late nineteenth century (Brewer, 1993). As early as 1891, British newspapers boasted that Trinity College of Music was organising examinations across the United Kingdom, Australia, New Zealand, South Africa, and India (Anon, 1891). Today, holding a Trinity certificate in India essentially functions as a qualification for being a teacher of western music. As noted in a recent study by Diana T. Dumlavwalla, more than one half of the teachers in India who were surveyed for an academic study listed a Trinity exam certificate as their highest level of music education (ranging from grades 6 to 8), and 95% of those surveyed confirmed that their students took Trinity exams. However, Dumlavwalla notes a certain level of pushback from Indian teachers who claim that India's piano teaching culture is too 'examcentric', in that it relies too heavily on advice from British examiners who still fly in to examine from the UK, rather than helping to foster the expertise of local teachers (Dumlavwalla, 2019).

In the nineteenth century, Victorians were fascinated by the possibilities for racial mixture in the administering of colonial exams, and this was a topic brought up in interviews of examiners as they returned to London. For example, in an interview with the London *Musical Times* in 1899, a 'Dr Cresser' noted that most of his examining work lay with the children of the white British population in India, although he also encountered 'Brahmins, Parsees, Persians, and others' (Anon, 1889). Cresser also indicated that the majority of classical music teaching at the time in India happened in private British schools. While Cresser is largely positive about the imperial examining project in his assessment of the candidates' musical abilities, conflicting comments from within the instrumental teaching profession in colonial India would become more mixed over the next two decades, particularly as the graded examinations became further entrenched within white settler communities. For example, a 1922 letter to the editor of the *Musical Times* from Heathcote D. Statham, a former organist of the Cathedral at Calcutta, noted that:

> The examinations themselves appear to me to be excellent; and they are admirably conducted by examiners of high reputation. But I am quite certain that the wholesale and indiscriminate examination by a College at home of pupils at centres abroad (or at any rate at Calcutta) is not only not of educational value, but is definitely detrimental to any real musical

advance in the centre. When I was a teacher at Calcutta almost every pupil I had was simply obsessed with the idea of passing a Trinity College examination (Statham, 1922).

This excerpt is an example of how the practice of graded examinations in colonial India was deeply linked to racial and social privilege (i.e. candidates in a colonial outpost could use the exams as a way to gain access to 'examiners of high reputation' sent all the way from Britain), and came to function as a form of cultural capital (examinees could participate in an assessment ritual that linked them to a fantasy of being like British students back in the imperial centre). Yet it also sparked concern from within the teaching profession that students often used the system as a means of social mobility, rather than for musical or creative reasons; thus, the growing market for examinations in colonial India was still met with some consternation precisely at the time when its popularity gained traction.

Case Study 2: South Africa

South Africa was the first colonial destination for the ABRSM in 1894 (Johnson-Williams, 2020). The chosen examiner for the first tour was Franklin Taylor (1843–1919), an established piano teacher at the Royal College of Music. Taylor's departure for South Africa was widely documented in newspaper reports and the ABRSM's official records. His impending voyage was a feature of the speeches at the Board's Fifth Annual Dinner in London on 16 July 1894, where RCM Principal Sir George Grove invited the departing examiner to speak, 'so that we shall have an opportunity of hearing [his] farewell accents from the chair which he is going for a few months to forsake us in favour of the black men' (Associated Board of the Royal Schools of Music Archives, 1894). This was an ironic statement considering that it is highly likely that all of the 346 candidates he examined in South Africa that year were white. It was not until a few years later when examiner Walter Parratt toured South Africa that mention of racial diversity in the ABRSM examinations appears, with Parratt writing to the *Royal College of Music Magazine* in 1904 that 'once I examined two [Black candidates] and tried hard to pass them, but without success' (Parratt, 1904: 7).

While the presence of the examinations in colonial South Africa received less official criticism than did the Indian Trinity exams, it is worth considering how the privilege associated with the British graded exams has continued to accumulate associations of whiteness in a country that was notorious during the Apartheid era for systematising racial divisions to an extreme degree. As recent studies have shown, the overwhelming culture of classical music education in twenty-first century South Africa is still mostly centred around costly private education, and those who continue to enrol for British examinations such as the ABRSM or Trinity are overwhelmingly white candidates (Pooley, 2016). It is therefore important to consider what possible future for diversification lies ahead, when potentially little has changed in the racial administering of graded examinations in South Africa since the nineteenth century, particularly when these systems struggle to create dialogues with Indigenous traditions.

Case Study 3: Canada

One of the most heated debates about music teaching and colonialism in London's musical press through the decade of the 1890s was the 'Canadian Controversy' of 1899. The issue at hand was the establishment of Canadian musical examinations, administered by music professors at Toronto University. These were a cheaper alternative to the ABRSM examinations that had been exported there from 1897. In contrast to India and South Africa, nineteenth-century Toronto was a highly flourishing, economically independent city with its own successful structures of music education and examining. Toronto's university had been established in 1827 (earlier than the foundation of the University of London in 1830), and the Toronto Conservatory of Music had been in existence since 1886 (earlier than the Royal College of Music or Trinity College of Music) (Horwood, 1936).

It is perhaps unsurprising, considering this level of colonial autonomy, that the introduction of expensive British examinations into nineteenth-century Toronto was not met with the same level of enthusiasm as had been felt in India and South Africa. Toronto's music industry and teaching profession had strong links with conservatoires in the United States of America, a location where there was very little adherence given to British music examining. It could be argued that a Canadian child candidate had potentially less to gain in terms of cultural capital from taking one of the British examinations, especially when the Canadian examining options were widely accepted in Canada as being just as good.

Yet such was the ABRSM's outrage about the spread of rival homegrown Canadian examinations that in March 1899 their Honorary Secretary, Samuel Aitken, published a 30-page tract entitled *The Case of the Associated Board*, which condemned the Toronto examinations and defended the right of the ABRSM to carry out their work in Canada (Aitken, 1889). Within two weeks of the publication of Aitken's tract, the Canadian Protesting Committee distributed a direct rebuke, entitled *An Account of the Canadian Protest Against the Introduction into Canada of Musical Examinations by Outside Musical Examining Bodies*. This document, amounting to nearly 50 pages, was circulated within both Canada and the United Kingdom. The Protesting Committee argued that 'under the Associated Board's regime in Canada, the Canadian musician is clearly outlined and well defined as a musical 'Colonist', and as such is expected to humbly submit to the imperious dictate of the Board' (Canadian Protesting Committee, 1889: 4).

The Canadian musicians therefore disputed the examining authority of an imperial exam board that limited their own evolution as a specifically Canadian profession of music teachers. It is worth noting, however, that in contrast to India and South Africa as discussed in Case Studies 1 and 2, the Canadian music profession was far more established by the end of the nineteenth century and teachers had less to lose by breaking most of their ties with the British examining systems. In Canada today, the domestic exams administered by Toronto's Royal Conservatory are still far more successful than British imports.

> ### Activity 1.4
> Find out about the history of graded exams or other forms of instrumental examinations in your country. How did they evolve? Did they grow from the Indigenous musical traditions of the country or were they imported from other musical settings or traditions. What was the process by which this took place? How have they changed in recent years? Do you think these changes have improved the examinations?

Contemporary Repercussions

How can this discussion help teachers today to navigate the complex world in which standardised music accreditation continues to grow across the non-western world – particularly in a competitive international market? As Banfield has noted with regard to the reach of the ABRSM in the twenty-first century: 'It flourishes as never before, indeed as though the Empire has never been disbanded' (Banfield, 2007: 77). Banfield's statement is challenging, and reflective of how associations of institutional and cultural elitism can risk limiting wider possibilities for participation. Indeed, if one were to view graded examinations as an ongoing form of capitalist imperialism in the postcolonial world, then the issue of how to help students negotiate these pedagogical spaces today becomes significant, particularly when taking into account sensitive issues around race, gender and authority.

In 2007, Kok (mentioned above) explored her memories of the postcolonial experience as the examinee in late twentieth-century Malaysia:

> I derived so much pleasure from playing the piano that by the age of thirteen, as I completed the final grade offered by the ABRSM, I was sure I wanted to become a musician (albeit without knowing what that meant or entailed). Perhaps the decision, born of a colonized imagination, represented a continued yearning to become "British". At this point I began to wonder if one could become a musician simply by passing examinations …? (Kok, 2007: 98).

This provocative quote leaves us with a set of questions for further research and exploration. Given the imperialistic history of British standardised examinations, what are the socio-cultural implications of the graded exam certificate, today, for examinees from minority groups? Can Victorian power structures be transcended by new frameworks for diversity and creativity? And by continuing to centralise examining power to Britain, do we risk the conflation – as seen in the quotation above – of proficiency in western classical music with being white, and British? Does the 'normalised standardisation' of western classical music teaching effectively put ideological pressure on the examination candidate to 'perform whiteness', and to ascribe to salvationist discourses about the aesthetic 'good' of western classical music – potentially at the expense of local and popular musical traditions with which students might also identify?

In the twenty-first century, British music exams are more popular than ever across the non-western world. As such, exam boards are now actively grappling with the political and racial legacies of how the standardised instrumental teaching of western classical music emerged from a set of historically-contingent values about what could and could not be included in the 'canon'. There are, however, signs of willingness to change: TCL have taken notable steps to diversify their syllabi and teaching and learning recommendations, and they include in their list of core values that 'our qualifications are accessible to candidates of all ages and from all cultures' (TCL, 2020). The ABRSM's website now also maintains, under the subtitle 'Knocking Down Barriers', that they plan to 'work more with organisations that reach beyond classical repertoire and have a focus on inclusivity and diversity' (ABRSM, 2020). While there is clearly still a long and challenging path ahead towards confronting imperial pasts and breaking down the cultural elitism that is associated with classical music teaching, these kinds of initiatives, if carried out with historical and cultural awareness, may help to pave the way for a more self-aware and inclusive future, where there might be room for teaching and examining practices to diversify.

Activity 1.5

Imagine you are asked to advise on the design of a new form of instrumental exam reflecting the diversity of instrumental learning in your country and setting. The new exam aims to serve a wide range of musical traditions and the different ways in which instruments are taught.

What are the key features of musical learning in your setting that the exam should recognise and reflect?

What are the potential pitfalls or barriers which a new exam system would need to overcome – are some of these unique to your setting?

What new or different types of assessment (e.g. live, digital, group, etc.) do you think would be most appropriate for learners in your setting?

References and Bibliography

Aitken, S. (1899) *The Case of the Associated Board*. London: Samuel Aitken.

Anon. (1889) A Musical Examiner's Experiences in India. *Musical Times* 40(682), p. 817.

Anon. (1891) The Great English Schools of Music. *The Magazine of Music* 8(4), p. 64.

Associated Board of the Royal Schools of Music Archives (1894). *Minutes of the Annual Dinners*. London: ABRSM.

Our reinvestment in music education *Associated Board of the Royal Schools of Music*. Available at: https://gb.abrsm.org/en/about-us/our-reinvestment-in-music-education/. Accessed 24 June 2020.

Baker, G. (2014) *El Sistema: Orchestrating Venezuela's Youth*. New York: Oxford University Press.

Banfield, S. (2007) Towards a History of Music in the British Empire: Three Export Studies. In: K. Darian-Smith, P. Grimshaw, and S. Macintyre eds. *Britishness Abroad: Transnational Movements and Imperial Cultures*. Melbourne: Melbourne University Press Academic, pp. 63–89.

Brewer, F. (1999) *Case Study Examinations of Independent Piano Instruction in India*. Ph.D. Thesis. University of Oklahoma.

Bull, A. (2020) *Class, Control, and Classical Music*. New York: Oxford University Press.

Canadian Protesting Committee. (1889) *An Account of the Canadian Protest Against the Introduction into Canada of Musical Examination by Outside Musical Examining Bodies*. Toronto: Canadian Protesting Committee.

Dumlavwalla, D. T. (2019) The Piano Pedagogy Scenes in India and the Philippines: An Introductory Cross-Cultural Comparison. *International Journal of Music Education*, 37(3), pp. 390–406.

Herbert, T. (2000). *The British Brass Band: A Musical and Social History*. Oxford: Oxford University Press.

Horwood, F. J. (1936) *The Toronto Conservatory of Music: A Retrospect (1886-1936)*. Toronto: University of Toronto Press.

Johnson-Williams, E. (2020) The Examiner and the Evangelist: Authorities of Music and Empire, c.1894. *Journal of the Royal Musical Association* 145(2), pp. 317–350.

Kok, R-M (2006) Music for a Postcolonial Child: Theorizing Malaysian Memories. In: S. Boynton and R-M. Kok, eds. *Musical Childhoods and the Cultures of Youth*. Hanover: Wesleyan University Press, pp. 89–104.

Trinity College London. https://www.trinitycollege.com/about-us. Accessed 24 June 2020.

McGuire, C. (2009) *Music and Victorian Philanthropy: The Tonic Sol-fa Movement*. Cambridge: Cambridge University Press.

Parratt, W. (1904) Reminiscences of South Africa. *The Royal College of Music Magazine* (1), pp. 5–8.

Rutland, H. (1972) *Trinity College of Music: The First Hundred Years*. London: Trinity College of Music.

Scharff, C. (2015) *Equality and Diversity in the Classical Music Profession: A Research Report*. ESRC and King's College London.

Statham, H. D. (1922) Trinity College Examinations in India. *Musical Times* 63(954), p. 574.

Wright, W. (2013) *The Associated Board of the Royal Schools of Music: A Social and Cultural History*. London: Boydell.

Chapter 2 Commentary

Randall Allsup and George Nicholson note in this chapter how Lucy Green's book How Popular Musicians Learn *(2002) prompted something of a seismic shift in some areas of musical pedagogy, with a focus on student-centred learning and outcomes and informal approaches to teaching and learning, etc. Green spoke with a range of popular musicians about their early musical experiences and challenges, discovering that their musical and instrumental development typically followed a very different path to that of most learners of western classical instruments. This gave rise eventually to initiatives such as Musical Futures in the U.K. and Australasia and the Modern Band Method in the U.S.*

But although Lucy Green's work had and has the potential for profound implications for the teaching and learning of all instruments and genres, not just popular music, how much difference has it actually made to instrumental teaching pedagogy? As the authors note, 'discourse is not the same as policy, research, or practice'. Put another way, academics can discuss, theorise, infer and propose all they like, but how do we, as a music teaching profession, ensure that the experience we offer learners is influenced and informed by current and new understandings of the business of learning music? In this sense the chapter that follows goes to the very heart of what this book is attempting to do.

The world of young people's learning described by Allsup and Nicholson is a very different one to that which we might assume was experienced by those young people living in the colonial world described in Chapter 1. Where, historically, approaches to music learning tended to focus on the specific set of skills required to play the western classical canon, modern approaches tend to take a more democratic view, giving learners more control over their learning and more say in what is learned. Attempts are made not only to level the playing field which has previously been tilted towards western classical music, but also to develop deeper and more relevant understandings of the enormous cultural variety which the musical world offers. But, as the authors note, 'Relevance, however, is always a moving target, and thus efforts must be sustained across conditions that both do not change (e.g. the colour of one's skin) and conditions that do (e.g. meanings and significations associated with sub-cultures and cultural artifacts/forms)'.

The authors suggest that in music education 'nothing has changed and everything seems to be moving too fast'. As you move through this chapter you might consider this statement in the light of your own teaching – what has changed and continues to change, and what stays the same?

2 The Changing Landscapes of Contemporary Instrumental Music Teaching: Policy and Practice

Randall Everett Allsup & George Nicholson

At the turn of the 21st century, a large-scale survey indicated that 21% of U.S. high school seniors, approximately 18 years old, enrolled in some kind of musical ensemble (Elpus and Abril, 2011), a statistic that has remained reliably stable for decades (Elpus and Abril, 2019; Hansen, 2004; Henry, 2005; Humphreys, 1995; Salvador and Allegood, 2014). Regarding concert bands and orchestras, recent data appears to have uncovered what was hiding in plain sight: that certain demographic groups are either more likely or less likely to have access to, or interest in, school-based instrumental music-making (Elpus and Abril, 2019). U.S. students who play an instrument are overwhelmingly white, speak English as their first language, come from wealthier families, and score higher-than-average on standardized tests (Ibid.). Put another way, the categories that are most correlated with large ensemble education bump up against the realities of privilege and structural forms of oppression: categories like race/ethnicity, gender, social economic status, parents' educational level, native language, math scores, and access to out-of-school arts experiences (Ibid.). As economic inequalities increase around the world (Sala-i-Martin, 2002), and as western classical art music remains the dominant form in many university music programs, this North American problem can be seen as an international music education problem writ large. Playing an instrument takes time, costs money, and requires an intricate support system for its teachers and learners.

This chapter will examine research and policy contexts, as well as the varied and various teaching practices of instrumental music education during the first two decades of the 21st century. Because of the important role that instrumental music plays as a marker of youth identity (Campbell, Connell, and Beegle, 2007), a special emphasis will be placed on issues of school access and inclusion.

Change: Too Fast? Too Slow?

From the Tanglewood Symposium of 1970 (Mark and Gary, 2007) to contemporary scholarship on the democratic possibilities of instrumental music education (Allsup, 2003) and its analogue critiques of gender (Abramo, 2011) and race (Butler, Lind, and McKoy, 2007; Hess, 2019), many researchers have grappled with the twin problems of who benefits from school-based instrumental music education (Allsup and Benedict, 2008) and why so many students seem to reject what these teachers have to offer (Williams, 2007). Today, most discourse in the field of instrumental music education sees change as inevitable, but occurring too rapidly or at a snail's pace. A *cris de coeur* erupted in 2014 when an exasperated university instrumental music educator declared that calls for change were unpersuasive and thus 'no default or reset [was] necessary' (Fonder, 2014). Writing for the largest and oldest practitioner journal devoted to music education, conductor Mark Fonder spoke in defense of continuing the North American concert band system unchanged:

> *These academicians [sic] would have us abandon the 20 percent–the most motivated and interested students–to accommodate the other 80 percent. They bandy the word democracy about . . . What is not democratic is forcing all students into a 'participatory experience' whether they want it or not, which is the stance of these academicians* (Fonder, 2014).

Fonder further contended that critics of band were overly represented by the research community and its network of journals. His commentary gave voice to the frustrations of a silent majority, those ensemble directors and instrumental music teachers who felt hurt by accusations that school band and orchestra programs were somehow non-educative, with academics calling the experiences they provide to their students as mostly passive (Scheib, 2006; Shively, 1989), pedagogically dubious (Mantie, 2012), unaware of their ethical dimensions (Allsup, 2012), resistant to technology (Brown, 2010), presentational, rather than participatory (Tobias, 2013) and uninterested in change (Kratus, 2007; Williams, 2011).

Many of the critics of large ensemble music education found dual inspiration in (1) the ways in which popular music appealed to young people, particularly their sense of identity, and (2) the ways in which popular musicians learn from each other and teach each other – so different than classical training, which is impossible to imagine occurring without the steady help of an adult teacher (Rodriguez, 2004). Furthermore, one cannot overstate the influence that Lucy Green's historic research on 'how popular musicians learn' had on the field of instrumental music education (2002). Green's groundbreaking study sparked intense discussions about relevance, informal learning, and student-centered or democratic curricula (Allsup, 2008; Allsup and Olson, 2012).

One might say that thanks to emerging popular music research in the field of music education (in contrast to the field of cultural studies where popular music research has a long history), ensemble directors, publishers, and instrumental music teachers were existentially pushed into conversations about what students want from their music classes.

Certainly, music educators have always talked about relevance. But it is worth recalling that prior to *How Popular Musicians Learn* (Green, 2002), there was almost no empirical research on popular music and music education. Many cite the Tanglewood Declaration as the original source for diversity in the field of music education, as well as for discussions of learner relevance. But Tanglewood was *only* a declaration, not a curriculum. The Yale Seminar (1963), the Comprehensive Musicianship Symposium at Northwestern University (1968), the Juilliard Repertory Project (1964–1970), the Manhattanville Music Curriculum Project (1966–1970), John Paynter's Schools Council Music Project (1973–1980) and other early scholarly efforts all emphasized creativity and diversity, but their authors were much more interested in 'new' or avant-garde music than jazz, multi-ethnic, or popular instrumental music. At the end of the 20th century, David Elliott's (1995) highly influential 'praxial' philosophy of music education was celebrated as open to multiple styles and genres, but his philosophy was adamantly non-prescriptive (he had, in other words, no preferred genre to which he advocated). As long as orchestra directors followed the historic norms of teaching string music, and jazz instructors followed the rules of learning and performing jazz, the praxial music teacher was not ethically compelled to change what they did best. It is important to acknowledge that popular music ensembles were thriving in Nordic countries as early as the 1970s. These instrumental music educators should have been early sources of inspiration. Unfortunately, nativist tendencies to prefer English language scholarship, coupled with the obvious lack of internet search engines, meant that teachers and researchers outside Scandinavia and Finland were largely in the dark about many of their considerable achievements (Kallio and Väkevä, 2017).

Yet there is truth to the idea (nay, truth to the *feeling*) that when one speaks about instrumental music education in the 21st century, nothing seems to have changed and everything seems to be moving too fast. Such an observation is certainly illogical until one considers that 'discourse' is not the same as policy, research, or practice. How a professional field understands itself is not universal, consistent, or necessarily rational. Is the concert band director wrong to fear the loss of a cherished art form? Would the 'truth' matter more, knowing that guitar courses in the U.S. serve only 3% of the school population (Elpus and Abril, 2019)? On the other hand, how can 3% be seen as adequate to any constituency? In Scandinavia, teacher-researchers worry that it might be unethical to focus too much on the teaching and learning of popular instruments (Georgii-Hemming and Westvall, 2010). Shouldn't students have access to music that is unfamiliar? With the 2008 collapse of the International Association of Jazz Educators, jazz educators are teaching with little professional support for their art form of choice. In such a policy context, advocacy thrives, and competition (both real and imagined) makes allies hard to find.

Rather than reinforce the adversarial nature of these debates, and preferring to dwell in a space of tension, it might be more helpful to recast the tropes that surround instrumental music education. What if we accept contradiction as an on-going condition, not something that needs resolution? Rather than thinking about the potential loss of resources, we might consider where opportunities for access and relevance lie. What if non-partisan inclusion were our foremost concern? The remaining subsections of this chapter outline pedagogical and musical trends in instrumental music education, seen through the potential to enlarge and diversify what we currently do.

Activity 2.1

Think for a moment about the teaching you experienced as a pupil and compare this with the teaching you are now offering to your own pupils. What has changed – and what has stayed the same? Try grouping these aspects under four headings: different and positive, different and negative, same and positive, same and negative. How do your lived experiences and positionality impact your categorization? Are the negatives within your control/influence and what might you do to address them?

Teachers in Search of New Music

Structural change, the type needed to upend systemic forms of exclusion, happens slowly; but the teacher is in a powerful position to make change, effectively working from the bottom up. One strategy for enlarging and diversifying instrumental music education has to do with representation, finding materials in which students can see themselves and their cultures. Richard Milner (2012) suggests that disparities regarding who participates in school, how and why, are a result of so-called 'opportunity gaps'. This reconceptualization moves teachers and directors away from those reoccurring conversations about achievement, competition, and excellence to talk more explicitly about pedagogies and curricula that embrace opportunity and openness; fundamentally, such a shift refuses to see minoritized students through a deficit lens, a lens which blames students of colour and their communities for discrepancies in school performance, music or otherwise.

Opportunity-thinking on the other hand, places emphasis on the structures that create those discrepancies, and seeks to make repair. Milner outlines five critical qualities to address the opportunity gap: 1) rejecting colour blindness; 2) understanding and transcending cultural conflicts; 3) understanding how meritocracy operates; 4) shifting low expectations and deficit mind-sets; and 5) the rejecting of context-neutral practices (Ibid.).

Applied to the context of instrumental music education, Milner is not suggesting that we do away with orchestras and concerts bands, only that we refuse to see them as colour-blind organizations, or as historically neutral. Thus, choice of diverse repertoire is a logical way to enlarge opportunities for attracting and supporting a more diverse student body. Indeed, some efforts are already underway, with instrumental method books that place *Boer er ligt een kip in 't water* next to *Tsuki* and Bartók's *Romanian Folk Dances* alongside a Piazzolla tango.

Selecting repertoire with context in mind, as Carlos Abril suggests (2010), provides a comfortable and orderly space for music teachers to explore cultural issues with students. However, Abril warns that such a move is likely to backfire if student dialogue is not an inherent part of an opportunity-thinking teaching process. Abril cites a case study whereby a good-intentioned non-Hispanic white music teacher created a mariachi band to enlarge and diversify her curriculum, but failed to change her director-centric teaching style to a more democratic arrangement. Mexican music was chosen by this teacher *for* the students, which resulted in culturally inappropriate mis-matches and hurt feelings. Unfortunately, this self-evident notion that curriculum is all that matters is reinforced across all stages of a teacher's education. The renowned university conductor H. Robert Reynolds famously claimed that 'repertoire *is* the curriculum' (2000). But any repertoire – even a multicultural repertoire – that is implemented without consideration for an inclusive and diversity-affirming musical experience, still puts the teacher at the centre of the classroom. Furthermore, because repertoire needs to be enacted, it can never simply *be* the curriculum. The 'how' of bringing a poem, march, or pop song to life *is* pedagogy, whether hidden, open, or something-in-between.

Juliet Hess (2013), a scholar long associated with research on social justice and music education, wrote about the perils of something-in-between spaces. Hess documented her own trials and tribulations when, as an early-career instrumental music teacher, she designed a Ghanaian drumming ensemble for her elementary classroom situated in a middle-class neighborhood near Toronto, Canada. The most immediate outcome of the curriculum change was the obvious acknowledgement of difference: the students were aware they were playing the music from 'somewhere else', and written by 'someone other than' themselves. Even though Hess founded the ensemble for purposes of exploring and reflecting on hidden stereotypes, many students found difference as something exotic, lacking appreciation for human complexity. For some students, performing on African drums reinforced superficial notions of racial identity. Further, those who were able to look beyond their initial biases saw the people of Ghana as the same as themselves, a kind of colour-blind privilege that can serve to erase the histories of rich and multiplex cultures. Hess acknowledged the need to speak more openly about her own positionality as teacher, disrupting the idea that a teacher and a curriculum must remain politically neutral (Ibid.).

The teacher-driven need for diverse programming in musical ensembles, particularly those that are culturally derived from western classical art models and European histories, presents other problems as well. A kind of informal scavenger hunt occurs both on-line and off as directors scramble to find 'one multicultural piece' to programme in their concerts (Rotjan, 2017). Also, the critical need for a more diverse concert repertoire has produced arrangements that often stray from their cultural originals, papering over nuanced understanding of difference and context (Olson, 2014). Consider the strange case of the female Japanese composer Keiko Yamada, who wrote pieces for middle school orchestra using lovely melodies evocative of Asian folk tunes. Yamada's titles include *Hotaka Sunset*, *Tales of the Kojiki*, and *Kon'nichiwa*, the latter of which is described in publishers' websites this way:

> *This piece is like saying 'hello', with a smile on your face. It is meant to be simply delightful for the youngest of string students. The melodic material is based on the pentatonic scale, and all of the material is within reach of students who have only played a short time. Keiko Yamada continues to offer exceptional pieces for the youngest of students* (Sheetmusicplus).

Orchestra directors rushed to buy works by Yamada; some integrated histories of Japan and discussions of Asian culture into their rehearsals; she was seen as an exemplar for budding female composers (Rotjan, 2017). Except that Keiko Yamada was neither female nor Japanese, but a pen name invented by a white male American composer with the real name of Larry Clark.

> **Activity 2.2**
>
> Take some time to conduct a survey, or audit, of all the music you are working on with your pupils. Consider various ways of categorizing this repertoire, perhaps recording the genre, nationality, period, style, etc. of the pieces. Also think about the composers – gender, ethnicity, etc. Do you think the balance you have is right – or do you want to make changes, and if so why?
>
> Then select one piece that in your context broadens the musical possibilities for your students and examine it. How did the composer write in relation to the historical and ethnographic context of the piece? What traditions of musical practice can be explored through this piece? What potential problems arise?

Teachers in Search of New Pedagogies

The reconceptualization of a music curriculum for instrumental music, one that is larger than representation or repertoire alone, asks 'music educators to recast beliefs and practices, rather than merely improving and refining traditional programs, materials, and organizational patterns of the field' (Barrett, 2007: 148). Going beyond tokenism or exoticism requires what Slattery (1995) terms a 'kaleidoscopic sensibility', whereby insights into how others see and hear the world shift and realign within a 'vast, interrelated web of ideas, texts, personalities, architectural structures, stories, and much more' (pp. 243-244). Ladson-Billings (2014), whose culturally relevant framework once suggested an essentialist understanding of race and ethnicity, now calls for greater attention to the fluid and dynamic nature of culture and identity.

Revising her early theory, she writes now with greater appreciation for intersectionality and change: 'in popular culture, there is always an expectation that someone or something will come along and move a cultural form to another level' (76). Whether we talk about culturally relevant pedagogy (Ladson-Billings, 1995), culturally responsive learning (Gay, 2018), or culturally sustaining teaching (Paris and Alim, 2017), consequence and applicability remain our *sine qua non*. Relevance, however, is always a moving target, and thus efforts must be sustained across conditions that both *do not* change (e.g. the colour of one's skin) and conditions that *do* (e.g. meanings and significations associated with sub-cultures and cultural artifacts/forms). This way of teaching is not easy, of course, considering that the majority of music teachers study, perform, and listen to music that is different from the tastes of their students (Kruse, 2015).

Perhaps the most significant pedagogical trend that emerged after the publication of *How Popular Musicians Learn* was the integration of informal learning processes into formal instrumental music curricula (Wright and Kanellopoulos, 2010; Green 2008; Westerlund, 2006). 'If there is any strength in the [informal] approach', Green writes:

> . . . *it must lie in the fact that the [pedagogical] strategies were developed by learners, through learning, rather than by teachers through teaching. They derive, not from a theory of learning drawn from an experimental or formal educational situation, or from an analysis of a musical outcome, but from the observation and analysis of real-life learning practices by musicians in the world outside formal education* (Green, 2008: 22).

At its core, efforts to include more aspects of informal learning in instrumental music pedagogies were aimed at the twin problems of identity and relevance, thus creating more opportunities for student access and inclusion. 'In order to more thoroughly or accurately reflect pupils' musical identities', Green writes, 'it seems appropriate to give pupils some autonomy to select curriculum content for themselves: that is, to choose the music they work on in class' (Green, 2008: 13). For Green, an immediate benefit of informal pedagogies in formal spaces is that

> . . . *pupil-selection of curriculum content breaks down the reproductive effects of many previous music curricula, which by ignoring the musical identities and tastes of vast numbers of pupils prevented many of them from demonstrating or even discovering their musical abilities* (Green 2008: 13).

Activity 2.3

With some or all of your pupils introduce a project where they are going to find a piece they want to play and learn to play it. They can use as many resources as they like – videos, self-help tutorials, music, etc. Explain that you will provide any support they ask for, but make it clear that this is their project, and you will not be assessing progress, nagging about practice, etc. Keep a diary with brief notes on their growth musically, socially, and holistically. In what ways did identity and relevance enter into this new pedagogical space? How did your role as teacher change? What value does this add to a music curriculum? What challenges arose?

Drawing upon sociological and anthropological principles, and combining these perspectives with extant research on informal learning, Green designed one of the largest and most innovative curriculum projects in the 21st century: Musical Futures.

Musical Futures

Musical Futures is a non-profit education provider in the United Kingdom that gives shape to Green's research through funding from the Paul Hamlyn Foundation, an 'independent funder working to help people overcome disadvantage and lack of opportunity, so that they can realize their potential and enjoy fulfilling and creative lives' (Musical Futures, 2019). In their words, they are promoting a 'tried-and-tested, yet innovative approach to music learning, based on a pedagogy that is driven by the musical culture of the participants' (Musical Futures, 2019). The organization partners with U.K. schools to provide support for music instruction, new learning systems, professional development, and physical resources – but Musical Futures is *not* described as a curriculum. Core values are defined as inclusive, absorbing, relevant, sociable, informal, varied, progressive, and respectful (Musical Futures, 2019).

In Musical Futures, the design of learning – not *teaching* – is structured around three levels. The *JustPlay* level is for children aged 8-14 years old. The teacher is described as a leader, but they are expected to foster musical exploration through a sound-before-symbol aural methodology, allowing for the growth of instrumental skills as they are needed by the student, not as they are directed by the teacher. Whole class instruction necessarily involves a great deal of group improvisation. The *Non-Formal Teaching* level is for learners aged 8-18, and while the approach still has a musical leader, the music that is made is co-constructed with students through a total immersion in listening and self-study. As students grow through the programme, they can become involved in the *Informal Learning* option, where the teacher's purpose is to 'stand back, empathize with learner goals, [and] act as a musical model and resource' (Musical Futures, 2019). On this level, the students are in almost complete control, choosing everything from the music they want to learn to the ways in which they want to rehearse and perform.

Inspired by Musical Futures, research on popular music, and the imperative to reach more students, a new phenomenon has recently emerged in North American instrumental music education often coined the Modern Band movement. Advocates of Modern Band bring popular music-making and informal learning processes into public schools as a way to enlarge, perhaps even compete with, the hegemony of the traditional North American concert band system. Recalling Milner's notion of opportunity-thinking, popular music has created an ethos of exploration and problem-solving, an ethos that stands in sharp contrast to the discourse of excellence that is prevalent in traditional band communities. Improvisation and composing, in particular, provide learners with greater experiences being autonomous and connected.

In a study by West and Cremata (2016: 80), learning popular music is haphazard and fun, but richly experienced according to participants.

> One time, we all messed up at the end – one instrument went out, a second instrument went out, and then they just all floated out at the end. And [Doug] was like, 'That was pretty cool!' And we all sat back and laughed and said, 'That was pretty awesome'.

For Wright and Kanellopoulos, 'the educational potential of improvisation is linked to the project of autonomy. Learning to set the rules through interaction and not through reference to some universal musical norm is what improvisation might offer to education' (2010: 80). The voices of their participants are compelling. 'When you are given due respect as a human being and as a personality, you can create from the simplest to the most elaborate piece of music' (81). For facilitators, the richest insights were not just 'learning to improvise on a variety of musical instruments, but most importantly, learning to improvise in [building] our relationship towards a child/student' (81).

Modern Band can also be considered in neoliberal terms, as a kind of 'disruption', a way to break apart what backers see as change-resistant traditional pedagogies and aesthetic forms. As a means to break the status quo, deregulation has become an essential ingredient in U.S. education policy reform, opening up space for private organizations to fix public problems. Similar to Musical Futures, independent non-profit providers are leaned upon to help schools make the change they can't seem to make themselves, circumventing research universities and the university's traditional role in regulating practice and certifying teachers. Little Kids Rock and their affiliates provide a cautionary example.

In 1996, after the loss of arts funding at his school, music teacher David Wish began to offer extra-curricular guitar classes to any child who wished to participate. Within six years, word of his student-centered and popular music-based curriculum spread. Wish gained support from well-known musicians like Carlos Santana, Bonnie Raitt, John Lee Hooker and others. Thus was Little Kids Rock formed. In 2014, Amp Up, a privately-funded non-profit organization, was initiated to move Little Kids Rock away from its free-wheeling extra-curricular roots to become a more systematic programme that New York City teachers could apply in K-12 music classes during the instructional day. To expand, Little Kids Rock and Amp Up partnered with the Berklee College of Music, accessing and promoting their online collection of popular music lesson plans and resource materials called Berklee PULSE. Amp Up's main objective is to provide their mostly classically-trained music teachers with training in classroom instruction and online technology, and help with learning popular music instruments. Teachers who work in low-income schools receive all resources, including a cadre of instruments, at no cost.

Amp Up's arrival in New York City schools coincided with a stinging report that unveiled the declining state of arts education in the city's public school system (Stringer, 2014). While the Department of Education places values on an arts education, it is largely because of its ability to teach so-called 21st century job skills, and the effects these creative skills bring to the vitality of the local economy. Also noted was the disparity of arts teachers in schools located in the poorest areas of the city. As a staggering statistic, more than 42% of the schools in the South Bronx and Central Brooklyn did not have a certified music teacher.

Amp Up has five core objectives: to redefine relevant educational programming, reach and engage more children in music education, provide teacher training and professional development, improve academic achievement and increase positive pathways for students, and to stabilize and systemize operations in New York City Department of Education music programmes. Their plan is rooted in children's knowledge of popular music forms such as rock, pop, blues, hip-hop, country, reggae, and R&B, while preparing teachers to offer classes that use Modern Band methods and materials. It should be noted, however, that in spite of its innovative content, Amp Up and Little Kids Rock have aligned their organizations with highly traditional policies that may prevent radical changes in pedagogy, such as the NYCDOE Blueprint for Teaching and Learning in Music, the Danielson Framework for teacher evaluation, and the National Arts Standards and Common Core Standards. PULSE, furthermore, has lists of objectives, standards, and assessments associated with each unit and level, focusing on traditional 'elements' like form, rhythm, melody, and harmony. Popular music argues for new pedagogies, multi-modal forms of learning, alternate visions of teacher quality, and new relationships to knowledge and learning. Fitting new content into existing frameworks does not automatically challenge the structural problems that prevent access and create learner relevance.

Lingering Thoughts

After the great disruption of popular music research and its gradual integration into schools and universities, it can be argued that a kind of professional calm has settled into the field of instrumental music education. Music teachers are still needed; large ensembles are stable, if not growing; and more music educators are comfortable working across styles and genres. It is a relief to report that popular music has not 'destroyed' our traditional programmes, but nor has it revolutionized pedagogy. If popular music is taught in the same teacher-directed, master-apprentice method that classical music seems trapped in, what have we gained beyond a change in course content?

Our questions are new and perennial: (1) Who gets access to a quality instrumental music education, and who does not? (2) How is what we offer culturally and personally relevant to those students who are currently not involved? (3) What role can universities and non-profits play in helping shape the aforementioned transformation? Alternate providers will continue to fill in gaps, as will teaching artists in large cities, but neither can scale up to reach all students everywhere. Global programmes like El Sistema and Musical Futures International will need continued research and programme evaluation as they adapt to the local communities in which they locate. Popular music, specifically hip-hop, might lead the way in helping design more sophisticated notions of teacher quality, learner criticality, and student-centred learning. Instrumental music educators must continue to insert more composition and improvisation into all classrooms and rehearsal spaces. And finally, no matter the genre, tradition, or school and community setting, we must constantly consider ways to include more students in music and to help them feel represented in the work they do.

Activity 2.4

A recurring theme in music education literature is the positive impact on learning that can be gained from giving learners more control and influence over their own learning. Try to place your own approach on a scale where 1 = my students' learning is set out and directed by me, and 10 = my students control their own learning which I facilitate. What particular activities from your lessons fall at the extreme ends of this scale? What do you think might be the benefits of giving pupils greater agency over their musical learning? What changes in pedagogy need to occur in order to effectively facilitate student-led activities?

References

Abramo, J. M. (2011) Gender differences of popular music production in secondary schools. *Journal of Research in Education*, 59(1), pp. 21-43.

Abril, C. R. (2010) Openings spaces in the instrumental music classroom. In: A. C. Clements, ed. *Alternative Approaches in Music Education: Case Studies from the Field* (3-14). Washington, D.C.: Rowman & Littlefield Education.

Allsup, R. E. (2003) Mutual learning and democratic action in instrumental music education. *Journal of Research in Music Education*, 51(1), pp. 24-37.

Allsup, R. E. (2008) Creating an educational framework for popular music in public schools: Anticipating the second-wave. *Visions of Research in Music Education*, 12(1), pp. 1-12.

Allsup, R. E. (2012) The moral ends of band. *Theory into Practice*, 51(3), pp. 179-187.

Allsup, R. E. and Benedict, C. (2008) The problems of band: An inquiry into the future of instrumental music education. *Philosophy of Music Education Review*, 16(2), pp. 156-173.

Allsup, R. E. and Olson, N. (2012) New educational frameworks for popular music and informal learning: Anticipating the second-wave. In: S. Karlsen and L. Väkevä, eds. *Future Prospects for Music Education: Corroborating Informal Learning Pedagogy*, Cambridge, UK: Cambridge Scholar, pp. 11-21.

Barrett J. R. (2007) Currents of Change in the Music Curriculum. In: L. Bresler, ed. *International Handbook of Research in Arts Education*. New York, NY: Springer International Publications, pp. 147-162.

Butler, A., Lind, V. and McKoy, C. (2007) Equity and access in music education: conceptualizing culture as barriers to and supports for music learning. *Music Education Research*, 9(2), pp. 241-253. https://doi-org.ezproxy.cul.columbia.edu/10.1080/14613800701384375

Brown, D. J. (2010) Band as Reflective Collaboration – Advancing an Alternative Rehearsal Paradigm. *The Finnish Journal of Music Education*, 13(2), pp. 8-16.

Campbell, P. S., Connell, C. and Beegle, A. (2007) Adolescents' Expressed Meaning of Music In and Out of School. *Journal of Research in Music Education*, 55(3), pp. 220-36.

Elpus, K. and Abril, C. R. (2011) High school music ensemble students in the United States: A demographic profile. *Journal of Research in Music Education*, 59(2), pp. 128-145.

Elpus, K. and Abril, C. R. (2019) Who Enrolls in High School Music? A National Profile of US Students, 2009-2013. *Journal of Research in Music Education*, 67(3) pp. 323-338.

Fonder. M. (2014) Another Perspective: No Default or Reset Necessary – Large Ensembles Enrich Many, *Music Educators Journal*, 101(2), p. 89.

Gay, G. (2018) *Culturally Responsive Pedagogies: Theory, Research, Practice*. New York: Teachers College Press.

Georgii-Hemming, E. and Westvall, M. (2010) Music education–a personal matter? Examining the current discourses of music education in Sweden. *British Journal of Music Education*, 27(1) pp. 21-33.

Green, L. (2002) *How Popular Musicians Learn*. Farnham, UK: Ashgate.

Green, L. (2008) *Music, Informal Learning, and the School*. Farnham, UK: Ashgate.

Hansen, R. (2004) *The American Wind Band: A Cultural History*. Chicago, IL: GIA Publications.

Henry, M. (2005) An analysis of certification practices for music educators in the fifty states. *Journal of Music Teacher Education*, 14(2), pp. 47-61.

Hess, J. (2013) Performing the "Exotic?": Constructing an ethical world music ensemble. *Visions of Research in Music Education*, 23.

Hess, J. (2019) *Music Education for Social Change: Constructing an Activist Music Education*. New York: Routledge Press.

Humphreys, J. T. (1995) Instrumental music in American education: In service of many masters. *Journal of Band Research*, 30(2), pp. 39-70.

Kallio, A. A. and Väkevä, L. (2017) Inclusive Popular Music Education? In: F. Holt and A. Kärjä, eds., *The Oxford handbook of popular music in the Nordic countries*, Oxford, UK: Oxford University Press, pp. 75-91.

Kratus, J. (2007) Music Education at the Tipping Point. *Music Educators Journal*, 94(2), pp. 42-48.

Ladson-Billings, G. (1995) But that's just good teaching! The case for culturally relevant pedagogy. *Theory into Practice*, 34(3), pp. 159-165.

Ladson-Billings, G. (2014) Culturally relevant pedagogy 2.0: aka the remix. *Harvard Educational Review*, 84(1), pp. 74-84.

Mantie, R. (2012) Bands and/as Music Education: Antinomies and the Struggle for Legitimacy, *Philosophy of Music Education Review*, 20(1), pp. 63-68.

Mark, M. and Gary, C. L. (2007) *A history of American music education*. New York: Rowman & Littlefield Education.

Milner, H. R. (2012) Opportunity gaps in education. *Journal of Black Studies*, 43(6), pp.693-718.

Musical Futures (2019) *Musical Futures*. Available at: https://www.musicalfutures.org

Olson, Nathaniel J. (2014) *The institutionalization of fiddling in higher education: Three cases*. New York: Teachers College Press.

Paris, D. and H. S. Alim (2017) *Culturally Sustaining Pedagogies: Teaching and Learning for Justice in a Changing World*. New York: Teachers College Press.

Reynolds, H. Robert (2000) Repertoire *is* the curriculum. *Music Educators Journal*, 87(1), pp. 31-33.

Rodriguez C., ed. (2004) B*ridging the Gap: Popular Music and Music Education*, Reston, VI: MENC.

Rotjan, M. S. (2017) *In-Between and Together With: Exploring the Complexity of Repertoire Selection with School Orchestra Teachers and Their Students*. Doctor of Education, Thesis. Teachers College, Columbia University.

Sala-i-Martin, X. (2002) The disturbing "rise" of global income inequality (No. w8904). National Bureau of Economic Research.

Salvador, K. and Kelly-McHale, J. (2017) Music Teacher Educator Perspectives on Social Justice. *Journal of Research in Music Education*, 65(1), pp. 6-24. https://doi.org/10.1177/0022429417690340

Salvador, K. and Allegood, K. (2014) Access to Music Education with Regard to Race in Two Urban Areas. *Arts Education Policy Review*, 115(3), pp. 82-92. https://doi-org.ezproxy.cul.columbia.edu/10.1080/10632913.2014.914389

Scheib, J. W. (2006) Lindy's Story: One Student's Experience in Middle School Band, *Music Educators Journal*, 92(5), pp. 32-36.

Sheetmusicplus. (2020) *Konnichiwa* Available at:
https://www.sheetmusicplus.com/title/konnichiwa-so0-5-sc-pts-sheet-music/21611508

Shively, J. L. (1989) Musical Thinking and Learning in the Beginning Instrumental Music Classroom. In: E. Boardman, ed. *Dimensions of Musical Learning and Thinking*. Reston, VI: MENC, pp. 169–184.

Slattery, P. (1995) *Curriculum development in the postmodern era*. New York: Garland.

Stringer, S. M. (2014) *State of the arts: A plan to boost arts education in New York City schools*. Available at: https://comptroller.nyc.gov/reports/state-of-the-arts-a-plan-to-boost-arts-education-in-new-york-city-schools/

Tobias, E. S. (2013) Toward convergence: Adapting music education to contemporary society and participatory culture. *Music Educators Journal*, 99(4), pp. 29–36.

West, C. and Cremata, R. (2016). Bringing the outside in: Blending formal and informal through acts of hospitality. *Journal of Research in Music Education*, 64(1), pp. 71–87.

Westerlund, H. (2006) Garage rock bands: a future model for developing musical expertise? *International Journal of Music Education*, 24(2), pp. 119–125.

Williams, D. A. (2007) What are Music Educators Doing and How Well are They Doing It? *Music Educators Journal*, 94(1), pp. 18–23.

Williams, D. A. (2011) The Elephant in the Room. *Music Educators Journal*, 98(1), pp. 51–57.

Wright, R. and Kanellopoulos, P. (2010) Informal music learning, improvisation and teacher education. *British Journal of Music Education*, 27(1), pp. 71–87.

Chapter 3 Commentary

So far in this book we have looked back to see what the past can tell us about instrumental learning and have looked at the changing context for that learning. Chapter 3 now goes on to explore some of the current research which is relevant to instrumental learning and how it might inform practice. A premise of this book is that there is much in music education research that could help teachers improve the experience of their pupils. However, it can be a challenge for teachers to access such research, to know where to look, and to be able to find areas of research directly relevant to their situation.

Like Allsup and Nicholson in Chapter 2, Andrea Creech raises some important challenges for instrumental teachers. In 2021 she suggested that research into instrumental music learning demonstrates 'a continuing preponderance of the traditional one-to-one master apprentice model, characterised by unidirectional teaching and somewhat passive learning'. The research covered in this chapter has predominantly taken place since 2012, giving a very contemporary view on how instrumental music teaching and learning has responded, or might respond, to some of the challenges learners and teachers now face.

Clearly the research field is huge, and it is beyond the scope of a single chapter to provide a comprehensive overview. The author helpfully structures the chapter under four headings to help orient the reader, broadly summarised as: student learning, relationships and collaboration, access and visibility, and teacher development. Under each heading Creech considers a number of current research perspectives with a brief summary of the findings of each and their relevance for teachers. She ends her chapter with a call to action in the 'critical questioning of the traditional master-apprentice approach in instrumental learning, for example focusing on facilitative teaching, creativity, collaboration, autonomy, self-regulation and even empowerment'. These concepts will emerge again in future chapters and provide an appropriate end point for Part 1.

Although there will be much to be gained from a through reading, the chapter may also be considered as providing a series of jumping off points for further enquiry. As such it might be something to return to again once you have read the other chapters. It also has a bibliography that provides useful pointers for teachers to some of the most important areas of research relevant to instrumental music learning. Towards the end of this chapter you will find a table that sets out some practical lesson activities which are related to each of the sections in the chapter, alongside an invitation to further populate this list with examples of your own. In this way the chapter demonstrates a clear link between academic research and classroom practice.

3 Instrumental Music Teaching: Contemporary Research Perspectives

Andrea Creech

Introduction

Although arguably still an under-investigated area of music education, in recent years researchers have paid increasing attention to instrumental learning and teaching. This chapter provides an overview of recent research in this domain, highlighting the implications for instrumental education. In doing so the chapter will introduce many of the main themes to be explored in the book's subsequent sections.

I begin the chapter with a brief discussion of some methodological approaches that researchers have taken in their efforts to contribute to knowledge concerned with how and why we learn to play musical instruments – and who has access to such learning. I follow this with a short summary of some of the themes and pedagogical issues that have been researched in the context of one-to-one instrumental learning and teaching over the past three decades. I then turn to the most contemporary perspectives, introducing the idea of 'transformational learning', which in recent years (e.g. since 2012) has gained much traction in research and pedagogy. The remainder of the chapter is organised around four principles that have been said to be fundamental considerations in transformative instrumental education, namely: 1) what is important to student learning within specific contexts, 2) relational issues within communities of learners, 3) making teaching visible, via accessible and achievable alternative pedagogical strategies, and 4) opportunities for professional growth among teachers.

In each of these sections, I use examples drawn from research concerned with instrumental learning across a range of contexts, including those concerned with school-aged pupils and adults as well as those concerned with more advanced students in tertiary music institutions. Arguably, instrumental teachers have themselves often come through tertiary music education and furthermore often teach in a number of different kinds of educational contexts (e.g. home studio, school, community groups, junior conservatoire, tertiary institution), transferring their pedagogical experience and practices from one context to another. Therefore, I conclude the chapter with some summary discussion points, pedagogical applications and reflective questions concerned with the broad implications of contemporary research perspectives that may have relevance across a continuum of contexts for instrumental learning and teaching.

Research Methodologies

As any instrumental teacher or learner knows, instrumental education occurs within diverse real-world contexts, subject to a myriad of environmental, social, cultural, interpersonal and intrapersonal variables. It is therefore perhaps appropriate that research in this domain is dominated by qualitative methodologies that seek to generate rich representations of processes and practices and that aim to represent the experience of teachers and learners alike, as well as the perspectives of families, educational institutions and policy. Within the broad 'qualitative' paradigm, researchers have increasingly exploited the possibilities offered by video observations of teaching and learning (e.g. Burnard and Dragovic, 2015; Coutts, 2018; Kooistra, 2016; Kupers et al., 2017; Miksza et al., 2018). Others have employed phenomenological approaches that aim for authentic representations of the perspectives and beliefs of teachers and learners (e.g. de Bruin, 2017; Roulston et al., 2015); narrative approaches to analyses of interview data that seek to understand instrumental learning in relation to participants' life stories (Laes, 2015); and thematic analyses of participant and researcher reflective journals (e.g. Coutts, 2018; Meissner, 2017).

Alternatively, intervention studies are typically designed in order to test participants' performance on an intended outcome (e.g. their proficiency in sight reading; creativity in composition tasks; aural skills; etc.) which is measured before and after the implementation of some 'new' pedagogical strategy (Baker and Green, 2013; Boucher et al., 2019; Miksza et al., 2018; Ritchie and Kearney, 2018). Correlational studies have also been carried out, where attitudes, beliefs or pedagogical practices or approaches to learning are measured at one point in time using a questionnaire approach (e.g. Hallam, 2013; Moscardini et al., 2013). Intervention or correlational studies, which are therefore concerned primarily with the collection of quantitative, numerical measures, often use some qualitative approaches to complement the quantitative data. These so-called 'mixed-method' approaches contribute to our deep understandings of the complex interrelationships between pedagogical processes and learning outcomes.

Participant observation where researchers observe the practices of a group in which they have participated (e.g. Andrews, 2013) and ethnographic research where researchers live for an extended period as one of the 'researched' community (e.g. as in Baker's 2014 ethnographic study of El Sistema), while less prominent in the research to date, offer great potential in relation to bridging research with practice concerned with instrumental education.

Finally, action research, where teachers engage in cycles of reflective practice in researching their own practice, usually with the intention of solving problems or developing new and innovative pedagogies (e.g. Blackwell and Roseth, 2018; Meissner, 2017), is a powerful representation of the quest to bring about transformational change in instrumental learning and teaching.

> **Activity 3.1**
>
> In this section you have read about three main research methodologies:
>
> ▶ Qualitative studies
> ▶ Intervention studies
> ▶ Participation studies and ethnographic research
>
> Begin by thinking carefully about the differences between these three approaches. Then consider how each approach might help you to address a question about learning and teaching in your own professional context.

The Contemporary Context for Research in Instrumental Education

In 2012 I argued that instrumental teaching had at that time changed very little, notwithstanding 'advances in our understanding of effective learning and teaching, changing patterns of engagement with music, growing cultural diversity and change relating to globalisation and technology' (Creech and Gaunt, 2012, pp. 694). At that point, research concerned with instrumental education, particularly within the western classical paradigm, pointed to a continuing preponderance of the traditional one-to-one master apprentice model, characterised by unidirectional teaching and somewhat passive learning. This focus on the master-apprentice approach had been reiterated by a corpus of studies including (for example) those exploring interpersonal (Gaunt, 2010; Presland, 2005) and motivational issues (McPherson and McCormick, 1999), deliberate practice (Ericsson, Krampe, and Tesch-Römer, 1993; Jørgensen, 2002), pedagogical approaches (Burwell 2006), beliefs about instrumental teaching (Mills, 2006), and parental involvement (Creech and Hallam, 2009).

More recently, Simones (2017: 254) highlighted a pressing need to consider how a transformational approach to instrumental learning might be articulated, 'which should include a vision for instrumental/vocal teachers considering: what they are, do in society and how they can achieve their mission'. Transformational learning is conceptualized here as a process involving the construction of knowledge through deeply reflective learning that supports critical thinking, resulting in fundamental and potentially profound changes in perspective (Nerstorm, 2017). The idea of transformational instrumental learning and teaching builds upon the work of Carey, Grant, McWilliam and Taylor (2013), who proposed four underpinning principles of pedagogical capacity-building in the domain of instrumental education: 1) what is important to student learning within specific contexts, 2) relational issues within communities of learners, 3) making teaching visible, via accessible and achievable alternative pedagogical strategies, and 4) opportunities for professional growth among teachers.

In this chapter – written pre-Covid-19 pandemic in December 2019 – I therefore address the question of where we have come since 2012. I provide an overview of the ways in which research concerned with instrumental education, framed by the principles proposed by Carey et al. (2013), has responded to Simones' (2017) call for action with regards to a transformational approach. Accordingly, in the following sections I identify some prominent research themes, and several corresponding key concepts and contexts that have been explored.

What is Important to Student Learning

Practising, self-regulation and self-directed learning

The idea that 'practice makes perfect' has long been critiqued and contested among researchers concerned with instrumental learning and teaching. Our understandings of the characteristics of effective practising have been shaped by the seminal research carried out in the 1990s concerned with deliberate practice and the associated constraints of time spent practising, resource, effort and motivation (Ericsson et al., 1993; Hallam, 1998; Sloboda, Davidson, Howe and Moore, 1996). Practising has continued as a prominent research theme, but with a shift in focus towards 'quality', including conceptual thinking, strategies and self-directed learning.

In this vein, much recent research concerned with practising has been underpinned by an increasing emphasis on the pedagogies that can support self-directed strategies (Uygun and Kilinçer, 2015; 2017) and autonomous learning in relation to motivation and student engagement. Complex relationships between quality as well as quantity of practice, time spent learning, motivation and expertise have been explored. For example, Hallam (2013) undertook a correlational questionnaire study involving 163 school-aged learners of a range of orchestral instruments. While reinforcing the importance of overall time spent learning and quantity of practice in relation to the development of expertise, Hallam raised some critical questions regarding the factors that may support self-directed learning.

Subsequent research has provided evidence in support of the view that support for reflective problem-solving approaches (Blackwell and Roseth, 2018; dos Santos, 2018; Nielsen, 2015) and intentional use of practice strategies (Mieder and Bugos, 2017) can enhance deeper cognitive engagement in instrumental learning.

Theoretical understandings of self-regulated instrumental learning have continued to be developed. Focusing on quality of practice, Miksza and Tan (2015) undertook a questionnaire study involving 241 higher education wind players and 52 teachers, highlighted the role of grit (referring to the capacity to complete short-term goals yet also persevere towards long-term goals), flow and reflection in the cyclical self-regulatory processes of forethought, performance, and self-reflection (McPherson and Renwick, 2001). In a later study, Miksza, Blackwell and Roseth (2018) adopted an in-depth microanalytic approach to studying music self-regulation, revealing learner profiles that varied in terms of affective, cognitive, and behavioral elements at each stage in the self-regulation cycle. The same authors highlighted that personalized coaching in self-regulation strategies could effect positive change in practising.

This study by Miksza and colleagues complements the work of Green (2012) concerned with individual learning styles and learning strategies, and Nielsen (2012) who explored tertiary learner profiles based on epistemic beliefs (i.e. beliefs about how knowledge and skills are acquired). A key finding from Nielsen was that learners who held 'sophisticated' epistemic beliefs, whereby ability is thought to be malleable and responsive to effort, were more likely to engage in metacognitive self-regulatory practices as compared with their counterparts who held 'naïve' epistemic beliefs that supported the view of fixed ability. Nielsen's study has important implications for teachers of school-aged pupils, as it is in the formative years of study that instrumental learners develop their epistemic beliefs, which are likely to be shaped by pedagogical models and approaches (López-Íñiguez and Pozo, 2014). Collectively, the studies discussed above point to the need for further research concerned with the nature of best practices in integrating musical self-regulation coaching into instrumental education.

> **Activity 3.2**
>
> The focus of this section has been on 'self-regulated' practice. In other words how instrumental learners organise their practice, remain motivated and make progress through individual practice that is not directly monitored by a teacher.
>
> What are the strategies that you adopt or the advice or techniques that you give your pupils to help them make the most of their individual practice time? Note these down.
>
> Try and gain access to one of the papers cited and read what it says about developing instrumental learners practice strategies and consider ways in which you might draw on these in your own context.

Inclusivity

The right to access music learning has been recognised internationally (UNESCO, 2010). In this vein, in England (for example) a focus on inclusivity has been articulated by the National Music Plan (DfE and DMCS, 2011) where the stated aim was to 'enable children from all backgrounds and every part of England to have the opportunity to learn a musical instrument; to make music with others; to learn to sing; and to have the opportunity to progress to the next level of excellence' (p. 9). Among the research community, questions have been raised relating to who has access to instrumental learning and what the optimal teaching processes are that meet the needs of all students (Laes and Westerlund, 2018; McCord and Watts, 2006).

However, there have been few studies focused specifically on inclusivity in instrumental learning, and yet some published evidence suggests that there continues to be under-representation of students with additional special needs in formal instrumental instruction. For example, Moscardini, Barron and Wilson (2013) surveyed 21 Scottish schools, revealing normative beliefs about musical achievement and explicit as well as 'hidden' recruitment and selection processes that may have excluded particular groups and explained for example why there was not one student with a physical disability among the 323 instrumental learners. This study lends support to the call for an 'expanded professionalism' that reinforces the idea that 'today's music teacher education cannot rely solely on normative teaching methods, both in terms of practice and in the conceptual thinking of expertise and professionalism' (Laes and Westerlund, 2018: 42).

Long term participation

Alongside an interest in inclusive practices has been a growing interest in the factors that may mitigate barriers to instrumental learning and therefore be predictive of continuing (even lifelong) engagement with music participation. The interest in continuing and inclusive participation in instrumental learning is in part linked to the wider social emotional benefits associated with learning musical instruments (Osborne, McPherson, Faulkner, Davidson and Barrett, 2016).

In addition to a great deal of research concerned with the learning outcomes associated with practice strategies, self-regulation, and creative, collaborative pedagogies (discussed elsewhere in this chapter), there is some evidence to suggest that affinity for music, value placed on music in the family home, and support for the development of a long-term musical possible self are significant predictors of continuing participation (Creech, Varvarigou and Hallam, 2020; Evans and McPherson, 2014; Krupp-Schleußner and Lehmann-Wermser, 2018; StGeorge, Holbrook, and Cantwell, 2014). For example, StGeorge et al. (2014) interviewed 17 primary school-aged instrumental learners, 17 tertiary music performance students, as well as 32 younger and older adults from the community who had learnt instruments at school. The researchers found that across all three groups, affinity for music was fostered through music-making with others and in turn had a positive influence on motivation. A later study (Krupp-Schleußner and Lehmann-Wermser, 2018) used a survey approach to explore the factors that may have contributed to continuing participation in instrumental learning among 529 German instrumental learners aged 11-12 years. The children were participants in a government-funded, school-based programme that aimed to enable children, irrespective of socio-economic status, to learn an instrument, express themselves through music and develop their musical identities. The researchers reported that 'affinity for music' and 'importance of music at home' (measured by questionnaire responses) were both predictors of continuation in learning an instrument and for overall musical involvement. However, children with migrant backgrounds were less likely to continue learning in secondary school, as compared with those without a migrant background, suggesting that:

> *In migrant contexts, musical participation and education might have to be promoted differently by integrating the families as well as their cultural backgrounds much more in the educational process. The deliberate integration of culturally relevant songs, music and instruments might additionally characterise a good music education programme* (Krupp-Schleußner and Lehmann-Wermser 2018: 45).

Therefore, while drop-out may be mitigated when lessons are organised around optimally challenging tasks that support a belief in competence, provide opportunities for peer relationships to flourish, and include the scope for students to experience autonomous decision making (Evans, McPherson and Davidson, 2013), research also suggests that the wider context, including family environment and cultural background, can influence or complement what is achieved between the learner and teacher.

Adult learners

The advent of lifelong learning (Smilde and Bisschop, 2016) has emerged alongside new knowledge about brain plasticity (Wan and Schlaug, 2010) and within a context characterised by extraordinary demographic change in the form of an ageing population (Beard et al., 2016). We are now considering the possibility that learning a musical instrument is no longer solely within youth-oriented contexts. Increasingly, we have seen examples of people learning instruments across the adult lifespan, fostering a growing interest in the idea that adults, irrespective of prior musical experience, have the capacity for musical development and for acquiring instrumental skills (Laes, 2015). Concurrently, there has been a growth in research concerned with how pedagogues might respond appropriately, focusing around questions concerned with how adults can best be supported in instrumental learning (Creech, Hallam, Varvarigou and McQueen, 2014; Roulston, Jutras and Kim, 2015).

Much of the literature concerned with adult learners, and in particular older adults, is positioned around the idea of music for health and wellbeing (e.g. Creech et al., 2014; Ellis, 2018). However, collectively, the research carried out to date touches on many themes that are represented in the literature concerned with instrumental teaching and learning more widely. In other words, issues that are salient with younger learners continue to be relevant, irrespective of the learners' ages.

For example, Perkins, Aufegger, and Williamon (2015) highlighted the value of high quality, personalised and flexible pedagogies, underscoring the importance of finding links to the learners' own past experiences and prior knowledge. Collaborative and dialogic student-teacher interactions were found to be an underpinning principle of efficacious piano instruction with adults, promoting the space for autonomous and self-directed learning (Coutts, 2018). In a similar vein, Laes (2015) has highlighted the capacity for older adults to learn rock band instruments through a democratic and flexible approach that allows opportunities for individuals to express musical agency.

Improvisation and playing by ear have been found to be instructional strategies associated with transformational learning among adult instrumental students (Hartz and Bauer, 2016). After eight weekly improvisation sessions, ten adult amateur musicians reported increased musical self-efficacy, enjoyment, and a deeper knowledge of musical structure. Finally, Ritchie and Kearney (2018) reported that adult instrumental learners, supported by a worksheet designed to encourage novice adult musicians to structure and implement self-regulated practice strategies, did engage in a self-regulatory cycle. In brief, the evidence to date supports the view that progressive approaches in instrumental teaching that focus on collaborative, personalized, creative, and self-regulated learning can support transformational learning among learners of all ages, across the lifecourse.

> ### Activity 3.3
> What do you think are the differences between teaching instruments to young people/children and adults? In your experience, what influences do past experiences have on adult learners' attitudes and approaches to and reasons for learning an instrument?

Making Teaching Visible – Alternative Pedagogical Strategies

Musicianship

A continuing strong emphasis on individual approaches to acquiring instrumental technique has been highlighted (Hallam, 2013) leading to potential gaps in our knowledge concerned with musicianship and the place of creative and collaborative activities in instrumental learning. It is not surprising then that increasing attention has turned to pedagogies that can support the development of musicianship.

Musicianship has been explored from a number of perspectives, for example highlighting the potential for singing to support instrumental learners in developing creative strategies and an interpretive voice (Wallace, 2014). Similarly, strategies for teaching expressive playing have been researched (Meissner, 2017), lending support for a model of efficacious pedagogical strategies that includes enquiry (asking open questions and promoting problem-solving) and discussion about musical character, alongside explanations of how to use technique to translate expressive ideas into sound. Research concerned with supporting expressivity in playing has also been framed by the idea that deep learning may require new ways of teaching and learning that involve the entire body in musical responses (Gruhn, 2021).

One predominant strand of research focuses on learning to play by ear (Baker and Green, 2013; Varvarigou, 2017). Ear playing strategies derived from the Musical Futures informal learning approach (Green, 2008), based on the idea of copying single lines from recorded music, were tested in an intervention study where students who learnt to play by ear were compared with matched peers who learnt from notation over a period of ten weeks (Baker and Green, 2013). This study, where the ear-playing students out-performed their peers on tonal awareness and rhythmic accuracy, points to the need for further research investigating the ways in which aural skills training could best be integrated into instrumental education.

A specific interest in the potential power of improvisation as a pedagogical tool in instrumental learning has emerged in recent research. The relationship between playing by ear and the development of rhythmic, harmonic and melodic improvisation skills has been demonstrated by Varvarigou (2017), who applied the informal learning ear-playing strategies reported by Baker and Green (2013) in group contexts with higher education western classical instrumental learners.

Others have focused on the place of improvisation in school and community contexts. For example, Wall (2018: 132) reported that through improvisatory activities, supported by a 'collaborative leader' whose role was to observe and guide, fifth-grade instrumental music students could articulate and develop personal and collective musical ideas. Similarly, the wider benefits of creative improvisatory approaches in the context of group instrumental learning in the community have been highlighted (Burnard and Dragovic, 2015). Within a 'democratic' pedagogy, students were empowered, for example being invited into decision-making processes and encouraged to take risks within a family-like community.

Activity 3.4
How do you use singing and playing by ear in your teaching? If you were to try and persuade a teacher who uses neither of these approaches, what would you tell them about the benefits to instrumental learning?

Music technology

Surprisingly few studies have focused on the use of music technology in the context of instrumental learning and teaching. The use of 'flipped learning' (video tutorials, to augment one-to-one lessons) in cello instruction has been explored (Akbel, 2018), pointing to some evidence that this could be an effective pedagogical approach for advanced students. With a similar focus on the use of technology to enhance self-directed learning, Hanson (2018) assessed the educational value of beginning instrumental music tutorials available via the video-sharing site YouTube. Flute, clarinet, trumpet, trombone, and snare drum videos were systematically evaluated by a panel of three judges according to their perceived credibility, efficiency, musicality, and overall value. Generally, although many videos achieved low ratings for musicality, overall they were found to be useful as a supplement to traditional instruction.

The use of technology, in the form of video feedback to enhance self-regulated practice, has been explored. Boucher, Creech, and Dubé (2019) reported that college-level guitar students who incorporated video feedback in to their practice routine over ten sessions developed an increasingly problem-solving attitude. Over time, these students, who reflected upon video-recorded performances of their progress prior to each subsequent practice session, focused increasingly on strategy use and specific revisions, while expressing less overall satisfaction with their playing. While this study was carried out with advanced-level students, it is clear that the use of resources such as video recordings may have relevance for developing the capacity for self-regulation among younger learners, many of whom have ready access to devices that can be used for this purpose.

Music technology has also been found to be an effective tool to support instrumental learners in creative improvisation activities (Rowe, Triantafyllaki, and Anagnostopoulou, 2015). The technology, which functioned as an electronic partner to the learner, responded to musical iterations produced by the learners, reflecting back in terms of the thematic material and the expressive qualities of their playing. Over six weeks, learners were supported in early steps as improvisers, becoming more reflective, spontaneous and exploratory in their improvisations.

Relational Issues

Collaboration in student-teacher interactions

The idea of instrumental learning outcomes residing in what teachers and learners achieve together (or not) has continued to fascinate researchers. Since 2012, there has been a growing interest in the complex and dynamic ways in which student-teacher and peer-to-peer interactions shape learning, in particular focusing on collaborative pedagogical approaches. Much of this research has taken place within tertiary education, but there is strong evidence that collaborative approaches may equally be fruitful with other cohorts of learners (Creech, Varvarigou and Hallam, 2021). As noted elsewhere in this chapter, the key messages emerging from research in advanced-level contexts may have implications for the instrumental teachers who emerge from such training in that their tertiary experience will in turn influence and shape the ways in which teachers subsequently engage with their younger learners in instrumental education.

In the context of conservatoire education, there has been specific interest in collaborative pedagogies that equip students appropriately for twenty-first century professional music careers. For example, Gaunt, Creech, Long and Hallam (2012) identified facets of mentoring and coaching in conservatoire student accounts of teacher support for integration into professional music careers. Similarly, in the context of conservatoire education Johansson (2013) highlighted the value of deeply reflective student-teacher collaboration in redefining learning obstacles as opportunities for professional identity development.

Research concerned with student-teacher interactions and its relationship with professional musical development has extended into jazz studies. In this vein, de Bruin (2017) undertook an in-depth phenomenological study of five expert jazz musicians and their students, applying dynamic systems theory to explain how micro-level moment-to-moment interactions shaped motor skill and audiative, imaginative and strategic development in jazz improvisation. The usefulness of collaborative conservatoire group lessons in relation to professional preparation has been explored in jazz, popular and classical departments (Rumiantsev, Maas, and Admiraal, 2017). The efficacy of these group lessons was found to be dependent upon transparency with regards to teacher intentions and student expectations, as well as space for dialogue and opportunities for equal active participation.

Some researchers have highlighted the delicate issue of dissonance in teacher-student relationships (Burwell, 2017) and the potential negative implications when there is a disconnect between the instruction that teachers deliver and student dispositions toward learning (Kupers, van Dijk and van Geert, 2017; Miksza and Tan, 2015). Others have sought to compare teacher-directed with constructivist, facilitative and informal pedagogies, with regards to support for autonomous learning. For example, focusing on school-aged groups of instrumental learners, Andrews (2013) compared teacher-directed approaches and informal learning approaches (Green, 2008) while Kooistra (2016) and McPhail (2013) researched the interpersonal facets of teaching that may support student autonomy in instrumental learning (Kupers et al., 2017). Still others have focused on the potential for peer learning to complement traditional approaches to instrumental learning. These studies have highlighted the positive implications for motivation and the development of rich musical understandings within a facilitative pedagogical relationship that allows for observation, exploration and interaction, while privileging the development of metacognitive strategies as opposed to monitoring skill acquisition.

With a similar interest in the ways in which learning may be shaped by facilitative pedagogical approaches, López-Íñiguez and Pozo (2014) demonstrated that student conceptions of learning were strongly influenced by their teachers, and that students who subscribed to a constructivist perspective tended to focus on learning processes and student autonomy. In contrast, their counterparts who held more traditional didactic conceptions of teaching and learning were outcome-focused and relied upon teacher instructions. These findings are complemented by Kupers et al. (2017) who revealed the interrelationship of autonomy and scaffolding and the idiosyncratic ways in which these concepts were related to change over time within teaching and learning dyads.

> **Activity 3.5**
> This section is about research into the importance of the relationship between teacher and pupil in instrumental learning. Sometimes these relationships are framed within particular pedagogical approaches including, for example, collaborative pedagogies. How do your teaching approaches promote the kinds of relationships you try and form with your pupils?

Collaboration in peer learning

The notion of peer learning has been positioned as an underpinning principle in informal learning approaches modelled on the ways that popular musicians learn (Hallam, Creech, and McQueen, 2017) as well as in non-formal extra-curricular orchestral programmes (Creech, González-Moreno, Lorenzino, and Waitman, 2013). Notwithstanding this, there has been limited research concerned with the practices and processes of peer learning within formal instrumental teaching and learning. However, Johnson (2017) demonstrated that school-aged students made gains in musical skills through working together in pairs, irrespective of whether they were paired in with others of similar or divergent ability. Within a higher education context, peer learning via video tutorials made by students for students has been found to foster a supportive and inspiring community of practice within which student expertise is celebrated and where peers act as role models and benchmarks for self-evaluation (Reid and Duke, 2015).

Teacher Professional Development

Deep thinking about how transformational instrumental education might be articulated requires a focus on the perspectives of teachers themselves. Some researchers have focused on 'expansive' developmental opportunities for teachers that encourage them to step 'outside of the box' and to widen their professional possibilities (Perkins et al., 2015: 81). For example, Draves (2017) reported that instrumental teachers who had participated in a four-day professional development course recognised creative activities as being motivating and empowering for students, and perceived collaborative professional development activities as being supportive of deeply engaged, reflective teaching and learning.

Teacher engagement in practice-oriented and action research approaches may represent a particularly powerful process by which pedagogical change can be supported. This is beautifully demonstrated by McPhail (2013), who carried out a small-scale action research study where he explored the possibility of translating informal learning approaches derived from Musical Futures (Green, 2008) into the context of one-to-one instrumental teaching. As McPhail (2013: 168) reports, reflection on feedback from a group of professional observers and listeners 'helped make explicit various aspects of my teaching approach and provided a stimulus for further exploration towards the aim of developing student autonomy. Within this context the observers were able to relate this to their own work. ... In this way, little knowledge is created. A strong connection was also made between theory and practice.'

The capacity for phenomenological approaches to research to support professional development, engaging teachers in reflection on practice (Yeh, 2018) and making explicit a wealth of tacit teacher knowledge has also been highlighted (Cheng and Southcott, 2016; Edgar, 2016). For example, Cheng and Southcott (2016: 55) interrogated the reflections of three expert piano teachers with regards to what motivated their students, reporting that effective teachers 'differentiate ... model enthusiasm ... are concerned about the quality of their teaching ... seek to foster in their students the three general needs which must be satisfied by individuals: competence, relatedness and autonomy'.

Similarly, Edgar (2016) engaged instrumental teachers in deeply reflective interviews focused around the idea of being facilitative teachers whose practice was underpinned by positive teacher-student relationships. From this perspective, teachers adopted a dialogic leadership style characterized by guiding and coaching students as they met new challenges, and encouraging student ownership of their learning. A key finding here was that 'being a facilitative teacher not only increased cooperation, but also productivity and musical performance quality' (Edgar, 2016: 249).

Conclusion

In this chapter I have organized recent research around the four principles for pedagogical capacity-building proposed by Carey et al. (2013), comprising 'what is important to student learning'; 'relational issues'; 'making teaching visible – alternative pedagogical strategies'; and 'opportunities for professional growth'. Table 1 sets out some potential practical applications, or possibilities for evidence-based practice, that emerge from the research discussed in this chapter.

Table 3.1: Possibilities for evidence-based pedagogies

Research theme	Practical applications
Promoting self-directed, autonomous learning	▶ Devote time to engaging learners in reflective problem-solving approaches. For example, use open questions and allow time for learners to explore, experiment and evaluate; and to learn through making mistakes. ▶ Support learners in developing their intentional use of practice strategies. For example, ask them to articulate specific goals in their practice. Ask them to video-record their own practice and then do their own analysis on how they have used their time, identifying alternative strategies for achieving those goals. ▶ In every lesson, support learners in recognising at least one point that reinforces the idea that their effort translates to musical development and musical ability.
Inclusion and supporting long-term participation	▶ Does your pedagogical practice reinforce a 'normative' version of an instrumental learner? Identify one thing you could change to meet the needs of a learner who may not fit into this 'normative' approach. Model alternative ways of doing familiar musical activities. ▶ Reach out to parents or wider support communities and involve them in the learning and teaching (for example, start an intergenerational group; or include music that is meaningful for family groups). ▶ Explore music and musical instruments that are culturally relevant and meaningful for your learners.
Musicianship	▶ Embed singing into instrumental learning, for example singing new pieces before learning them on the instrument, or singing well known pieces to explore expressive possibilities. ▶ Encourage active listening with activities focused around learning by ear (e.g. listening and copying melodic lines or harmonic progressions; listening and identifying different instruments; listening and copying different ways of solving technical problems or different musical interpretations).

Research theme	Practical applications
Musicianship *(cont.)*	▶ Use music and movement to explore and develop embodied musical expression. ▶ Include improvisation activities, where learners are free to learn through exploration and risk-taking. ▶ Use technology to support improvisation (e.g. using iPad applications such as Thumbjam) and exploration of harmony, melody and timbre. This learning can then be transferred to acoustic instruments, or could be used in tandem with acoustic instruments, for example creating loops or backing tracks.
Collaborative learning	▶ Experiment with collaborative rather than directive approaches to one-to-one teaching and learning. For example, explore and discuss new repertoire together; encourage learners to experiment with problem-solving; use open rather than closed questions; ask learners what they would like feedback on. ▶ Expand teaching to include peer learning. This could be with pairs or small groups of learners of similar ability who explore, create or solve a problem together; or it could be with pairs of 'helped and helper', where the 'helped' can benefit from 'proximal' and accessible role models, while the 'helper' benefits from the experience of sharing or scaffolding the learning (in either case, peer learning should be prepared for, with ground rules pertaining to interpersonal dynamics, as well as specific strategies for scaffolding).
Professional development	▶ Identify one issue that you would like to develop, solve or change, in your pedagogical practice. Engage in practice-oriented enquiry or action research, focused around this issue (e.g. McPhail, 2013; or see https://methods.sagepub.com/video/what-is-practitioner-inquiry).

In summary, a majority of the research cited in this chapter responds to the question of how transformational learning may be articulated, with a focus on individual practice-specific skills and strategies, creative pedagogies, as well as relational issues that are important for student learning. In accordance with the idea that transformational learning involves fundamental and profound change in knowledge and beliefs, the emergent themes discussed here convey an increasing interest in how students can be supported in deeply engaged, self-directed and analytical learning. These themes intersect around critical questioning of the traditional master-apprentice approach in instrumental learning, for example focusing on facilitative teaching, creativity, collaboration, autonomy, self-regulation and even empowerment.

In relation to a vision and mission for instrumental teachers, some research has been concerned with the roles and responsibilities of teachers, for example focusing on pedagogies that support holistic, personal development (Edgar, 2016). Another emergent strand of research has investigated barriers to learning that may contribute to drop-out (Evans et al., 2013), and conversely, the conditions that may contribute to long-term (possibly lifelong) instrumental learning and participation (StGeorge et al., 2014), with all its attendant benefits (e.g. Osborne et al., 2016). The very idea of 'instrumental learner' has begun to shift, for example with a growing literature concerned with adult learners (Creech et al., 2014). However, there is a clear need for further research that advances understandings of the meaning of inclusivity and the ways in which inclusive practices can be embedded in instrumental education. In this vein, Laes and Westerlund (2018: 34) have argued that 'music teacher education needs to transform its professional discourses to fully address the issues of inclusion and diversity'.

References

Akbel, B. A. (2018) Students' and Instructors' Opinions on the Implementation of Flipped Learning Model for Cello Education in Turkish Music. *Journal of Education and Training Studies*, 6(8), pp. 1–11.

Andrews, K. (2013) Standing "On Our Own Two Feet": A Comparison of Teacher-Directed and Group Learning in an Extra-Curricular Instrumental Group. *British Journal of Music Education*, 30(1), pp. 125–148.

Baker, G. (2014) *El Sistema: Orchestrating Venezuela's Youth*. Oxford: Oxford University Press.

Baker, D. and Green, L. (2013) Ear Playing and Aural Development in the Instrumental Lesson: Results from a "Case-Control" Experiment. *Research Studies in Music Education*, 35(2), pp. 141–159.

Beard, J. R., Officer, A., de Carvalho, I. A., Sadana, R., Pot, A. M., Michel, J.-P., Chatterji, S. (2016) The World report on ageing and health: A policy framework for healthy ageing. *The Lancet*, 387(10033), pp. 2145–2154. https://doi.org/10.1016/S0140-6736(15)00516-4

Blackwell, J. A. and Roseth, N. E. (2018) Problem-Based Learning in a Woodwind Methods Course: An Action Research Study. *Journal of Music Teacher Education*, 28(1), pp. 55–69.

Boucher, M., Creech, A. and Dubé, F. (2021) Video feedback and the self-evaluation of college-level guitarists during individual practice. *Psychology of Music*, 49(2), pp. 159–176.

Burnard, P. and Dragovic, T. (2015) Collaborative Creativity in Instrumental Group Music Learning as a Site for Enhancing Pupil Wellbeing. *Cambridge Journal of Education*, 45(3), pp. 371–392.

Burwell, K. (2006) On musicians and singers. An investigation of different approaches taken by vocal and instrumental teachers in higher education. *Music Education Research*, 8(3), pp. 331–347. https://doi.org/10.1080/14613800600957479

Burwell, K. (2017) Feeling and Thinking about Studio Practices: Exploring Dissonance in Semi-Structured Interviews with Students in Higher Education Music. *British Journal of Music Education*, 34(2), pp. 189–202.

Carey, G., Grant, C., McWilliam, E. and Taylor, P. (2013) One-to-one pedagogy: Developing a protocol for illuminating the nature of teaching in the conservatoire. *International Journal of Music Education*, 31(2), pp. 148–159. https://doi.org/10.1177/0255761413483077

Cheng, Z. and Southcott, J. (2016) Improving Students' Intrinsic Motivation in Piano Learning: Expert Teacher Voices. *Australian Journal of Music Education*, 50(2), pp. 48–57.

Coutts, L. (2018) Selecting motivating repertoire for adult piano students: A transformative pedagogical approach. *British Journal of Music Education*, 35(3), pp. 285–299. https://doi.org/10.1017/S0265051718000074

Creech, A. and Gaunt, H. (2012) The changing face of individual instrumental tuition: Value, purpose and potential. In: G. McPherson and G. Welch eds., *Oxford Handbook of Music Education*. Oxford: Oxford University Press, pp. 694–711.

Creech, A., González-Moreno, P., Lorenzino, L. and Waitman, G. (2013) *El Sistema and Sistema-inspired programmes: A literature review*. London: Institute of Education, for Sistema Global.

Creech, A. and Hallam, S. (2009) Interaction in Instrumental Learning: The Influence of Interpersonal Dynamics on Parents. *International Journal of Music Education*, 27(2), pp. 94–106.

Creech, A., Hallam, S., Varvarigou, M. and McQueen, H. (2014) *Active Ageing with Music: Supporting wellbeing in the Third and Fourth Ages*. London, UK: Institute of Education Press.

Creech, A., Varvarigou, M. and Hallam, S. (2021) *Contexts for music learning and participation: Developing and sustaining musical possible selves*. Palgrave.

de Bruin, L. R. (2018) Shaping Interpersonal Learning in the Jazz Improvisation Lesson: Observing a Dynamic Systems Approach. *International Journal of Music Education*, 36(2), pp. 160-181.

Department for Education and Department for Media, Culture and Sport (DfE and DMCS) (2011) *The importance of music: A national plan for music education*.
Available at: http://publications.education.gov.uk

dos Santos, R. A. (2018) Ways of Using Musical Knowledge to Think about One's Piano Repertoire Learning: Three Case Studies. *Music Education Research*, 20(4), 427-445.

Draves, T. J. (2017) Instrumental Music Educators' Experiences in a Professional Development Course. *Update: Applications of Research in Music Education*, 35(3), pp. 38-45.

Edgar, S. N. (2016) Approaches of High School Instrumental Music Educators in Response to Student Challenges. *Research Studies in Music Education*, 38(2), pp. 235-253.

Ellis, B. (2018) Music Learning for Fun and Wellbeing at Any Age! *Australian Journal of Adult Learning*, 58(1), pp. 110-124.

Ericsson, K. A., Krampe, R. T. and Tesch-Römer, C. (1993) *The Role of Deliberate Practice in the Acquisition of Expert Performance*. (No. 0033-295X; pp. 363-406).

Evans, P. and McPherson, G. E. (2014) Identity and practice: The motivational benefits of a long-term musical identity. *Psychology of Music*, 43(3), pp. 407-422. https://doi.org/10.1177/0305735613514471

Evans, P., McPherson, G. E. and Davidson, J. W. (2013) The Role of Psychological Needs in Ceasing Music and Music Learning Activities. *Psychology of Music*, 41(5), pp. 600-619.

Gaunt, H. (2010) One-to-one tuition in a conservatoire: The perceptions of instrumental and vocal students. *Psychology of Music*, 38(2), pp. 178-208. https://doi.org/10.1177/0305735609339467

Gaunt, H., Creech, A., Long, M. and Hallam, S. (2012) Supporting Conservatoire Students towards Professional Integration: One-to-One Tuition and the Potential of Mentoring.
Music Education Research, 14(1), pp. 25-43.

Green, L. (2008) *Music, informal learning and the school: A new classroom pedagogy*.
Aldershot: Ashgate.

Green, L. (2012) Musical "Learning Styles" and "Learning Strategies" in the Instrumental Lesson: Some Emergent Findings from a Pilot Study. *Psychology of Music*, 40(1), pp. 42-65.

Gruhn, W. (2021) Chapter 6: Musical Processing Across the Lifecourse. In: A. Creech, D. Hodges, and S. Hallam eds. *Routledge International Handbook of Music Psychology in Education and the Community*. Routledge.

Hallam, S. (1998). The Predictors of Achievement and Dropout in Instrumental Tuition. *Psychology of Music*, 26(2), pp. 116-132. https://doi.org/10.1177/0305735698262002

Hallam, S. (2013). What Predicts Level of Expertise Attained, Quality of Performance, and Future Musical Aspirations in Young Instrumental Players? *Psychology of Music*, 41(3), pp. 267-291.

Hallam, S., Creech, A., McQueen, H. (2017) Can the adoption of informal approaches to learning popular music in school music lessons promote musical progression?
British Journal of Music Education, 34(2), pp. 127-151.

Hanson, J. (2018) Assessing the Educational Value of YouTube Videos for Beginning Instrumental Music. *Contributions to Music Education*, 43, pp. 137-157.

Hartz, B. and Bauer, W. (2016) The Effect of Ear Playing Instruction on Adult Amateur Wind Instrumentalists' Musical Self-Efficacy: An Exploratory Study. *Contributions to Music Education*, 41, pp. 31-51.

Johansson, K. (2013) Undergraduate Students' Ownership of Musical Learning: Obstacles and Options in One-to-One Teaching. *British Journal of Music Education*, 30(2), pp. 277-295.

Johnson, E. (2017) The Effect of Symmetrical and Asymmetrical Peer-Assisted Learning Structures on Music Achievement and Learner Engagement in Seventh-Grade Band. *Journal of Research in Music Education*, 65(2), pp. 163-178.

Jørgensen, H. (2002) Instrumental Performance Expertise and Amount of Practice among Instrumental Students in a Conservatoire. *Music Education Research*, 4(1), pp. 105-119. https://doi.org/10.1080/14613800220119804

Kooistra, L. (2016) Informal Music Education: The Nature of a Young Child's Engagement in an Individual Piano Lesson Setting. *Research Studies in Music Education*, 38(1), pp. 115-129.

Krupp-Schleußner, V. and Lehmann-Wermser, A. (2018) An Instrument for Every Child: A Study on Long-Term Effects of Extended Music Education in German Primary Schools. *Music Education Research*, 20(1), pp. 44-58.

Kupers, E., van Dijk, M. and van Geert, P. (2017) Changing Patterns of Scaffolding and Autonomy during Individual Music Lessons: A Mixed Methods Approach. *Journal of the Learning Sciences*, 26(1), pp. 131-166.

Laes, T. (2015) Empowering Later Adulthood Music Education: A Case Study of a Rock Band for Third-Age Learners. *International Journal of Music Education*, 33(1), pp. 51-65.

Laes, T. and Westerlund, H. (2018) Performing Disability in Music Teacher Education: Moving beyond Inclusion through Expanded Professionalism. *International Journal of Music Education*, 36(1), p. 34. https://doi.org/10.1177/0255761417703782

López-Íñiguez, G. and Pozo, J. I. (2014) Like Teacher, Like Student? Conceptions of Children from Traditional and Constructive Teachers Regarding the Teaching and Learning of String Instruments. *Cognition and Instruction*, 32(3), pp. 219-252.

McCord, K. and Watts, E. H. (2006) Collaboration and Access for Our Children: Music Educators and Special Educators Together. When Music Educators and Special Educators Work Together, All Students Are Likely to Benefit. *Music Educators Journal*, 92(4), p. 26.

McPhail, G. J. (2013) Developing Student Autonomy in the One-to-One Music Lesson. *International Journal of Music Education*, 31(2), p. 160-172.

McPherson, G. E. and McCormick, J. (1999) Motivational and Self-Regulated Learning Components of Musical Practice. *Bulletin of the Council for Research in Music Education*, (141), pp. 98-102.

McPherson, G. E. and Renwick, J. M. (2001) A Longitudinal Study of Self-regulation in Children's Musical Practice. *Music Education Research*, 3(2), pp. 169-186. https://doi.org/10.1080/14613800120089232

Meissner, H. (2017) Instrumental Teachers' Instructional Strategies for Facilitating Children's Learning of Expressive Music Performance: An Exploratory Study. *International Journal of Music Education*, 35(1), pp. 118-135.

Mieder, K. and Bugos, J. A. (2017) Enhancing Self-Regulated Practice Behavior in High School Instrumentalists. *International Journal of Music Education*, 35(4), pp. 578-587.

Miksza, P., Blackwell, J. and Roseth, N. E. (2018) Self-Regulated Music Practice: Microanalysis as a Data Collection Technique and Inspiration for Pedagogical Intervention. *Journal of Research in Music Education*, 66(3), pp. 295-319.

Miksza, P. and Tan, L. (2015) Predicting Collegiate Wind Players' Practice Efficiency, Flow, and Self-Efficacy for Self-Regulation: An Exploratory Study of Relationships Between Teachers' Instruction and Students' Practicing. *Journal of Research in Music Education*, 63(2), pp. 162-179.

Mills, J. (2006). Performing and teaching: The beliefs and experience of music students as instrumental teachers. *Psychology of Music*, 34(3), pp. 372-390. https://doi.org/10.1177/0305735606064843

Moscardini, L., Barron, D. S. and Wilson, A. (2013) Who Gets to Play? Investigating Equity in Musical Instrument Instruction in Scottish Primary Schools. *International Journal of Inclusive Education*, 17(6), pp. 646-662.

Nerstrom, N. (2017) Transformative Learning: Moving Beyond Theory and Practice. *International Journal of Adult Vocational Education and Technology (IJAVET)*, 8(1), pp. 36-46. https://doi.org/10.4018/ijavet.2017010104

Nielsen, Siw G. (2015) Learning Pre-Played Solos: Self-Regulated Learning Strategies in Jazz/Improvised Music. *Research Studies in Music Education*, 37(2), pp. 233-246.

Nielsen, Siw Graabraek. (2012) Epistemic Beliefs and Self-Regulated Learning in Music Students. *Psychology of Music*, 40(3), pp. 324-338.

Osborne, M. S., McPherson, G. E., Faulkner, R., Davidson, J. W. and Barrett, M. S. (2016) Exploring the Academic and Psychosocial Impact of El Sistema-Inspired Music Programs within Two Low Socio-Economic Schools. *Music Education Research*, 18(2), pp. 156-175.

Perkins, R., Aufegger, L. and Williamon, A. (2015) Learning through Teaching: Exploring What Conservatoire Students Learn from Teaching Beginner Older Adults. *International Journal of Music Education*, 33(1), pp. 80-90.

Presland, C. (2005) Conservatoire student and instrumental professor: The student perspective on a complex relationship. *British Journal of Music Education*, 22(3), pp. 237-248. https://doi.org/10.1017/S0265051705006558

Reid, A. and Duke, M. (2015) Student for Student: Peer Learning in Music Higher Education. *International Journal of Music Education*, 33(2), pp. 222-232.

Ritchie, L. and Kearney, P. (2018) Adult Beginner Instrumentalists' Practice, Self-Regulation, and Self-Efficacy: A Pilot Study. *Journal of Education and Training Studies*, 6(5), pp. 1-9.

Roulston, K., Jutras, P., and Kim, S. J. (2015) Adult Perspectives of Learning Musical Instruments. *International Journal of Music Education*, 33(3), pp. 325-335.

Rowe, V., Triantafyllaki, A. and Anagnostopoulou, X. (2015). Young Pianists Exploring Improvisation Using Interactive Music Technology. *International Journal of Music Education*, 33(1), pp. 113-130.

Rumiantsev, T. W., Maas, A. and Admiraal, W. (2017) Collaborative Learning in Two Vocal Conservatoire Courses. *Music Education Research*, 19(4), pp. 371-383.

Simones, L. L. (2017) Beyond Expectations in Music Performance Modules in Higher Education: Rethinking Instrumental and Vocal Music Pedagogy for the Twenty-First Century. *Music Education Research*, 19(3), pp. 252-262.

Sloboda, J. A., Davidson, J. W., Howe, M. J. A. and Moore, D. G. (1996) The role of practice in the development of performing musicians. *British Journal of Psychology*, 87(2), pp. 287–309. https://doi.org/10.1111/j.2044-8295.1996.tb02591.x

Smilde, R. and Bisschop, B. (2016) Lifelong Learning and Healthy Ageing: The Significance of Music as an Agent of Change. In: *Kulturelle Bildung; Vol. 52. Forschungsfeld Kulturgeragogik: Research in Cultural Gerontology*. München: Kopaed Verlag, pp. 205–220.

StGeorge, J., Holbrook, A. and Cantwell, R. (2014) Affinity for Music: A Study of the Role of Emotion in Musical Instrument Learning. *International Journal of Music Education*, 32(3), pp. 264–277.

UNESCO. (2010) *The Seoul Agenda: Goals for the development of arts education*. Retrieved from http://www.unesco.org/new/fileadmin/MULTIMEDIA/HQ/CLT/CLT/pdf/Seoul_Agenda_EN.pdf

Uygun, M. A. and Kilinçer, Ö. (2017a) Developing a Scale for Strategies Used during the Practice and Learning of Instrumental Music. *Educational Research and Reviews*, 12(8), pp. 518–530.

Uygun, M. A. and Kilinçer, Ö. (2017b) Examination of Strategies Fine Arts High School Students Use during the Practice and Learning of Instrumental Music. *Journal of Education and Training Studies*, 5(4), pp. 178–189.

Varvarigou, M. (2017) Promoting Collaborative Playful Experimentation through Group Playing by Ear in Higher Education. *Research Studies in Music Education*, 39(2), pp. 161–176.

Wall, M. P. (2018) Improvising to Learn. *Research Studies in Music Education*, 40(1), pp. 117–135.

Wallace, K. (2014) When Instrumentalists Sing.
International Journal of Music Education, 32(4), pp. 499–513.

Wan, C. Y. and Schlaug, G. (2010) Music Making as a Tool for Promoting Brain Plasticity across the Life Span. *The Neuroscientist*, 16(5), pp. 566–577. https://doi.org/10.1177/1073858410377805

Yeh, Y.-L. (2018) An Investigation of Taiwanese Piano Teachers' Reflection on Teaching Challenges and Pupils' Learning Difficulties. *Music Education Research*, 20(1), pp. 32–43.

Part Two:
Music Learning, Development and Progress

Chapter 4 Commentary

The word 'musical' can have a wide range of meanings. We might hear a parent claim 'he's very musical' or another adult confess 'I'm not very musical', or an examiner remarking on 'a very musical performance'. It's a word we all use widely and whereas we can probably define what we personally mean by it, there is perhaps a lack of a shared understanding of what defines someone or something as musical? The challenge of definitions becomes even more tricky when it comes to 'gifted', 'talented', and 'able' – words that are frequently used when referring to learners of musical instruments. Arriving at better understanding of these terms is not a semantic nicety. They are words which are used to make judgements about both the current and future needs of young learners, so it is vital that we have a clear understanding of the concepts that underpin them.

Alison Daubney helps us to build an understanding of these terms by first considering music making by very young children, whose worlds are 'alive with music' and who demonstrate that 'humans are musically capable and creative from a very young age'. She then goes on to look at the critical place of fluency, contrasting the fluency, passion, and communication of a singing football crowd, with the sometimes stilted and halting performances given by young learners on instruments. There is much here that should make us as instrumental teachers consider carefully the repertoire we use with our students to ensure that they have the opportunities to explore and express their own musicality with fluency, passion, and communicatively. Going further, Daubney considers the ways in which we, as teachers, can help our students feel musical, arguing that we might benefit from a rethinking of our teaching approach, putting the aim of supporting students to feel musical at the heart of what we do.

In the second half of the chapter, Daubney tackles the thorny issues of musical ability, aptitude, giftedness and talent, offering us some helpful definitions as well as considering some factors that are influential in the development of talented individuals. She considers how learners view themselves and others, and how, if well handled, this can contribute in very significant ways to their musical development. To support this, she offers a structured activity for teachers to conduct with their students.

In conclusion, she encourages us to reassess our teaching in the light of these understandings about musicality and musical ability because, as she says: 'A big part of the responsibility for nurturing students to thrive musically falls to us'.

4 What Does it Mean to be Musical? Musical Ability and Learning in Instrumental Education

Alison Daubney

Introduction

The question 'what does it mean to be musical?' lies at the heart of all music education and drives (or should drive) decisions around pedagogical approaches, assessment and questions of diversity, access and inclusion. This chapter seeks to address this question in the context of instrumental music education through consideration of what musicality is and how it can be promoted throughout teaching to engender musical learning. It considers the terms 'ability', 'talented' and 'gifted' and the importance of considering the role of psychological, as well as musical, flexibility. Primarily, it places the importance of *feeling* musical at the heart of musical engagement and learning.

It is crucial that instrumental teachers are open to exploring these important issues as they play a vital role in helping students to flourish as lifelong musical learners.

What Does it Mean to be 'Musical'?

At an Aussie Rules match the home team have a shot on goal. The interest from the fans rises and from behind the goal the away team supporters strike up the music, perhaps a strategy in part aimed at trying to distract the players. A young boy stands on his chair and beats a rhythmic pattern on large drum. The crowd nearby respond with a known chant; around the stadium the team's flags wave as this 'call and response' is repeated with more and more voices joining in with every repetition. As anticipation and tension build, the volume and speed of the music increase. Watching the ball soar over the goal for six points, the musical moment passes to the home team's supporters as they cheer, punch the air and their team's theme song erupts spontaneously around the stadium in a moment of celebration.

In this brief two-minute ritual, thousands of people were immersed in a participatory musical experience. Nevertheless, in other contexts many of the same people might say 'I'm not musical' or use other phrases such as 'I'm tone deaf' and 'I don't have a musical bone in my body'. And yet, in that moment, these people were playing, chanting, singing their hearts out and were fully involved in the musical culture and rituals of the match.

Perhaps, then, what we need to explore is the idea that how we feel about ourselves musically is bound up in the processes we engage with, as well as the context. In order to answer the question 'what does it mean to be musical?' we should also give due consideration to what makes people feel musical, or indeed, to feel unmusical.

Terminology relating to 'being musical'

There is little consensus about definitions related to 'being musical'. This quote, from Hallam (2006: 93) offers an overarching view of related terminology, providing an important starting point to explore these terms:

> *The adjective 'musical' is often attached to a range of other terms, for example, ability (defined as capacity or power), aptitude (natural propensity or talent), talent (a special aptitude or faculty), and potential (coming into being or action, latent). In the literature these terms are often used interchangeably, although there has been a tendency for the term 'musicality' to be adopted in considerations of whether being musical is a species-specific characteristic of human beings.*

Activity 4.1

Take some time to explore your own perspective in relation to the question 'what does it mean to be musical?' Jot down your thoughts. Then talk to some of your students and ascertain their thoughts on what it means to be musical, how they relate themselves to the constructs they identify and how they would define small steps in their own development to reach the next stage. Their own view of the constructs will give you an insight into their perspectives and are very likely to differ in part from yours and also from each other.

Exploring musicality

In order to explore 'musicality' it is interesting to think about our early musical lives. Parnutt (2009: 219) reminds us that musical development starts pre-birth:

> *Pre-natal music development involves the acquisition of perceptual, cognitive, motor and emotional abilities and information that may influence later musical development.*

From observing infants' engagement with their sound world we can identify tenets of musical development emergent over time. As Trehub (2009: 229) describes, 'their world is alive with the sound of music'. Pre-verbal children are musically curious, spontaneous and creative; they interact with, engage and react to sounds, speech and timbres physically and in verbal ways that contribute to speech development and communication with their world. This embodied, encultured learning does not follow a set pattern or a specific set of rules, yet it embeds some of the fundamental building blocks of music (both in terms of musical behaviours and developing understanding relating to how music is constructed, adapted and performed – including the social sharing of music).

Like the acquisition of spoken language, infants' early musical learning comes from a combination of factors including, for example, social learning, immersion, listening, repetition, playfulness and, to a much lesser degree, targeted teaching, all of which contribute to the development of new knowledge (including skills) and increasingly applying these to new situations and contexts. We can conclude from this that humans are musically capable and creative from a very young age. We can also see that musicality is not something to put in a box that is exclusive to music; it has transferable value. For example, think of a dancer of any style and how the timing, gesture and nuance of their movement is linked to a deep, integral relationship with the music.

This small snapshot of early childhood research provides evidence of the complexity of musical development and the multiplicity of the processes involved, as well as the recognition of the importance of the roles played by communication, contexts and relationships. Returning to Parnutt's findings, we could consider aspects of perceptual, cognitive, motor and emotional learning to be important to notions of musicality. Watching and listening to very young children as they communicate through sound, pulse, rhythm, movement and gesture with their mother (see Malloch and Trevarthen's work on 'communicative musicality', 2009) could be considered central to their 'engaging performance', placing the role of emotional connectivity and communication firmly in the frame when we consider aspects of musicality.

Emotional connection to and communication through music are by no means limited to our experiences in early childhood. As the 'Aussie Rules match' vignette at the start of this chapter demonstrates, being involved in making music, and engaging as a listener are two (of many) situations which potentially evoke emotional connection, response and communication. A considerable amount of research on music and emotion has been undertaken (e.g. see Juslin and Sloboda, 2010). The emotional/aesthetic and communicative aspects of musicality merit attention within an instrumental learning context. For example, music played with convincing and persuasive emotional communication is an important aspect of musicality. Even in the earliest stages of learning, much fun can be had with exploring storytelling through music so that a student experiences first-hand that they, as the performer, have the authority to make decisions about how the music is communicated, and their role is not simply to mimic what has come before. Such playful exploration helps them to understand that a piece of music, even when written as notation on a page, is not a precise instructional manual. There is also much to be gained from helping students to understand the historical, cultural and social context of the music they learn, particularly as they become more technically advanced. Approaching emotional communication in playful ways helps students to recognise that they are not seeking one 'correct' way to perform, whether they are playing music written by others or their own music. Instead, instrumental teachers could use a variety of creative ways to cultivate their students' understanding that the uniqueness, character and creativity we personally bring to any music are important components of musicality.

The importance of musical fluency

In the musical examples above – both at the Aussie Rules match and the musical exchanges between mothers and babies – the participants are socially-engaged and the musical episodes are part of a musical discourse. Additionally, musical fluency is evident – one of the three principles of music education (along with 'care for music as discourse' and 'care for the musical discourse of students') postulated by Keith Swanwick:

> *Musical fluency takes precedence over musical literacy. It is precisely fluency, the aural ability to imagine music coupled with the skill of handling an instrument (or the voice) that characterises jazz, Indian music, rock music, music for steel pans, a great deal of computer-assisted music and folk music anywhere in the world* (Swanwick, 1990: 56).

Imagine this scenario. Think of the song 'Happy Birthday'. A student has read the simplified notation and memorised the notes for the melody, but plays them all at equal length with no regard for the time signature or rhythm. It has one of the building blocks of music – the melody. But it isn't 'musical' – it lacks the musical fluency. Yet, at a birthday gathering in many places around the world, this same child could join in with the singing of this melody and be musically fluent and even musically playful. We could compare this reading of music with a child learning to read a sentence – sounding out the letter using phonemes and graphemes and eventually making whole words. Their reading lacks flow and possibly even understanding, through the atomisation of discrete sounds and then individual words. If reading every sentence during a normal conversation, there would be a distinct lack of fluency and sense of flow.

The Happy Birthday example demonstrates the importance of musical fluency whilst also highlighting some of the potential pitfalls of an over-reliance on musical literacy. It may be important to some extent to develop practical use of written musical 'language' in order to decode and encode using symbols, but this is only one aspect of musical learning (and we should be mindful that it is not universally used in all musical cultures around the world). In designing musical learning for our students of any age, whether in a group or individually, we should remember the importance of Swanwick's mantra 'fluency first and last' and ensure that students are immersed in genuinely musical learning environments. Purposeful aural development, helping students to understand and recognise the relativity of the notes, and playing by ear, are some important skills for developing musically. In paying attention to learning music in this way, teachers help students better understand the relationship between sounds and symbols, giving meaning to notation when it is appropriately used and, importantly, providing them with a wider range of ways to access and engage with music. Immersion in the act of musicking through playing, singing, improvising and aural development are important for this development of musical fluency and improvising technical skills so that students learn to control and adapt these skills in the context of 'being musical'.

The importance of *feeling* musical

Somewhere along the way we can lose sight of the overwhelming evidence that music is intrinsic to being human and to our relationships with each other and the world. The complex nature of musicality may also get lost. Sometimes this unfortunately gives way to a view that is perpetuated in some societies in which music is seen as something only *special* people can do and therefore distancing some people from meaningful and positive engagement with music; even those who may be more actively involved at some points in their lives are sometimes led to question how 'musical' they really are and may develop musical insecurities that lead them to give up, feeling 'unmusical'. As Ruddock (2018: 2) points out:

> ...it is important to consider how misconceptions of musicality lead to widespread denial where both overt and subtle effects of misconceived language use lead musical beings to 'learn' that they are not musical.

Laird (2009) postulates that in order to maintain and grow our interest in music, as well as providing mechanisms that we benefit from to live our lives healthily, we need 'musical nourishment'. Instrumental teachers have a significant role to play in providing this nourishment. Even when working within systems, cultures and establishments that potentially perpetuate the gulf between opportunities for and approaches to learning, we personally can be a positive influence that nurtures students to feel musical. This relies on us constantly reflecting on the impact of our work; identifying and being willing to change practices that lead to some students feeling temporarily or permanently 'unmusical', as well as signposting diverse pathways and opportunities to students that nourish their motivations and musical preferences.

Recognising that the term 'musician' is value laden and personal, it is important for instrumental teachers to consider what it is that makes their students 'feel musical' and for teachers to be mindful of the language they use and the messages they purposely or inadvertently communicate. It sounds obvious to say that this means that instrumental teachers need to be flexible and malleable in their approaches, the curriculum, and pedagogic choices they make. Perhaps there is an argument that the ways in which we personally approach teaching would benefit from some serious reflection and adaptation in order to make us more effective at keeping a greater proportion of students 'feeling musical'. There are constant pressures within the systems in which many instrumental teachers work (including, for example, time pressures, parental and school expectations) and, as with all teaching, there is a strong case to be made for instrumental teachers to constantly reflect and adapt their approaches so that students are nurtured to 'feel musical' as much as possible. For some teachers the flexibility required and the need to explore new ideas and potentially adapt ways of working might initially seem daunting, but finding other professionals to share ideas with (e.g. through online networks or in person), or through seeking professional development opportunities, can often be beneficial to both the teacher and the students.

Activity 4.2
Think of three students with different levels of experience you have taught recently. Write a list of all the ways you have helped them to 'feel musical' in each lesson. Then, identify ways in which these strategies can become even more embedded in your future approaches to teaching and learning with these students.

Exploring 'Musical Ability'

Hallam and Prince (2003) asked 415 people from a range of different backgrounds and age ranges, some of whom were actively involved in music, to complete the sentence 'Musical ability is...'. The result yielded the following:

> *Overall, musical ability was most strongly perceived as relating to a sense of rhythm, followed by the ability to understand and interpret the music, express thoughts and feelings through sound, being able to communicate through sound, motivation to engage with music, personal commitment to music, and being able to successfully engage musically with others. Least important were having technical skills, being able to compose or improvise, being able to read music, and understanding musical concepts and musical structures.*

Unsurprisingly, there were also marked differences in perceptions between different age groups and those with differing degrees of engagement with music. Those with a greater level of engagement in music gave much more detailed and nuanced responses. These responses can be broadly categorised as technical, analytical, interpretative, communicative and personal (and to some extent, creative), but failed to identify psychological constructs or actions, which are also crucial to musical ability and being able to thrive as a musician.

However, a somewhat narrow view of musical ability prevails in many societies (Levitin, 2012) which is almost exclusively centred on playing musical instruments and performing music composed by others, often that of the western classical canon, despite the commodification of an eclectic range of music from around the world. If you ask people about how they perceive a 'musical' person, the chances are that playing a musical instrument, singing and performing will be high up on their list, with relatively little attention paid to other creative processes such as improvising or composing.

Just as in general education, we need to be wary of how we use and think of the term 'ability' as often what we are referring to is a person's attainment (e.g. passing certain graded examinations), not their ability. There is an unfortunate propensity across all education to label students as 'more able' and 'less able'. The use of such language can lead to the so-called Pygmalion (or Rosenthal) effect, where teachers' expectations and in turn their actions and judgements of students are influenced by pre-conceived ideas and sometimes even by unconscious bias. This can lead to students adapting their expectations of themselves, ultimately impacting on how students see themselves musically. We need to be aware of this within our teaching and work to mitigate the impact, ensuring we are adaptable in our approaches and do not unwittingly create glass ceilings.

Musical aptitude, talent and giftedness

The term 'musical aptitude' sits at the heart of discussions about the extent to which our musical development is influenced by environmental and genetic factors, i.e. the balance between the influences of nature vs nurture.

> *Aptitude is a measure of one's potential to learn, and achievement is a measure of what one has learned ... What is known is that regardless of the level of musical aptitude a child is born with he must have favourable early informal and formal experiences in music to maintain that level of potential* (Gordon, 1980: 3).

There has long been controversy surrounding the use of musical aptitude tests. The complexities of musical learning and musical ability point to problems with musical aptitude tests having ecological validity. And yet, with society's desire to 'measure' and assess, musical aptitude tests have been, and in some cultures continue to be, used as the basis for selection of certain students to access musical learning experiences whilst denying opportunities to others.

For example, there are many examples of children in western cultures being selected to play musical instruments and given opportunity over others based on the outcome of aural perceptions tests such as Seashore's (1919) *Measure of Musical Abilities* or Bentley's (1966) *Musical Aptitude Test*. With hindsight and much research in music education from a broad range of psychological and sociological perspectives it is easy to spot the pitfalls in basing musical learning opportunities on the limited dimensions upon which a range of musical aptitude tests are founded (Bentley's test had four sections – pitch discrimination, tonal memory, chord analysis and rhythmic memory). We must accept the harsh reality that sorting out people into those that 'can' and those that 'can't' access music education through crude measures such as these, have, in many cases, contributed to people's negative perceptions about themselves as musical beings that they take with them into their adult life.

The terms 'gifted' and 'talented' are also problematic in music education, and indeed in education *per se*. The lack of clarity about the potential purpose of identifying students as 'gifted' or 'talented' is not a new issue, as pointed out by McPherson (1997: 65):

> *The terms 'gifted' and 'talented' are often used in music, but what do they imply? More importantly, how can music education serve the needs of highest achievers? In some ways these questions have been answered by the great pedagogues of our time, including Dalcroze, Orff, Kodaly, and Suzuki, who argue that all children are talented and that it is only a matter of degree...*

Gagné's (2003) definition of 'gifted and talented' is widely cited, proposing the following:

> *Gifted students are those whose potential is distinctly above average in one or more of the following domains of human ability: intellectual, creative, social and physical... Talented students are those whose skills are distinctly above average in one or more areas of human performance.*

This implies that giftedness relates to a person's 'natural or innate *potential to achieve* what is distinctly above average' whereas 'talent can be used to describe someone who can demonstrate superior performance as a result of some type of systematic training in a specific field' (McPherson, 1997: 67, 68). However, Gagné also acknowledges that the terms gifted and talented are a 'terminological conundrum'.

There are numerous issues relating to the identification and education of students in relation to being gifted or talented. As already noted, the identification of 'giftedness' can be problematic in the first instance, particularly given the very narrow scope of musical aptitude tests. Sometimes there is a tendency to gloss over the exceptionally hard work that goes into developing high level musicians (or any other domain, e.g. sport, chess playing, visual artist); and just because someone is identified as being 'gifted' doesn't mean that the opportunities and environment will sustain them to reach their potential.

Young people and adults identified as either 'able' or 'talented' by others are likely to be those who have had the experiences in music education that others haven't. Clearly, this is problematic as it shows the discrepancy of opportunity and shines a light for us to examine the extent to which access to learning a musical instrument is inclusive across different cultures and societies. Another ongoing issue is the narrow way in which talent is often perceived in music, where a performance culture takes central stage over many other equally valid musical skills, such as, for example, improvising, composing and playing by ear.

Gifted and talented students amplify the need for meaningful differentiation and adaption of what we teach and how we teach, which can be one of the greatest challenges for a teacher of any subject and particularly in music, where opportunities to learn are far from equal. Whether teaching on an individual basis, working with small groups, whole classes or ensembles, it is important that we are aware of the need for everyone to thrive. A skilful instrumental teacher will develop ways for everyone to have appropriate challenge and mitigate the risk of isolating one group or another. This might be through ensuring that students don't feel bored at the lack of challenge or through the pace being too fast/the material too difficult, and instead ensuring that students are able to access the learning through ways which offer challenge that is personally appropriate. Teachers who philosophically believe in the importance of music education for all pupils, not just privileging one group, are vital to developing inclusive music education.

Some Key Considerations for Developing Talent

Some other significant points of interest for instrumental teachers come from widely-cited work studying the talent development of 120 'immensely talented individuals' from across a range of different domains including music, art, sport, mathematics and science, carried out by researchers with specialist knowledge in each field (Bloom, 1985). Bloom presented the approaches through three stages, covering the earliest stages of learning right up to professional levels of training and thus each of these stages covers many years. Whilst much work has been undertaken on notions of giftedness and talent since Bloom's study, the very practical application of the findings still resonate strongly.

Whilst there is a need to recognise the limitations of the body of work this is drawn from, particularly the narrow range of the situations included and the focus on individual learning, it nevertheless provides plentiful food for thought across instrumental teaching. These include the curriculum, pedagogic approaches and assessment choices, as well as our relationship with students and parents. Some key points stand out which give rise to a number of considerations. Firstly, accessible opportunities to learn must be there for all young people in the first instance — through wide possibilities for musical engagement in schools and communities, as well as access to learning instruments, being playful with music and being part of social learning. The environment is crucial, and in the early stages of learning, 'talent development is initially viewed by the child as play and recreation' (Bloom, 1985: 508). With the pressures of time and sometimes the external pressures set by others, it is easy to forget the value of playfulness and its contribution to musical learning. It is worth exploring ways in which you and your students could be even more playful with the approaches to musical learning, with the music itself and even with exploring psychological concepts such as how they think of themselves as learners and cope with the psychological demands of musical engagement. Secondly, recognising our own progress regularly and feeling positive about ourselves as learners through positivity from others is important for motivation and self-determination. With a focus on musical fluency through processes and outcomes, this adds to the quality of the music produced and created. This is crucial no matter where you are in your musical learning journey, and as teachers, finding regular and supportive ways to provide diagnostic feedback and increasingly to help students learn the skills to see this for themselves benefits their learning.

Additionally, whilst Bloom identified these points from models of exceptional talent, there is much here that could help more students to engage initially and to stay as engaged learners for longer, thriving in their own development and being fulfilled in their musical learning even if they are not striving to be professional musicians. This relies as much on teachers helping their students to develop musical flexibility as well as psychological flexibility, which we will explore in the final part of this chapter.

Activity 4.3
(adapted from Daubney, 2017)

Complete a 'personal construct' exercise with your students. Through discussion, gather their ideas in response to the following question:

'What are the attributes of a great... (e.g. clarinettist, singer, bass guitarist etc.)?'

Try not to prompt them! This is about what they think and aims to give you an insight into their perspective. Everyone's list will be different!

Now identify the opposite:

(e.g. 'looks up when singing' ↔ 'Looks down when singing')

(e.g. 'clear diction' ↔ 'mumbles')

These create bipolar scales. Against each scale from 0 to 10 (where 10 is the 'good' attribute and 0 is the opposite, ask them to say where their own current level is (e.g. 'I think I'm a 7').

Discuss what this score means. Then ask what the next number up will look like and how they will get to it (i.e. target setting). The power in this exercise often arises from the discussion, rather than the numbers, and students' understanding is always surprisingly nuanced.

A very clear and visual way to show these is to fill in a polar graph such as the one on page 82. This chart is something you can keep returning to periodically to help students have an active role in their own self-development.

Figure 4.1

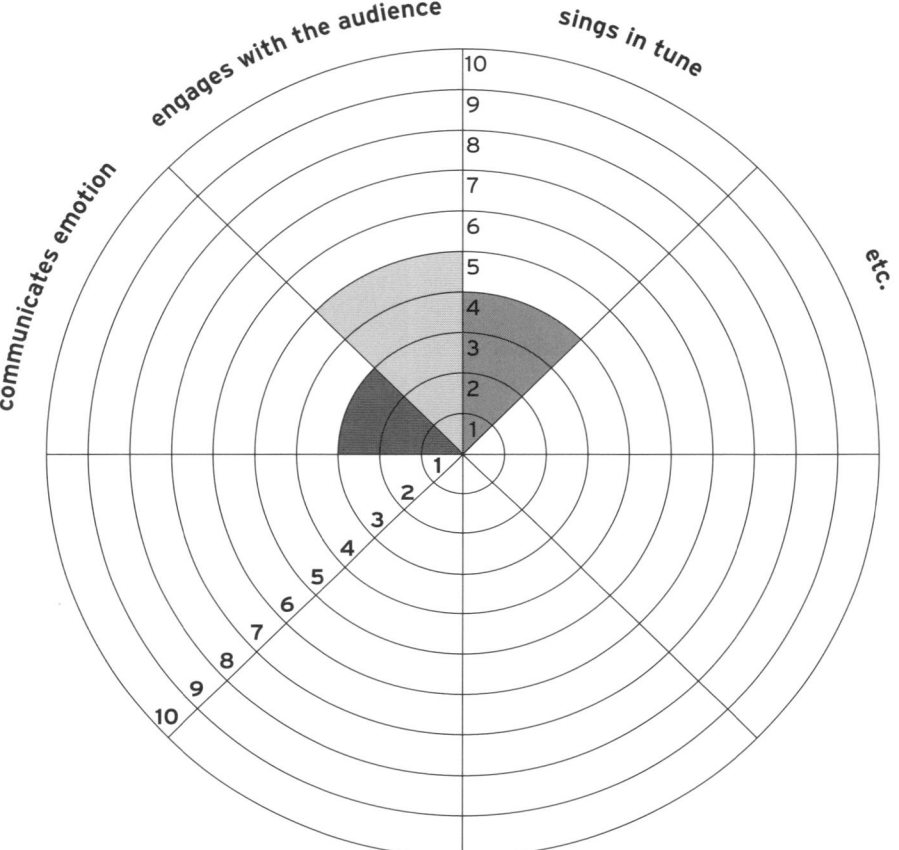

The Importance of Developing Psychological Flexibility on Nurturing Musicality

The ideas explored in this chapter have demonstrated how musicality relies on the development of a broad range of musical knowledge (including skills), supportive and appropriately challenging environments and conditions that promote meaningful engagement, aesthetic connection to the music and ways to communicate musically. Psychological aspects of musical learning are also crucially important to the development of musicality. This final part of the chapter briefly explores the importance of psychological flexibility in music education and considers some practical implications for instrumental teachers. In terms of musical development, the term 'psychological flexibility' refers to the ability of oneself to hold ones own emotions and thoughts very lightly in order to continually create the right internal environment to persist in taking creative risks without being held back by unhelpful thoughts, feelings and behaviours that could otherwise stifle musical engagement.

Social comparison

One area in which psychological flexibility can be most helpful is within the sphere of social comparison, where the influence of others needs to be modified by our own internal psychological processes. Social comparison is something many of us naturally do in many aspects of our lives. It can be helpful, but very quickly this can become unhelpful and leave us feeling inadequate, and can drain our self-esteem and motivation. Unhelpful social comparison in musical learning can potentially lead to poorer performance and music performance anxiety. For example, comparing themselves to siblings or friends with a greater level of musical experience, or those who started at the same time but appear to be making faster progress, can make students feel unmusical. As Hargreaves and Lamont (2017: 44) note:

> *The ways in which we see ourselves, and evaluate our own skills and competencies, form a key part of the development of our identities, and these self-assessments influence our developments in general.*

Therefore, ways to see our own skills and competencies in a positive light through social comparison is an important potential strategy for students who would benefit from improving their own self-efficacy.

The following task, adapted from 'Play: A psychological toolkit for optimal music performance' (Daubney and Daubney, 2018) uses peer comparison in ways that are healthy and motivating. When completing this task, you could either use an example from your own musical life, or complete this exercise with a student who has a propensity to negatively engage in social comparison.

Activity 4.4

Take a blank piece of paper and draw two stick people side by side. The first one is you (or your student). Label this one as you and provide the stick person with your musical instrument and the attributes you have. This is the stick person on the left-hand side of your page.

The second stick person is someone in your peer group who you consider is able to do something better than you at this point in time. This can be for any reason – it can be that you feel they are generally better than you at everything or maybe a very specific thing. Make a list of the attributes that you see this person displaying that make you think they are better at something. Highlight as many of those attributes as you can and include physical, psychological, technical and communicative elements. Try to be as precise as possible about each of those attributes and what each one looks and sounds like. Now give that person a mark out of ten (where 1 is the lowest and 10 the highest) for each of those attributes that person displays.

Next, consider where you are on that same ten-point scale, essentially, how far behind them are you? Try to think about why you are putting yourself at that number and why they are at their number. Once you have done this, insert these details into a table like the one on page 85. Then, consider how you could move yourself up to the next rating on the scale and use the final section of the table to specify when you will evaluate whether you have moved towards your peer's rating.

Table 4.1

Attribute	Peer rating	Evidence for peer rating	My rating on this attribute	Evidence for my rating	How I can move to the next rating	When I will evaluate my movement
Great posture	8	Always has good posture when playing	6	I hunch over when I'm playing and this inhibits my movement and then the sounds that come out of my instrument	Make my posture a more prominent part of my routine before I start playing	Video myself doing a practice performance at the beginning of every month
Plays with a lot of emotion	9	Their performances are always really interesting and it is commented on in their exams, with higher grades awarded	3	I play the notes in time but I don't have any emotional connection with the music	Using a piece I know well and can play easily, try to think about what the music is trying to convey. Create a story that expresses the different parts of the music	Make a recording of me playing it now and one next week once I have worked on the storytelling
They seem to be able to really thrive on performing	9	They always look confident, relaxed and they consistently play well	2	Nerves get the better of me. It doesn't seem to show in my playing but how I feel inside is really distressing	Try to embed a range of suitable strategies into my life and musical activities	See how these are going every two weeks

Conclusion – Thinking Artistically

Having considered the importance of context and how we, as music teachers, can help people to feel musical, perhaps the ultimate goal for us to work towards is as Eisner (2002) describes here:

> ...one of the highest compliments one can pay is to call someone an artist within their own field, whether it's language, arts, mathematics, science, history, or the social studies. Given the value we accord artistry in our work, we might even say that the major goal of education is the preparation of artists, people who can think artistically about what they do, who can use their imagination, who can experience their work as it unfolds, who can exploit the unexpected, and who can make judgments about its direction on the basis of feeling as well as rule. That would not be an outrageous goal for education.

It is clear there is a lot to consider, and we must accept that the development of 'musicality' is not founded on a specific recipe. A big part of the responsibility for nurturing students to thrive musically falls to us. As educators, we should strive to be the best we can, to question our approaches and impact, and to seek out new challenges and ways of doing and thinking about music and music education.

From hip hop artists to Tabla players, orchestras and big bands to singer-songwriters, musicality is evident. It isn't something exclusive to one culture or tradition and the tenets of it – particularly musical fluency – underpin this. If we are to help our students to develop as musical beings, we need to open their ears and provide opportunities for a wide range of ways to engage in genuine musical endeavours in order to encourage us and our students be interactive, proactive and reactive musicians (Welch, Ockelford and Zimmermann, 2009). We need to get to know our students, their perceptions of what it is to be musical, and to understand their experiences, cultures and motivations in order to find ways for them to develop. A supportive, creative and appropriately challenging environment is crucial. And we need to enjoy ourselves, for this is vital, and if this is evident across our work, hopefully our students will enjoy themselves too.

Underpinning this, or perhaps holding this back, is our willingness to change too; to reflect on the impact and actions of our teaching and to redouble our efforts to model the values, behaviours, traits and attitudes into our teaching that we strive to instil in others. Playfulness and student autonomy are key to this, along with the recognition that we influence only part of a student's musical life and that we must respect the diverse musical endeavours that they bring in other ways without suggesting a hierarchy. It is also so important to promote the musical and psychological flexibility students need to take their next steps towards thinking and acting musically, no matter their current age, experience or trajectory. As Eisner laments, these would be not outrageous goals for music education. We ignore this at our peril, but we should also remember that, as music teachers, our actions can weave the magic of music education through our students' world and enrich their lives well beyond the classes or ensembles that they attend. Our work offers considerable potential to positively influence the development of growing musicianship and encourage people from all backgrounds, levels of musical experience and dispositions across the lifespan to thrive in their music learning endeavours, whatever they may be, and to live their lives feeling more musical.

References

Bloom, B. (1985) *Developing talent in young people*. New York: Ballantine Books.

Daubney, A. (2017) *Teaching Primary Music*. London: Sage.

Daubney, G. and Daubney, A. (2018) *Play: A psychological toolkit for optimal music performance*. Incorporated Society of Musicians. Online at: https://www.ism.org/play

Eisner, E. W. (2003) The arts and the creation of mind. Language Arts, 80,5., *Imagination and the Arts*, pp. 340-344. Online at: https://acurriculumjourney.files.wordpress.com/2014/04/eisner-2003-the-arts-and-the-creation-of-mind.pdf

Gagné, F. (2003) Transforming gifts into talents: The DMGT as a developmental theory. In: Colangelo, N., Davis, G. A. (Eds.), *Handbook of gifted education*, 3rd ed., pp. 60-74. Boston, MA: Allyn & Bacon.

Gordon, E. (1980) *Learning sequences in music: Skill, content, and patterns*. Chicago: G.I.A. Publications.

Hallam, S. (2006). Musicality. In: G. E. McPherson, ed. *The child as musician: A handbook of musical development*. Oxford: Oxford University Press, pp. 93-110.

Hallam, S. and Prince, V. (2003) Conceptions of musical ability. *Research Studies in Music Education*. 20(1), pp. 2-22. https://doi.org/10.1177/1321103X030200010101

Hargreaves, D. J. and Lamont, A. (2017) *The Psychology of musical development*. Cambridge: Cambridge University Press.

Juslin P. and Sloboda, J. eds., (2010) *The Handbook of music and emotion*. Oxford: Oxford University Press.

Laird, S. (2009) Musical hunger: A philosophical testimonial of miseducation. *Philosophy of Music Education Review*, 17(1), pp. 4-21.

Levitin D. J. (2012) What does it mean to be musical? *Neuroview*, 73(4), pp. 633-637. DOI:https://doi.org/10.1016/j.neuron.2012.01.017

McPherson, G. E. (1997) Giftedness and talent in music. *The Journal of Aesthetic Education*, 3(4), pp. 65-77.

Malloch, S. and Trevarthen, C., eds. (2009) *Communicative musicality: Exploring the basis of human companionship*. Oxford: Oxford University Press.

Parnutt, R. (2009) Prenatal development and the phylogeny and ontogeny of music. In: S. Hallam, I. Cross and M. Hault eds., *The Oxford Handbook of Music Psychology*. Oxford: Oxford University Press, pp. 219-228.

Ruddock, E. (2018) *On being musical: Education towards inclusion, Educational Philosophy and Theory*, 50(5), pp. 489-498, doi: 10.1080/00131857.2016.1198248

Swanwick, K. (1990) *Teaching Music Musically*. London: Routledge.

Trehub, S. (2009) Music lessons from infants. In: S. Hallam, I. Cross and M. Hault, eds. *The Oxford Handbook of Music Psychology*. Oxford: Oxford University Press, pp. 229-234.

Welch, G., Ockelford, A. and Zimmermann, S. (2009) The Sounds of Intent project: Modelling musical development in children with learning difficulties. *Psychology of Music*, 37(3), pp. 348-370.

Chapter 5 Commentary

Elsewhere in this book the case is made for approaches to teaching which put the learner at the centre of the educational interaction; not merely in terms of teaching which is relevant to the needs of the individual, but a more fundamentally democratic approach which puts learners in control of their own learning. But who is this learner? What do we and can we know about them? Can research into children and young people's general and musical development help us understand them better and tell us something about how to support them in developing their own musical identities? It is these concepts that Kim Burwell will explore in this chapter.

In parts of the world where graded music exams are popular, they provide a ready means of identifying the performance standard of a developing musician. But do they tell us everything we need to know about musical development? As Burwell points out, 'we have all seen children ... enjoying the sheer physicality of playing without any particular concern for the sound they are making; or pupils with good aural skills, who play what they expect to hear rather than the detail of what is written'. Such children often demonstrate high levels of musical skill which fall outside the rather narrowly defined definitions enshrined in the graded exam. Perhaps a better understanding of the stages of both general and musical development might help us with broader definitions and understanding of musical progress.

Burwell suggests that 'development involves a continuous interaction between innate capabilities that we expect to emerge of their own accord, and abilities that are learned'. This statement recognises that children have a range of powerful influences in their development that may have nothing to do with us as teachers and simply emerge and develop through children's interactions with their musical worlds. She will explore these within the context of children's general development and then more specifically within their musical development. This chapter is necessarily a brief summary of a huge area of study, but there are many prompts for further study which interested readers might follow.

5 Development and Instrumental Learning
Kim Burwell

Round the village stands out in my mind as a problem piece because I almost never had problem pieces. I was progressing quickly at the piano by the age of 9 or 10. I remember once learning ten new pieces in a week (and yes, wondering vaguely whether the material might be too easy for me). But I could not get on with *Round the village*. It was (uncharacteristically) bristling with chromaticism; looking at it now I can see a dominant 13th implied in bar 1, resolving via an appoggiatura 9th in bar 2. I loathed it. In my lesson I would pick out individual notes until I got stuck, and then wait – eyes front, feigning reading – until the teacher named the next note for me. I struggled to grasp the tune in my mind, though of course, I never actually heard it. Eventually the melody began to stick, but I never mastered the rhythm: the search for notes had dissolved any sense of pulse in bar 1, so I just played bar 2 slowly and hoped for the best.

It turns out that *Round the village* is not a gauntlet of unpredictable sharps: there's just one problem motif, seven times. It sounded new because of the chromaticism, and felt new because of the 1-2-1-2-1 fingering. We should have picked that out first, and played it as a game, transposing it all over the keyboard. The left hand has an easier part but it's always recalcitrant: we should have taken its two-bar pattern separately and noticed how many times it repeats itself. And it would have been worth singling out that appoggiatura 9th, embracing the dissonance and enjoying the resolution. A few minutes of prep could have paved a smooth path to music-making.

In the event, *Round the village* came to a stalemate: we quietly abandoned it, and moved on. But it occurs to me now that for my sister, who dropped out of piano lessons and remembered them with disdain, too many new pieces must have felt like *Round the village*.

The problem with situations like this is not, or is not limited to, a lack of strategic knowledge about approaching new material. Coaching undergraduates who are learning to teach their own instruments, I've seen that a surfeit of knowledge can be equally problematic. These young teachers, in the (admirable) spirit of ensuring that their pupils have a better experience with music than they once had, and hoping to avoid omissions and prevent problems before they arise, sometimes deliver so much information – details, rationale, caveats – that their pupils can barely function. In such cases, I ask them to consider proceeding on a 'need-to-know' basis. The principle is captured concisely by John Dewey in *My pedagogical creed* (1897): method in teaching 'is ultimately reducible to the question of the order of development of the child's powers and interests'. Thus the starting point for the instrumental lesson is not knowledge of 'how to play the instrument', 'how to play *Round the village*' or even 'how to make music'. The teacher has all of that knowledge, but the starting point for the lesson is the learner herself: what she understands and what she can do – now, and next – and with what kind of help from the teacher.

The scholarship of development can be invaluable to instrumental teachers who are constantly dealing with these questions, by providing a sense of context for each pupil's trajectory: not only what the pupil is like at any one time, but what she is becoming. The answers are complex because development is heterogeneous, and child development, of course, is a huge and rapidly expanding field of study. This chapter offers some sketches and highlights, that I hope will be of interest and value to studio teachers. It begins with the earliest emergence of aural perception and capabilities, and broadens into the multi-dimensional background of development through early and middle childhood and adolescence, before turning to the specifically-musical enculturation of children who enjoy specialist music education.

Fundamentally, development involves maturation (otherwise discussed in terms of nature, development, genetics, or biology) as well as enculturation (nurture, ecology, instruction, or environment). In short, development involves a continuous interaction between innate capabilities that we expect to emerge of their own accord, and abilities that are learned. Often, because individual trajectories are the product of the two variables, scholars are reluctant to define them in terms of age or distinct stages of development. Even so, there are changes expected from the cradle onward. Pitch perception is one. As adult musicians we tend not to notice, or we forget, that each musical note is a combination of frequencies that our brains 'process' as one pitch: normally babies are able to do this by about seven months of age (Laurel Trainor, 2005: 263). They begin to discern contours of pitch around the same time, with increasing refinement: by age five they can detect out-of-scale notes, and by age seven they can detect out-of-harmony notes, though detecting changes that are within-scale and within-harmony takes longer. Trainor (2005) points out that the earliest sensitivities are basic to our auditory and musical systems, while culture-specific features are learned later; so, for example, an apprehension of harmonic structure is developed gradually in western cultures through middle childhood or the primary school years. Coinciding with this attunement, children lose some of what David Hargreaves calls their 'open-earedness', or their tolerance for a wider range of musical styles (Hargreaves and Lamont, 2017). Thus, an initial grasp of convention comes at a cost, though there is often a recovery of flexibility, later.

Activity 5.1
Think back to your own development as a young musician. Make a table with two columns, entitled maturation and enculturation, then note down the key factors in your musical development under these headings. Thinking about your students, are there differences in the way their development is supported by enculturation (e.g. differing parental support, conducive environment, encouragement, etc.)? What can you do as a teacher to support those students whose musical development might be hampered by less advantageous developmental environments?

Arguably, there are basic musical elements that emerge even earlier than pitch perception, with babies engaging in imitation and turn-taking: adults speak to them in short, sing-song phrases and babies respond by moving and vocalising (Marsh and Young, 2015). Increasingly, the movements can be coordinated with the adult, and the vocalising becomes 'babbling', which effectively lays the foundations for verbal communication through song. From the adult's responses to them babies come to know what their own babblings mean (Dewey, 1897), and infant-directed speech can signify emotional expression, perceived as early as 5 or 6 months (Daniel, 2006). The interpretation of emotion in music seems to develop relatively slowly, however. In a review of the literature, Corrigall and Schellenberg (2015) report that usually children can perceive the emotional tone of music by the time they start school, but they tend to rely on tempo for cues – fast being happy, and slow, sad. These features are culture-general, and seem to prevail through middle childhood, though some culture-specific cues are also learned – like major keys happy, and minor, sad. Perhaps surprisingly, there is little evidence suggesting that musical training can accelerate the development of this kind of discernment, and Hallam (2001: 21) having observed 55 young string-players each practising a new piece, noted that they did not attend to interpretative matters like dynamics unless they had attained previously 'a quite high level of expertise'. Learning psychologist Lev Vygotsky (1896–1934) asserted that learning precedes development (1978), but it seems that some aspects of music-making, and indeed life, are more susceptible to early training than others.

Multiple Dimensions in Development: The Evolving Self

Aside from the fundamental dichotomy of maturation and enculturation, development can be divided among several dimensions – emotional, behavioural, psychomotor, and cognitive – and these progress at different rates, presenting the child with a range of developmental tasks. Middle childhood, coinciding roughly with the primary school years, is typically the time for starting instrumental lessons, and for good reasons.

After rapid growth during infancy – particularly of the brain, which reaches 90% of its mature weight by age five (Daniel, 2006) – middle childhood is a relatively quiet period developmentally, with growth slower and steadier, and this provides a tremendous window of opportunity for learning. By age seven we expect children to have learned a degree of self-regulation, cognitively (with improvements in attention and concentration) and emotionally (so they can play well with others). These characteristics are required for, and consolidated by, formal schooling, which also opens a new world to children, beyond the home environment.

The partial separation from parents invites independence, and is associated with a drive for competence: it is no accident that classic children's literature features 'plucky, clever children who outsmart and outperform adults' (Gilmore and Meersand, 2015) – from Enid Blyton's Famous Five (1942-1962) through to Roald Dahl's Matilda (1988) and J.K. Rowling's Harry Potter (1997-2007). There is also a drive for order, and a passion for rule-based games, plans and projects (Gilmore and Meersand, 2015; Schofield, 2006). Children begin to perceive themselves differently, as having permanent dispositions, and often they are keen to measure those against others, becoming sensitive to feedback (Shiner and Caspi, 2003) and seeking confirmation from adults that they are correct (Kegan, 1982). In the context of instrumental lessons, Gary McPherson (2009) has shown that children quickly form lasting impressions of themselves as musicians, and that parents can play a crucial role in fostering their feelings of competence. The instrumental teacher has an important role to play in this too, because children typically compensate for the partial separation from their parents by seeking reliable relationships with other familiar adults (Mercer, 2018).

> Tony was probably 9 when, late in one of our piano lessons, I had an unexpected glimpse into his evolving sense of self. We had dealt with the opening section of a new piece, and we were trying to decide how much more he should learn for next time – one more section (his preference), or two (mine). I tried chivvying him along – 'Come on Tony, you're a clever chap!', and I was surprised that he did not laugh and give in.
>
> Rather, he paused, pondering, and said, 'Really?' – and when I pressed him a little further, his quiet response was, for me, like dropping a bombshell: 'Sometimes I think I'm stupid'. He was sitting very still, sincere and concerned. I knew from some of our previous chats that one of Tony's friends had become leader of the school orchestra, another was clearly outdoing him at football, and he was becoming conscious of how his school grades compared with his brother's.

> My instinct was to chivvy Tony along even more enthusiastically, dismissing the notion of stupidity and confidently announcing that he had better do THREE sections for next week. *Now* he laughed. Even so, by the following week, he had those three sections absolutely sorted; and in the following months, Tony turned himself into a very competent young pianist.

It can be challenging for us to monitor and support our pupils in developmentally-appropriate ways, because the multiple dimensions of development evolve at different rates, and at any given age, each child will present with a different developmental profile. We know for example that some infants are more school-ready than others, by age five; some will cope with the transition smoothly, while others may struggle, and it is around the time of school entry that learning difficulties or behavioural problems are exposed. A further transition occurs with the shift into adolescence, when the variety among individuals is still more dramatic. Cognitive development now is closely linked to age and experience, whereas puberty – marked by a rapid growth and reconfiguration of the body – is linked to maturational changes in arousal, motivation and emotion (Steinberg, 2016). The stakes of independence are raised again, as the child is thrown (emotionally ready or not) toward adulthood, and faces a raft of new expectations regarding self-regulation and autonomy.

Erik Erikson (1968) famously characterised adolescence as a time of identity crisis, and age 14 is the peak period for the onset of mental disorders (Gilmore and Meersand, 2015); but many adolescents navigate its challenges successfully, with sensitive support from teachers and caregivers. Susan Bailey (2006) recommends an authoritative approach, quite distinct from authoritarianism, that includes 'warmth, structure and support for autonomy'. Peer groups can provide empathy and social support, though conversely, the drive to conform to group expectations can be powerful for young people who become 'exquisitely aware' of how they compare with one another (Gilmore and Meersand, 2015). Relationships with adults shift as teenagers vary increasingly in their ability to recruit the attention of others (Kegan, 1982). Their repositioning at home and at school can be a lengthy process, and while puberty begins as early as age nine or ten, adolescence can be extended as young people often remain dependent on their parents into their early 20s (Bailey, 2006). Through this transition, the continuity of one-to-one instrumental lessons can be deeply significant for adolescents, first because they can support a private passion that may (but need not) tie in with group activity, and second because of the opportunity to work with a sympathetic adult who knows them well, and who can tailor a course of musical engagement to suit their evolving strengths and interests.

> **Activity 5.2**
> Think of two or three of your students across the age range from middle childhood to adolescence. Write a short vignette of each student, identifying how they exhibit the developmental traits outlined above. How do you, or could you, adapt your teaching to reflect the needs of students at these differing stages?

Musical Development

The grounds for musical development are laid in early experience, through the interaction of evolving capabilities, participation and exposure to music. Infants respond to music through social engagement with others, and their musical play typically combines singing and movement (Marsh and Young, 2015). On the basis of such enculturation, children become more attentive to music, gaining an intuitive grasp of its global features – whether it is fast or slow, loud or soft. With specialist training, they can acquire a more formal understanding, noticing patterns and how they are put together (Bamberger, 1991; Gardner, 1993). Since the work of Howard Gardner (1993) on multiple intelligences, musical intelligence has been recognised in its own right, though it can be divided among further abilities – psychomotor, aural, cognitive, expressive – that sometimes overlap other domains of learning. Edwin Gordon (1980) used the word 'audiation' to describe components specific to music, involving not only aural perception but the understanding, imagination and memory involved in making sense of it. In practical terms, the various components can develop at different rates: we have all seen children leading with their psychomotor skills – enjoying the sheer physicality of playing without any particular concern for the sound they are making; or pupils with good aural skills, who play what they expect to hear rather than the detail of what is written; and sometimes pupils who rely so closely on their cognitive skills that they do not recognise well-known tunes while they're reading them.

Problems with the multiple processing of psychomotor, aural and cognitive skills are most likely to emerge when children are working alone. Thus Hallam (2001), in her observations of children's violin practice, reported a gap between previous examination results, presumably achieved in collaboration with their teachers and perhaps parents, and what they were able to accomplish independently. Vygotsky (1978) explains this gap in terms of the 'zone of proximal development': what children can grasp or do is extended when they have the opportunity to interact with more expert others. With experience in this kind of joint activity, children gradually internalise skills, concepts and strategies, their zones of proximal development shifting as their solo activity becomes more sophisticated. This casts light on Hallam's (2001) finding that when the children were practising alone, their years of previous experience learning an instrument were a better predictor of success than their level of strategy use. Cognitive strategies can be explained and rehearsed in lessons, but children need to accumulate a certain amount of expertise in the musical domain before they can take responsibility for monitoring and regulating those strategies effectively. Interestingly, it seems that among the components of self-regulation, control can be cultivated deliberately, but monitoring is maturational – it comes with time; while on the other hand, and returning to the idea that learning precedes development, regulatory abilities can begin domain-specific before becoming generalised around the age of 14 or 15 (Zachariou and Whitebread, 2019). This might suggest that there is a balance to be struck, between allowing children time to mature in terms of self-regulation, and using specialised training to stimulate its development within the music domain in particular.

Activity 5.3

Think of one of your pupils. At this particular point in their development, can you ascertain the role that music has in your pupil's sense of self? Can you identify areas where they feel competent – or could, with your help? Can you locate their motivation to come to lessons, to practise, or to learn particular pieces? Can you identify any personal passions? Any of these might give you insight and access to the drive that can be harnessed to their individual journeys in music.

There is a balance to be struck, too, in the development of reading skills. Reading is an essential skill for anyone learning to play score-based repertoire, and although its importance is largely specific to western cultures, it is not limited to 'classical' music. The aspiration may be to routinise reading skills early, so that they pose no obstacle to performing and understanding. The best readers I have known read a lot of music as young children, with ex-choristers, for example, demonstrating remarkable levels of ease and fluency. Often, musicians who learned to read late – typically because they were able to achieve a good deal as singers or guitarists before having to tackle literacy – bitterly regret missing the early start that might have facilitated their performing as adults. As Dewey (1897) points out, reading provides tools that economise effort. On the other hand, and as Dewey also emphasises, the order of child development begins with the active side, not the passive; the starting point for lessons is the child's current powers and interests, not what we think she may find meaningful some years hence; and literacy skills presented for their own sake may remain 'a mass of meaningless and arbitrary ideas' (80). Fortunately, a balance can be struck for each child, and the imagination and enterprise of sympathetic teachers can be supplemented by ideas from scholarly literature, imaginative tutor-books, and the formal methodologies particularly of Kodaly (1882–1967) and Dalcroze (1865–1950).

> Through my family and students, I have had the pleasure of observing some highly constructive, developmentally-appropriate preparation for literacy, in early childhood music classes. Some outstanding examples include:
>
> The five lines of the stave are shown in the carpet, or painted across the floor, and the children play games that involve stepping or leaping onto a line or a space, or finding the right line or space when the teacher calls out its letter-name.
>
> Whole body movements are used to distinguish pitches from one another – stretching up for 'high' notes and down for 'low'. As the children become more confident the movements are replaced gradually by 'secret code signs' – the hand turned this way for high, that way for low.
>
> Stepping games introduce the principles of rhythmic patterns, with the children responding to musical prompts with lumbering semibreves, stately minims, walking crotchets or running quavers, whether they are named or not.
>
> All of these felt concepts gradually become more explicit, so that when the notated score is introduced in instrumental lessons, the transition is smoothed: from their first formal studio lessons, children quickly become comfortable with the concept of the stave, the use of symbols for pitch, and the characterisation of rhythm.

The strategies used by clever early childhood teachers prepare for literacy through activity, and this is complemented by the modern catch-phrase 'sound before symbol', which counteracts a tendency for reading to dominate early studio lessons. This need not imply a two-dimensional approach: learning by ear or by rote is congenial for young children, but it is not incompatible with learning through reading (Gardner, 1993). Rather, taking a cue again from Dewey, literacy should be taught as one of the mutually-embedded skills that make music what it is: reading, playing by ear, playing from memory, improvising, and playing rehearsed music. Early engagement with this rich range of skills has been linked to student success (McPherson, Davidson and Evans, 2015). Fundamentally, it ensures that the student's experience, and her relationship with her instrument, remain musical.

Activity 5.4
Gary McPherson (2015) proposes five essential skills of music: reading, playing by ear, playing from memory, improvising, and playing rehearsed music. Given the potential for these to help one another, and yet develop at different rates, how are each of your students faring in each skill at this particular point in their development? And how can you feed the areas that need more nourishment?

Epilogue: *Round the Village*

The discussion above, like the scholarly literature on development, has tended to emphasise perceptual and cognitive matters, though the order of development among the child's powers and interests includes psychomotor and motivational issues that pose further challenges. Returning now to *Round the village*, for example, I am struck by the 1-2-1-2-1 fingering given for the chromatic motif: why not use the standard fingering 1-3-1-3-1? Presumably adjacent numbers and fingers were thought to be better suited to the cognitive development of a child; but alternating 1 and 3 sets the hand rocking, minimising the emphasis on fingerwork by drawing on macro-muscular control, the basis of rotary technique. For children, with physical activity salient in their early development, such gestures come easily and feel good. What children do spontaneously can give us clues, too, about their motivation, particularly when there are differences between formal lesson activity and what they do independently. In that light, I am struck by the fact that we attempted *Round the village* when we did: it came from a tutor book that moved through well-judged incremental steps as a rule, but this one was an aberration, abruptly introducing a cluster of new challenges at once. My course of study at that time was dictated by the book, not my developmental profile; but my learning was driven by my motivation – by the extra-curricular activity that I did at home, as I continually listened, read, played by ear and 'messed about' in ways that (I think) my teacher never suspected. What my teacher saw in lessons was only part of the musician I was becoming.

No music was made in my encounter with *Round the village*. On the face of it, that might have been because reading was prioritised over music-making; but reading was not being learned, either – the teacher was doing that work for me, in a drip-feed process of naming one note at a time; and literacy is not merely a matter of naming notes, anyway – it's understanding what's going on. At that time in my development, what I needed from the teacher was a different kind of help. The alternative approach that I suggested above analyses the task and divides it into manageable components before putting them back together, and that is exactly what adult performers do when we approach new music.

Children can participate in this authentic kind of approach too, if the teacher – the more expert other – is there to help them notice shapes and patterns, so that they gradually learn how music is put together. In the long term this provides the means to proceed through repertoire of increasing complexity, because *this* is how literacy economises effort. In the short term it provides better lesson experiences, which engage the developmental capabilities of the child. The multi-dimensional nature of development and of music-making, each pupil presenting an individual, shifting profile, means that helping children to navigate their musical zones of proximal development is itself a sophisticated practice; and for instrumental teachers, the scholarship of development and of musical development in particular can guide us in our exploration of how lessons can embrace and support the learning of the whole child, the whole musician.

References

Bailey, S. (2006) Adolescence and beyond: twelve years onwards. In: J. Aldgate, D. Jones, W. Rose and C. Jeffery, eds. *The developing world of the child*, London, Philadelphia: Jessica Kingsley.

Bamberger, J. (1991) *The mind behind the musical ear. How children develop musical intelligence*. Cambridge, MA, London, UK: Harvard University Press.

Corrigall, K. A. and Schellenberg, E. G. (2015) Music cognition in childhood. In: G. McPherson, ed. *The child as musician: a handbook of musical development*, 2nd edn., pp. 81–101. Oxford: Oxford University Press.

Daniel, B. (2006) Early childhood: zero to four years. In: J. Aldgate, D. Jones, W. Rose and C. Jeffery, eds. *The developing world of the child*, London, Philadelphia: Jessica Kingsley.

Dewey, J. (1897) My pedagogic creed. *The School Journal*, 54(3), pp. 77–80.
http://www.infed.org/archives/e-texts/e-dew-pc.htm

Erikson, E. H. (1968) *Identity, youth and crisis*. New York, London: Norton.

Gardner, H. (1993) *Frames of mind. The theory of multiple intelligences*, 2nd edn. London: Fontana.

Gilmore, K. and Meersand, P. (2015) *The little book of child and adolescent development*. Oxford Medicine Online: Oxford University.

Gordon, E. E. (1980, 1993) *Learning sequences in music. Skill, content, and patterns. A music learning theory*. Chicago: GIA Publications.

Hallam, S. (2001) The development of expertise in young musicians: strategy use, knowledge acquisition and individual diversity. *Music Education Research*, 3(1), pp. 7–23.

Hargreaves, D. and Lamont, A. (2017) *The psychology of musical development*. Cambridge: Cambridge University Press.

Kegan, R. (1982) *The evolving self. Problem and process in human development*. Cambridge, London: Harvard University Press.

Marsh, K. and Young, S. (2015) Musical play. In: G. McPherson, ed. *The child as musician: a handbook of musical development*, 2nd edn. Oxford: Oxford University Press, pp. 462–484.

McPherson, G. (2009) The role of parents in children's musical development. *Psychology of Music,* 37(1), pp. 91-110.

McPherson, G. E., Davidson, J. W. and Evans, P. (2015) Playing an instrument. In: G. McPherson, ed. *The child as musician: a handbook of musical development*, 2nd ed. Oxford: Oxford University Press, pp. 401-421.

Mercer, J. (2018) *Child development. Concepts and theories*. Los Angeles, London, New Delhi, Singapore, Washington, Melbourne: Sage.

Shiner, R. and Caspi, A. (2003) Personality differences in childhood and adolescence: measurement, development, and consequences. *Journal of Child Psychology and Psychiatry*, 44(1), pp. 2-32.

Steinberg, L. (2016) Cognitive and affective development in adolescence. In: B. Maughan and M. Little, eds. *Child Development*, Abingdon: Routledge, pp. 111-116.

Trainor, L. J. (2005) Are there critical periods for musical development? *Developmental psychobiology,* 46(3), pp. 262-278.

Vygotsky, L. S. (1978) *Mind in society. The development of higher psychological processes*. M. Cole, V. John-Steiner, S. Scribner, and E. Souberman, eds. Cambridge MA, London: Harvard University Press.

Zachariou, A. and Whitebread, D. (2019) Developmental differences in young children's self-regulation. *Journal of Applied Developmental Psychology*, 62, pp. 282-293.

Chapter 6 Commentary

'How do I get my students to practise' is an often-heard plea from instrumental teachers through the ages, and if there was a 'magic bullet' in the research literature which would provide a solution it would have been patented long ago! However, what current research does suggest is that where learners feel they are in control of their learning, are making progress, and are recognised for their achievements, then they tend to be more motivated in what they do.

One of the central implications of the master-apprentice model of instrumental teaching is that the 'apprentice' is striving to achieve the skills that the 'master' already has. Practice in this context is likely to involve the teacher setting work for the student to complete between the lessons – after all they are the expert, so they understand the skills the student needs to develop and the order in which they need to attempt them, right? Well, perhaps, but if we are going to challenge some of the established models of instrumental learning, we might do well to re-examine what supports students' motivation and what environments it thrives in.

In this chapter Nick Beach argues that looking at some of the theories that underpin student motivation might help support more learners to continue with their instrumental learning. All of us as teachers want our students to be intrinsically motivated – to want to learn for the sheer joy of making music on the instrument. But how often do we resort to the extrinsic – rewards, threats, fear, ridicule, withdrawing approval, peer comparison, etc. Sometimes it seems as if we take a student's lack of motivation as a personal affront – we have put in so much effort, why is this not matched by the student?

In what is often an emotionally charged area this chapter gives us the opportunity to step back and look at motivation and practice in a new light. Perhaps if we ask some questions about how to encourage the feelings of achievement and success that often go hand in hand in highly motivated learners we might help more of our students experience these.

6 Sustaining Interest and Motivation: Agency and Self-regulation

Nick Beach

Most children who start to learn a musical instrument do not continue playing through into adult life. In one of the largest longitudinal studies of those beginning a musical instrument (McPherson, 2012), 27% gave up in the first two years and only 41% continued for five years. We might ask whether it is simply the way of things that children will try a range of activities and select for greater focus and effort the ones that excite them, or are we losing children who had the potential to gain a great deal from learning an instrument? When a child walks into their first instrumental music lesson there are a range of expectations at play: from the teacher, parents, other adults, peers and of course the child themselves. There will be many reasons why children in McPherson's study gave up in the early stages, but it is reasonable to assume that, for many, the motivation to overcome the challenges of learning an instrument waned over time. In this chapter we will look at some broader research into what motivates learners and how that motivation can be sustained. By motivation we might mean the motivation to persevere, to practise, to prioritise instrumental playing over other competing demands or to succeed, however success might be defined, but overall we will be considering how teachers and others can help create situations and environments where students can thrive.

One way of thinking about motivation is to consider the difference between intrinsic motivation, where motivation grows from the activity itself, and extrinsic, where it comes from external factors.

In the former, the student perhaps wants to play a particular piece really well or get good enough to play something they really like. In the latter, motivation stems from goals, rewards or punishments outside the activity. Our instinct as musicians is that intrinsic musical motivations are more desirable than extrinsic ones, and we hope that learners who have been externally motivated will eventually become intrinsically motivated to some degree. However, there is often little consideration given to the conditions which can support the development of intrinsic motivation in music learning and how these can be fostered. Motivating factors can also be thought of as either goal achieving (my mum will be pleased, I'll get a good grade) or discomfort avoiding (my mum will be cross if I don't, I don't want to mess up in the concert). Once again, we might have an instinct that positive motivators might be more effective and desirable than discomfort avoiding ones.

> **Activity 6.1**
>
> Talk to some of your students about what motivates them and make a list of motivational factors. Think about the characteristics of these: are they intrinsic or extrinsic, are they about making positive things happen (my mum/teacher will be pleased) or about avoiding negative things (my mum/teacher will be cross if I don't). Draw a box with four quadrants and plot your list of motivating factors as follows:
>
> | Extrinsic Positive e.g. I want to get a good mark in my exam. | Intrinsic Positive e.g. I really want to be able to learn that piece. |
> |---|---|
> | Extrinsic Discomfort Avoidance e.g. I don't want my mum to be cross. | Intrinsic Discomfort Avoidance e.g. I don't want to be the one that gets in the way of the band giving a great performance. |

Most of us as instrumental teachers will think of motivation and practice as being inextricably linked. One of the most commonly cited reasons for a child giving up learning a musical instrument is that they find practice a chore or a source of stress (McPherson, 2012). It is perhaps understandable that the excitement a learner feels on starting a new instrument may dim somewhat when obstacles are met – this is the norm with the learning of any new skill. But as so many children in McPherson's study dropped out of learning giving practice issues as a reason, perhaps we might try to understand better some of the motivational factors at play along with the theory that underpins them.

The Russian psychologist Vygotsky imagined learning taking place in the area between that which a learner could achieve on their own without support of any kind, and that which a learner can achieve with a teacher or more able peer (Vygotsky, 1978 in Blair, 2009). This concept of the 'zone of proximal development' (ZPD) helps us understand and identify that sweet spot for a learning goal which is just above what the learner knows or can do already, but not so difficult as to be unachievable, or only achievable with teacher support. This latter point is important when it comes to instrumental practice. Arguably the ZPD for a learner in a lesson with a teacher is different from that for that learner when they are practising at home alone. In the lesson the teacher will be offering advice, guidance, analysis and prompts to help the learner achieve more than they could on their own. In their practice at home, they seldom have such support, and practice can become a negative experience where the learner feels they are not achieving to the level they did in the lesson, becoming discouraged and demotivated.

> **Activity 6.2**
> Look at the practice goals you have set for your students over the past week. Think about these in the context of Vygotsky's ZPD. Looking back would you change anything?

In this chapter we will look at three well understood concepts in educational and psychological theory that are closely linked to motivation. We will ask some questions about how these might apply in the context of learning a musical instrument and attempt to draw them together into a set of approaches that might have practical implications for instrumental teachers and their learners.

Self-efficacy

The concept of self-efficacy is most extensively explored by Bandura who defines it as: 'people's beliefs about their capabilities to produce designated levels of performance that exercise influence over events that affect their lives' (Bandura, 1994: 2). Key to this definition is that a person's perceived level of self-efficacy is determined by their belief in their ability, not an empirical or other external measurement of their ability. In the educational context, learners who have high levels of self-efficacy believe that they have the ability to overcome obstacles, solve problems, deal with situations, etc. Such learners are more likely than others to be successful in their endeavours. They see tasks as 'challenges to be mastered rather than threats to be avoided' (Bandura, 1994: np). In contrast, when learners with low self-efficacy are faced with difficult tasks they tend to 'dwell on their personal deficiencies, the obstacles they will encounter and all kinds of adverse outcomes …' Bandura, 1994: np)

A further impact of low self-efficacy is stress, anxiety and low self-esteem resulting from a perceived lack of ability to conquer tasks. Learners with low self-efficacy view their inability to overcome a problem as resulting from their own inadequacy, leading to feelings of anxiety and stress. Learners with high self-efficacy tend to attribute failure to external influences and don't 'take it personally'. A natural human instinct in stressful situations is to remove oneself from the source of that stress, so it is easy to see how instrumental learners with low self-efficacy will be tempted to give up in order to avoid those negative feelings.

Although some personality types tend towards higher levels of self-efficacy, much of a learner's level of self-efficacy is influenced by the experiences they have had and the interactions with others they have experienced. Bandura identifies four sources of self-efficacy:

Mastery experiences – the learner has experienced success overcoming obstacles in the past so has the confidence to assume they will overcome further obstacles in the future. Key here is the level of the obstacle they have overcome, and at what stage they are in their learning. In order to build self-efficacy the tasks the learner overcomes must be challenging enough to provide a sense of achievement, but not so challenging as to generate a high risk of failure.

Observation of successful peers – the learner sees people they view as of similar ability to themselves successfully overcoming obstacles, and gains from this the confidence to do it themselves. This requires careful handling and a sensitivity to how learners view each other.

Social persuasion – that one has the required skills – this might come from the teacher, parent or peers. This is an area where many teachers are particularly gifted though it is sometimes hard to see how they have the positive impact they do. Again, caution is required, as Bandura states: 'It is more difficult to instil high beliefs of personal efficacy by social persuasion alone than to undermine them' (71–81).

Personality traits and emotional states – some learners are simply more determined and more self-confident than others. Psychological and emotional states also play a part, as does mood. But even here learners possessing different degrees of self-efficacy will react in different ways. The learner with high levels of self-efficacy will often view the stresses involved in performance preparation as a positive and energising motivator. Whereas the learner with low self-efficacy may find this stress debilitating and an inhibitor to success.

Self-efficacy is closely linked to motivation as it suggests that learners who succeed in tasks which are of value to them will be motivated in future tasks. One might summarise the impact of self-efficacy on motivation through the old axiom: 'success breeds success'. This concept explains to some extent the upward and downward spirals that many teachers see in their learners. Child A has early success, is praised and recognised by teacher, parent/carer and peers, feels confident in their ability so works hard to achieve again. Child B hits a challenge, feels they cannot overcome it, gets discouraged, practises less, doesn't respond well to coercion to practise and gives up. Self-efficacy theory would suggest that building the learner's belief in their ability to overcome obstacles offers one way to reinforce positive spirals.

Activity 6.3
Thinking about Bandura's four sources of efficacy, make a list under each heading of the sorts of activities instrumental teachers might do with their students that might improve the students' feelings of self-efficacy.

Agency

Learner agency describes the degree to which learners have, or feel they have, control or influence over their own learning. Maehr (2002) outlines how self-determination theory suggests that learners who are responsible for their actions and free to make choices are likely to be more intrinsically motivated. Giddens (1976) describes agency as an understanding that the world does not have a predetermined future and that learners have choices which will impact that future. In music learning Swanwick (1999: 53-4) describes agency as the natural energies that sustain spontaneous learning: 'curiosity; a desire to be competent; wanting to emulate others; [and] a need for social interaction'. Agency is context specific and highly dependent on relationships between individuals and in particular the societal structures that produce and sustain the relationship.

It is useful here to consider the power balance in the relationship between instrumental teacher and instrumental learner. The instrumental teacher is power-full – they often have high status (at least as perceived by their students), tending to be seen by their pupils as having high levels of expertise, technical skill and experience. In contrast the learner is relatively power-less – they often perceive themselves to be dependent on the teacher for their wisdom and guidance. This power imbalance can result in learning which is fully directed by the teacher, with the learner as recipient, or even supplicant.

> ... *highly skilled musicians/instrumental teachers are viewed as 'masters' that expect respect and obedience from their students. The teacher is regarded as a possessor of the tradition and if the student shows her/ himself worthy of it, the master can share the tradition with him or her, but only a little piece at a time* (Rostvall and West, 2003: 222).

Supporting the development of agency in instrumental learners requires placing the learner at the heart of their own learning, and as Westerlund argues, the whole purpose of music education should be in the learner, not the subject matter (Westerlund, 2002). So it is vital, therefore, that as teachers we are able to develop a deep understanding of why it is that our students are engaging with music learning and what their musical aims and goals are. Only through this understanding can we build a sense of agency in our students, so that they feel in control of learning which is geared towards their own ambitions.

In taking the lid off the Pandora's Box of learners' own aims we should be prepared for the fact that these may require real change in the teacher's approach. Often the choice offered to learners is illusory: Would you like to play this piece or that one? Which options will you choose for your exam? Which piece shall we start with? These are often merely presentational choices that don't impact on the curriculum that the teacher has set for their student. Referring to Green's (2002) work, learners in popular music often had little regard for a progression of pieces leading from the simple to the hard. They would frequently dive straight into harder music without playing simpler pieces first, and because of their determination and passion for the music they succeeded. This might suggest a rather different role for the instrumental teacher as the person who enables and supports the agency of the learner, providing information, guidance and expertise when requested by the student, but not imposing their own view of what musical progression should look like. Understanding of students' wider musical loves is important – a learner who is struggling with motivation to practise may still consider other aspects of music extremely important in their lives. Perhaps this broader understanding of the drivers that lead our students to engage with music might help us as teachers to understand them as musical agents.

> ### Activity 6.4
> Add to the survey you conducted in the first activity in this chapter, either with the same students or different ones. Explore the following ideas with your students:
>
> Think back to before you started learning – can you remember why you chose this instrument? What were you most looking forward to?
>
> Have your aims changed or are they the same?
>
> What excites you most about learning this instrument? What are you most looking forward to being able to do?
>
> Use this conversation to start to build a profile of your student and what they want to achieve. Then consider whether your current curriculum is serving these aims and, if not, what changes you would like to make.

Flow

> *I remember some of my own lessons as a learner, and later as a teacher, where the clock seemed to stand still – have we really only had ten minutes of the lesson! But on other days I remember lessons where we were so totally absorbed in the music that it was only the knocking on the door that reminded us that time was up.*

It is this latter experience which is described by the Hungarian-American psychologist Mihaly Csikszentmihalyi as flow: a state of consciousness where a person is totally absorbed in a task. Flow is a deeply enjoyable state, in which the outside world and its distractions are excluded and the activity at hand has a person's full attention. There are a number of factors that Csikszentmihalyi (Nakamura and Csikszentmihalyi, 1991) identifies as features of flow experiences:

Balance of challenge and skill – the task is one which uses and stretches our skills. It is not so challenging as to be unachievable, nor so easy as to be boring.

Clear goals and feedback – in order to experience flow, we must feel that we are getting somewhere, and that the goal we are reaching is one which is important to us.

Concentration – the level of challenge will require full concentration on the task at hand, with no room for other thoughts.

Distortion of time – people experiencing flow frequently lose track of the time spent on the activity.

Autotelic experience – defined as an activity which is an end in itself, in which doing the activity is its own reward and doesn't require or contribute to some external or future benefit.

Although flow can be experienced in any form of human endeavour, it is particularly prevalent in music. It is common to hear musicians talk about being 'in the zone', 'lost in their music', etc. But it need not be something which is reserved for the expert musician.

Fig 6.1

Adapted from Csikszentmihalyi (1991)

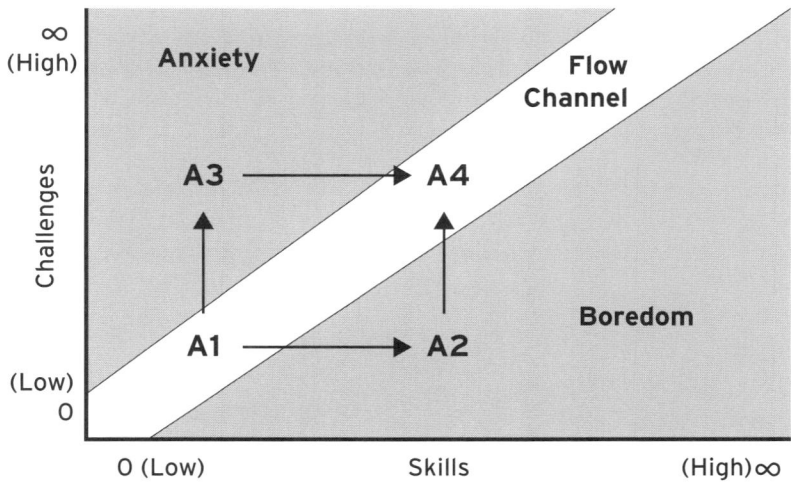

In the figure above A is for Asha, who learns the piano. At A1 Asha is just starting out, playing simple pieces. She can still experience flow as it takes a great deal of concentration to use her emerging skills. However, if she continues with these pieces, she will gradually move to A2, where boredom sets in and she moves out of the flow channel. Alternatively, her teacher might push her too quickly onto new pieces for which she doesn't have the skills (A3). A2 and A3 are uncomfortable places for Asha and her inclination will be to remove herself from them, either by simply not engaging, or in extreme cases by giving up. The skilled teacher will be constantly in dialogue with Asha to help her reach A4 and ensure that her music-making takes place in the channel in which flow is most likely to be experienced.

A case study in flow

Whilst writing this chapter I have been renovating an old mill in the West of England – this has involved learning a great many new skills. My motivation to get down to work and stick at it varies enormously. Some tasks, flooring for example, I have learned to do well and will happily spend hours getting it just right and feel the reward as it comes together. In others, such as dry-lining the ceilings, my current skill level doesn't produce a rewarding finish so I am much more likely to evade getting going and stop early. However, a well-placed word of encouragement from one of our many visiting professionals can change that in an instant and have me beavering away again!

Activity 6.5

Use the graphic on page 107 to track one of your pupils over the coming weeks. How will you judge where they are on the graph? How will you try to move them into the flow channel? Make a note of the strategies that are successful.

Motivation and Musical Instrument Learning

At first glance the concepts explored above might seem the very opposite of the approach which characterises the master/apprentice model which, as explored elsewhere in this book, underpins many traditional approaches to instrumental teaching and learning. In such approaches the course of study is usually determined by the teacher as a kind of path to enlightenment which, if the student stays the course, will result in them becoming a violinist, pianist, or whatever. This goal may well be shared by an ambitious parent, but it is frequently unclear whether it is shared by the learner.

There is a strong research base that suggests that the three concepts explored in this chapter are positive factors in motivating learners. There is, of course, some degree of overlap between them but some general themes emerge:

Challenge vs skills – both self-efficacy and flow theories emphasise the criticality of balancing challenges to existing skills. In the instrumental teaching context it is important to remember that this balance changes with context. The challenges a learner can overcome in a lesson with the scaffolding and support provided by the teacher may well seem overwhelming during their personal practice when this support is removed.

Learner empowerment – agency and flow theories make strong cases for the benefits of learners setting their own goals and monitoring and assessing their progress toward these. This suggests that the teacher in this context may not be the person that sets out the course of study, but might instead be the guide who helps the learner identify their goals and the skills they will need to achieve them.

Feedback – in the context of self-efficacy and flow theories, feedback comes to mean something rather different from straightforward appraisal. Developing self-efficacy requires feedback that builds confidence and the belief that challenges can be overcome. A state of flow might be best supported by the occasional well-placed word of encouragement. Or, feedback may not be external at all, but provided by the learner seeing their efforts producing a result that they find valuable and rewarding and that they are progressing towards reaching their own goals.

It is interesting to contrast for a moment the more traditional ways of learning with the way music is learned in the digital space. The YouTube piano tutorial for Christina Perri's *A Thousand Years* (2011), has had 34 million views. We know very little about the way in which people are engaging with this material and the field of online musical instrument learning is under-researched. But it is reasonable to assume that these learners are to some extent behaving in some of the ways as explored by Lucy Green (2002): learning through listening and copying, learning from peers, low focus on technique as something distinct from playing, irregular (though often extensive) practice, and frequently coming to a theoretical understanding of music much later. The musicians Green studied were motivated to a large extent by their desire to emulate and copy their musical heroes, but we could also hypothesise that their motivation is further supported by positive factors in areas of challenge vs skills, learner control and feedback.

Learning a musical instrument to any degree of success is highly likely to involve independent personal activity beyond the lesson – it is hard to imagine a rewarding musical experience for the student being based on lessons alone. The student's motivation to undertake this work is, therefore, a critical factor in them having a satisfying musical experience. The research we have considered in this chapter suggests that a student's motivation is not fixed but can be influenced by a number of factors over which the teacher has some control or influence. Taking action in this way, perhaps we might find that we do have some influence over the percentage that give up and that the percentage of drop outs in McPherson's 2012 study is not a given.

References and Bibliography

Bandura, A. (1994) Self-efficacy. In: V. S. Ramachaudran, ed.
Encyclopaedia of Human Behavior (Vol. 4). New York: Academic Press, pp. 71-81.
Available at: https://www.uky.edu/~eushe2/Bandura/BanEncy.html

Bandura, A. (1995) *Self-efficacy in changing societies*. Cambridge: Cambridge University Press.

Blair, D. (2009) Learner agency: To understand and to be understood.
British Journal of Music Education, 26(2), pp. 173-187.

Csikszentmihalyi, M. (1991) *Flow: The psychology of optimal experience*. New York: HarperPerennial.

Csikszentmihalyi, M. (2009) Flow Theory and Research. In: *The Oxford Handbook of Positive Psychology*, 2nd edn. Oxford: Oxford University Press.

Daniel, B. (2006) Early childhood: zero to four years. In: J. Aldgate, D. Jones, W. Rose and C. Jeffery, eds. *The developing world of the child*. London, Philadelphia: Jessica Kingsley.

Giddens, A. (1976) *New Rules of Sociological Method*. Stanford, CA: Stanford University Press.

Green, L. (2002) *How popular musicians learn*. London: Routledge.

Hallam, S. (2002) Musical Motivation: Towards a model synthesising the research.
Music Education Research, 4, pp. 225-244.

Karlsen, S. (2010). Immigrant students' development of musical agency – exploring democracy in music education. *British Journal of Music Education*, 27(3), pp. 225-239.

Karlsen, S. (2011) Using musical agency as a lens: Research music education from the angle of experience. *Research Studies in Music Education*, 33(2), pp. 107-121.

Maehr, M. L., Pintrick, P. R. and Linnenbrink, E. A. (2002) Motivation and Achievement. In: R. Colwell and C. Richardson, eds. *The New Handbook of Research on Music Teaching and Learning: A Project of the Music Educators' National Conference*. Oxford and New York: Oxford University Press, pp. 348-372.

McPherson, G. (2012) *Music in our Lives*. Oxford: Oxford University Press.

PlutaX, Peter (2015) *A Thousand Years – Easy Piano Tutorial* Accessed on August 14th, 2022, Available at : https://www.youtube.com/watch?v=y5JUV825IVA

Rostvall, A. and West, T. (2003) Analysis of interaction and learning in instrumental teaching.
Music Education Research, 5(3), pp. 213-226.

Swanwick, K. (1999) *Teaching Music Musically*. New York: Routledge.

Westerlund, H. (2002). *Bridging experience, action and culture in music education*. Helsinki: Sibelius Academy.

Part Three: Practices and Pedagogies

Chapter 7 Commentary

When you think instrumental musician, do you think artisan or artist? Is learning to play the instrument more akin to learning a craft, with a fixed and clearly defined set of skills, or is it an outlet for the imagination? A creative endeavour? In this chapter, Jennie Henley will explore creativity and imagination in instrumental learning, arguing that unlocking the imagination is the key to success in learning an instrument.

Creativity as a concept is much studied – and much argued over. Is it a process or a product? Is it innate or learned? Does it necessarily mean producing something new? Is it about composition and improvisation or is it wider than that? It can also be highly divisive, as Jennie points out: 'The myth of the creative genius … perpetuates the idea that some are gifted, and some are not'.

Henley argues here that perhaps we would be better advised to think in terms of musical imagination and how this can be unlocked in our students. We can probably all remember occasions when our musical imaginations took flight – perhaps it was in that musical fragment that we played over and over again, perhaps it was a particular concert or group of musicians. Henley talks to a number of practising teachers about what they think of as creativity and musical imagination showing how their experiences and opinions relate to the research literature. She argues that a musical imagination is something that can be unlocked in every child – it is not the preserve of the gifted few or the creative genius. Henley urges teachers to use their own imagination and take a flexible, exploratory approach to their teaching – imaginative and creative teaching promotes imagination and creativity in our students.

7 Creativities in Instrumental Teaching and Learning: Unlocking Musical Imaginations

Jennie Henley

Introduction

Can you remember the first time your musical imagination was brought to life? For me, it was discovering how to flutter tongue on my flute. This took me into a different sound world and fired my interest in exploring different ways of playing, allowing me to move between different musical worlds. For my daughter, it was playing Mussorgsky's *Pictures at an Exhibition* with her youth orchestra and then experimenting with finding the lowest possible note her French horn could play. My son's imagination was ignited when working out how to play music from the game *Undertail* on his keyboard, then finding a way to notate it to play on his trombone. For my former students, the stimuli for their musical imagination ranged from: learning *A Whole New World* from the Disney film, *Aladdin* and realising that it is ok to learn to play 'Disney songs' in a flute lesson; discovering that notation can be used as a guideline when learning Adele's *Rolling in the Deep*; learning Ian Clarke's *The Great Train Race* and discovering extended flute techniques; and finding freedom in writing a cadenza for a Mozart flute concerto through 'playing around' with style that might be considered as fixed and untouchable. Although seemingly diverse examples, the commonality in these musical discoveries is that they resonated with the player for some reason but, most importantly, they unlocked musical imaginations and opened up a whole new world of musical possibilities, deepening musicianship along the way, and consolidating their love of music.

Through the stories of different teachers and their students, this chapter will explore how instrumental teachers unlock musical imaginations through working with their students in creative ways. Runco (2008) suggests that imagination is fundamental to the production of original ideas, and original ideas are a necessity for creativity. Furthermore, creative potential can be defined as the ability to use imagination and produce original ideas. I will propose that teaching should focus on creative potential and therefore involves developing the musical imaginations of both the student and the teacher. To begin with, I will consider what being creative means, including how it has been described and discussed.

Being Creative

Defining what it is to be creative is a difficult task. As Craft (2001) acknowledges, definitions of creativity are elusive and encompass a 'broad spectrum of activity which can be described as creative' (13). On reviewing the literature on creativity in education in 2001, she grouped common definitions of creativity into two broad categories – 'high' creativity and 'ordinary' creativity. These two groups recognise the difference between 'publicly acclaimed creativity which changes knowledge and/or our perspective on the world' (13) and 'the creativity of the ordinary person' (14). She notes that definitions of 'high' creativity imply that only those with a special talent are creative, whereas in notions of 'ordinary' creativity, every person can be creative. However, for many, creativity still remains undefinable (Humphreys, 2006) and it can be difficult to reconcile the two categories and decide where we as teachers lie in the spectrum of creativity. However, rather than being a problem, Hanson (2015) sees the multiple definitions and theories of creativity as a potential strength. He suggests that creativity should be seen as an ideology – a framework of ideas that underpin our teaching. Viewing creativity in this way might enable teachers to work with multiple and changing ideas of creativity and also address tensions produced by assumptions surrounding creativity such as those discussed in this chapter – creativity as a special talent, the issue of perfection, and creativity as non-conformity. Moreover, it enables the teacher to understand creativity as it applies to their particular social and cultural context.

Why is thinking about creativity important?

Creativity as an important aspect of education has gained prominence in the past two decades becoming increasingly seen as a key commodity of learning. In order to improve the way students are prepared for the workplace, Singaporean schools are 'now focusing on learning for life, embracing holistic education, and developing its young people to think critically and creatively' (Ng, 2017:41). Similarly, the Australian National Curriculum identifies critical and creative thinking as a general capability across curriculum subjects[1] and national initiatives such as the *Creative Schools* initiative in Sweden[2] have sought to build children's engagement in creative activities. Creativity in education does not just apply to arts subjects, but extends to mathematics, language, science and across the humanities. Creativity in mathematics has been explored in various ways. For example as underpinning problem solving, finding new ways to reach an end point, imagining new end points, predicting and then experimenting with different possibilities – all fundamental to

---

[1] https://www.australiancurriculum.edu.au/f-10-curriculum/general-capabilities/critical-and-creative-thinking/
[2] https://en.unesco.org/creativity/policy-monitoring-platform/creative-schools-initiative

mathematical thinking (Viladot et al., 2017). The aim of developing the whole creative child through creative thinking is common to many school curricula, but how does this apply to instrumental teaching?

It is easy to assume that music as an arts subject is creative by its very nature, and this argument has been used to justify music as a subject in many contexts. However, some argue that it depends what type of music and musical activity a person engages in as to how creative that person is being or is allowed to be. Frith (2012) says that musical creativity 'means different things in different musical settings' and 'all humans are musical but only sometimes creative' (70). Clarke (2012) argues that 'not all performance takes creativity as its aim' (17). Therefore for many instrumental teachers where the focus is on performance, being creative may not necessarily be the aim of the lessons. However, there is a difference between creativity that requires a product or an outcome, such as composing, and original thinking that forms part of the creative process (Hargreaves, MacDonald, and Miell, 2012). This is in line with Runco's (2008) distinction between theories and definitions that focus on creative products and those that focus on creative potential. He argues that theories relating to the creative product 'say nothing about potential nor about students who have potential but are not yet in a position to produce anything of social significance' (2). Thinking about creativity through the lens of creative potential offers one way of conceptualising all students as potentially creative producers.

To understand the different ways instrumental teachers define creativity, I asked some teachers what being creative meant to them.

> Creativity is contextual: Justin is a trumpet teacher and teaches secondary music. His background is as a military musician. For him creativity 'depends on style. It can be teaching somebody the Blues. Creativity can be improvisation. If you are playing in a certain style and you want the student to be creative you say, "it's not actually written on the music but what could we do that fits the style, what happened in the Baroque period?" It is about knowing the context and working with that to interpret the notation.'
>
> Creativity is expression: Laura teaches French horn and performs as a soloist, for theatre productions and in orchestras. Laura's understanding of creativity is that it is 'the ability to express myself without boundaries. Making sounds and colours and express feelings. I think the reason why you pick up an instrument is so that you can express yourself in a different sort of way. It gives you the freedom to be cross or happy without actually having to dance around the room or scream or shout, you can do that through your instrument.'

Creativity is connecting with sound: Jon teaches violin. He is also a composer and conductor working with youth and adult orchestras. Jon describes the moment one of his students connected with her sound through an improvisation activity. 'For the student it was the realization that the freedom in playing wasn't being tied to the notes [notation]. Suddenly this student was playing with a tone they had never played before, they were freed up, their bow was beautiful, the sound was flowing, it was just that freedom and that imagination, the difference in the way they played was amazing.'

Creativity is possibilities: Fiona is a pianist who mainly teaches from home. Before she retired from teaching in schools, she mentored beginning piano teachers. Fiona explains creativity in interpretation. 'It's very tempting as a teacher to say, this is how it should be, that is how it should be, Beethoven should always be like this, Chopin should always be like that. But occasionally it's good to say how would you do it? or what do you think? or what if we tried this? what if we tried that? what if we tried it a different way?'

Creativity is dealing with mistakes: Steve teaches drum kit. His performance work spans pop and rock, brass bands and orchestral percussion. Steve says 'sometimes you've got to make mistakes just to see what comes from it, and it's trying to encourage the student to keep going if they do make a mistake and explain that we make mistakes as well. Sometimes those mistakes lead to something new.'

Creativity comes from the student: Tholly teaches violin in a school. He is a composer and a performer, often mixing acoustic and electronic sound. Tholly explained how he worked with a student who didn't want to practise and began misbehaving in lessons. 'I found out that he really likes Pink Floyd. So we started learning *Another Brick in the Wall*, just simple fingers. It has quite complex rhythms but because he knows how it goes that's fine for him. After a few weeks he was almost running to his lesson. He was playing at home and his mum said she was happy because he wanted to play. And I just thought, that's so cool, that's so great, he was just so keen. I drilled into what has fired him up, and then brought him back.'

Activity 7.1
What does creativity mean to you as a teacher? Think of some examples of lesson activities which you think were creative, or encouraged your students to behave creatively. Use these to develop your own brief definition of creativity. Revisit this definition at the end of the chapter to see if it has changed or developed in any way.

For these teachers, creativity in instrumental teaching is about understanding context and style as parameters for creative action. It is being free to express oneself, it is having the ability to use a 'mistake' positively, it is thinking about different possibilities and making musical choices, it is about finding the student's musical personality, and it is about recognising that music, musicianship and musical playing are much more than simply about how music is notated and slavishly realising that notation. However, within these definitions there still lie tensions between understanding creativity as a product or outcome and understanding creativity as a process. For example, Justin has a distinct understanding of the differences between technical learning and creativity, seeing creativity being activities such as composing and improvising and a need for technique to come before creative activities, whereas Tholly interprets creativity as the musical thinking process and asked, 'how is music not creative?'. A second tension lies in the use of examinations and competitions to measure progress and competence whilst wanting to develop students' individuality. All the teachers I spoke to referred to the problems arising from the formal examination of performance, leading to set ways of playing particular pieces, leaving little room for creative interpretation; the perception being that because they are being marked against assessment criteria there is a right way and a wrong way to perform them.

Hill tells us that 'if we want to enable a greater range of creative activities amongst a larger population, we need to begin by challenging many of the notions we take for granted about musical creativity' (2012: 101). Therefore, in order to explore these tensions, I will look at some of the assumptions and myths that surround them.

Dispelling the Myths of Creativity
Composing is a special talent
Creativity has been described by Clarke (2012) as being both the mental processes or ideas that lead to a new solution, as reflected in Tholly's view of creativity being the musical thinking processes, but also as coming up with something new, reflected in Justin's view of creative products. Frith (2012) tells us that 'creativity is not a special sort of human activity for people with

special powers' (62) and suggests that the long-standing idea of the composer as the creative genius has resulted in composers being put on a pedestal with performers being viewed as mere technicians. This does not just exist in the classical world and there are artists in the pop world who are happy to preserve the myth of the artistic genius in order to sell their music. The myth of the creative genius then perpetuates the idea that some are gifted, and some are not (Henley, 2015). The problem with this is that if creativity is defined only as a product or outcome of composing, and composers are revered as creative geniuses, teachers themselves may feel that they are not able to be creative.

Once we address what Runco (2008) calls the productivity bias – the idea that only those who produce significant outcomes such as the genius composer are creative – instrumental teachers can begin to see how they can use activities such as composing and improvising processes in their teaching. There are two ways of doing this. The first way is that as students develop their technique they can begin to learn how to compose and improvise; as the student's technique develops they can move from being confident in making small adjustments to beginning to learn how to improvise within a given style. This is important for several reasons, as explained by Fiona.

> Fiona: 'We've got to work using improvisation – you can play that piece there but can you play it an octave higher, can you play it an octave lower, what happens if you play that piece fortissimo, what happens if you play it piano? It goes from being a soldier's march to a lullaby, or what if you just put a couple of flats in there? Suddenly it becomes sad. And you can see the student's eyes light up and they're involved in the process and that's what you want. Because slowly but surely when they are involved in the process, they are understanding the piece more.
>
> Then, if you can improvise you can get yourself out of all sorts of holes when you are sight reading or you are accompanying. If you have got that confidence to have a go and know what the style is, it can get you out of all sorts of troubles.'

The second way to approach improvisation and composition is as part of the process of *teaching* technique. Laura explains that as a French horn teacher she needs to find ways of developing students' ability to feel the notes physically as well as listen to their sound, to develop breath control and to explore the range of the instrument, all without worrying about splitting or missing notes. She uses imagination to create musical stories so the student can focus on a particular technique related to embouchure, air speed, pitching and harmonics, etc. and develop their muscle memory and muscle control. As well as a forum for experimentation to find the best way for the student, the story gives the student their own aide memoir for the particular physical technique needed to produce the sound – the student's imagination mediates between the sound created and the technique needed to create it.

> Laura: 'We start by doing warm ups on open harmonics, and so we start to feel where the notes are, and we move around and it doesn't matter if we catch another note – it's not necessarily wrong. Then we begin with very simple tunes, making up their own tunes without any notated music. Just really gently, because it's quite hard with the horn, it's really challenging to control. When I've got younger students, we imagine a soundscape and we do soundscape stories and that's quite fun. We'll make up a story first and then make sounds to it, it can be just one note or rhythms, and if we can keep the instrument under control, and just find the right sort of sound to produce, that's great.'

This has always been my approach with teaching technique too. My own experience is that introducing new articulations, new fingerings, moving into a different register, or experimenting with rhythms, meters or embouchure are far easier to do away from notated music. Over the years I have developed a number of different ways of doing this, ranging from story soundscapes as Laura describes to building up improvisations using the scales we are learning but gradually adding new elements. As well as removing the complexity of having to realise notation at the same time as dealing with a new physical technique, working away from the notation enables the teacher and student to look directly at each other, which is important on both a pragmatic and social level. Often, it is only when you step away from the music stand that you can see where a tweak in posture or hand position or embouchure could make a marked difference to the student's playing. In addition, being creative with the student enables the teacher/student relationship to develop and helps the student develop ensemble and communication skills.

> Fiona: 'I love improvising duets and you start and you set them a challenge and you say, "this time you've got to put in three acciaccaturas" and they look at me and they put their three in and they look at me again and they sneak another two in, their eyebrows go up and they smile, and I say 'that was cheeky wasn't it?'

Activity 7.2

In this section we have explored two types of creativity: one where creative activities reflect the technical level a student has reached, and the other where creative activities are used as a means of developing technique. Develop one example of each which you could use in your teaching.

The issue of perfection

Frith (2012) recounts an anecdote where a session musician hears a radio interview with a producer whilst on his way to a recording session with that producer. In the interview the producer described session musicians as 'robots'. All the musicians had heard this and when the session started the musicians responded by playing in a purely mechanical way. When the producer asked what they were doing they replied that they were simply playing what was written. This anecdote highlights the fact that there is more to musical playing than technical precision and raises questions as to where creativity in performance lies.

> *Justin: 'Is sitting down playing something that's written down precisely, is that creative? It's creative for the person who wrote it, but I don't know if it's creative for the person playing it. I think it can be creative if the person is playing with interpretation skills and musicianship, I think that they can make something beautiful for other people to appreciate.'*

As well as questioning the notion that playing something 'perfectly', i.e. with precise technical accuracy, is creative, Justin also highlighted the issue of interpreting perfection as an exact replication, whether using notation or learning aurally. He notes how most things that young people listen to are highly manufactured, produced and packaged, and as a result they do not value things unless they are presented as a polished, exact performance. When the students do not value anything other than this kind of perfection, they set themselves an impossible target in their own playing that causes anxiety and stress.

> *Justin: 'When you ask young people why music should be perfect, they'll tell you, "well you wouldn't want to listen to it if it wasn't perfect". And I ask why their performance with a little mistake is not worth the same as a perfect recording. I point out that one is live and the other might have been recorded 50 times by someone 20 years older than them and in fact be a mixture of those 50 different recordings.'*

Perfection as defined by Justin's students is achieved by not 'making mistakes'. However, being free to make mistakes is crucial to developing as a musician. Burnard, Boyack, and Howell (2017) say that risk-taking is fundamental to music learning, but a student will not take a risk if they fear making a mistake. Steve explains why accommodating mistakes is important in developing creativity in performing as well as being a vital performance skill.

> *Steve: 'Trying to get them to play through their mistakes is important because they might say "oh actually I quite like that", and I tell them that if they do that, to do it again straight away. If they are going to go around the kit and they slightly fill a bit differently, while they are still thinking about what just happened, try and create it again and imagine that fill.*

> And I think that with a music exam you might lose points for going wrong, but you might get most points back for putting yourself right. So you are not going to lose all the marks, or they might let it go altogether because they can see that you can cope with the mistake.'

Steve points to the tension caused by focusing on how many marks you might lose for playing a wrong note. Freeing students from the idea that the notation is fixed is crucial to Tholly for both musicianship and technique.

> Tholly: 'The more you know about what the symbols really mean then the more you've got to draw on. Just because it says *p* it doesn't really tell you how to play it. Right it means soft but on the violin there are so many different ways of playing soft. So I get them to think about whether the soft thing is someone whispering in your ear right next to you, that's a very different kind of quiet than if you hear bells ringing three miles away over the hill, that's quite a distant thing. So that will be where the bow is.'

These anecdotes refer to a perception that notated music needs to be strictly interpreted otherwise the piece is somehow 'wrong'. However, notation serves different purposes in different musical styles and traditions. My own experience of playing Javanese gamelan has taught me that notation can serve different functions for different instruments in the same ensemble. In the early stages of my learning, I felt that I was cheating if I used the notation. This came from my assumption that Javanese gamelan is a purely aural tradition whereas in reality there are various forms of cypher and notation. As I began to understand the music, I realised that the notation provides the performer with structural and modal information. Each performer uses the notation to make musical choices as their instrument and the tradition of Javanese gamelan requires and allows. The knowledge of what the instrument does within the gamelan, how it behaves musically, where in the piece you are, and what the purpose of the piece is (song, dance, dramatic) is fundamental to knowing what information the notation is providing, what choices that information presents, and therefore to making musical choices. In short, rather than prescribing a set course of musical action, the notation helps the performer to realise the different possibilities that exist within the music and within their own instruments (Henley, 2009).

Activity 7.3
Would you rather hear your students giving a performance which is true to the score but lacks creativity or imagination, or one which has flaws and blemishes, but which is musically engaging? Do you think instrumental teachers are encouraged to work towards the former because of external pressures, exams, etc.? Thinking about Tholly's example, design and try out an activity for one of your students which aims to help them get beyond the instructions in the score. Write a brief description of how well it works.

Creativity Means Not Conforming

What is described in the previous section is an approach to teaching that is holistic. Through using their imaginations students are developing their technique, their theoretical understanding, their aural ability, and their expressive playing as well as exploring different possibilities and gaining confidence in their musicianship. They are developing resilience when making mistakes and they are learning that music is temporal, physical, communicative and social. Many instrumental teachers have been influenced by the idea of simultaneous learning – teaching in a way that combines different elements of musicianship rather than compartmentalising the lesson so that aural, scales, repertoire, and sight-reading are disconnected and taught separately (Harris, 2008). Often simultaneous learning is justified by referring to the notion that creativity is a 'right brain activity' and joining technique with creativity joins both sides of the brain. Dietrich (2007), however, argues against using simplistic ideas of creativity, such as this, as they fail to take account of recent advances in cognitive neuroscience, claiming that these ideas are outdated. Hill (2012) suggests that being creative means not conforming to predetermined or pre-existing models, but this also is too simple a definition. As stated at the start of this chapter, multiple definitions of creativity exist. Many models of the creative process have been developed to articulate these, but research has highlighted the complexities of attempting to map out creative processes against one model of creativity (Gooderson and Henley, 2017). Moving away from the ideas that creativity is a simple cognitive process, and that creativity cannot encompass conformity helps to work through some of the tensions between the need for both divergence and conformity in music (Hansen, 2015). For the instrumental teacher it helps to reconcile the tensions that arise between creativity in instrumental teaching and assessing performance through examinations and competitions.

Fiona raised the issue of rigidity of approach of examination repertoire and how she approached helping students to understand creativity within performance.

> *Fiona:* 'I have a new pupil who is doing grade 8. He's got all distinctions so far and so he's got to get a distinction for grade 8. He said, "I've got the CD from the exam board so I know what they should all sound like". I thought I can't let that pass. And we get YouTube out and we listen to all different interpretations of his Chopin Nocturne and the look on his face was wonderful. He said, "but he's a really great pianist", and I said "I know", and he said, "but he's not playing it like the exam board CD", and I say, "no he isn't is he?", and then I find a Lang Lang video, "listen to what Lang Lang's doing and listen to what Voladol is doing", and I remember the look on his face when he realised that four different great pianists whose names he knew were playing it different to the CD. And then he realised that he didn't have to play it like the CD.'

All of the teachers I spoke to agreed that creativity, whether leading to a product or as part of a process, involves having original ideas and they all highlighted that this created a tension with the assumption that performance, particularly in an examination or a competition, is either right or wrong. Laura explains that if you use your creative teaching then you can help students understand why certain things in music need to be the way they are written but still bring them to life.

> *Laura:* 'There is a right and wrong and most students understand that, but you have to teach out of the notation rather than teach into it. You can use the ideas that you've been doing without the music, "we know this rhythm has to be right, let's find some words to fit this rhythm", or "this is what's happening in the tune, she's really cross, she's stomping around, this arpeggio is her marching up the steps. She doesn't want to fall down stairs, she doesn't want to hurt herself, so they've got to be right". You build into your bank of things that you've already done, so they can say "yes we've got to play the right notes", but there's still some sort of creativity or meaning as we go.
>
> *Exam pieces are pieces, just because someone is being marked they still can be full of story, full of life, and actually if you do make a mistake, if the character that you are trying to portray is there because you've thought about it and we've talked about it, then mistakes are much less important. The notes don't have to be so important, it's about telling a story rather than getting every single note right.'

With this approach the students are still conforming to the stylistic parameters and syntax of the piece, but there is a creative approach underpinning that conformity coming from the student's imagination.

A final perspective that brings together the issues raised in relation to the composer, making mistakes, and ideas of right and wrong comes from Jon.

> Jon: 'As a composer, one of the most interesting things is when someone takes your music, another orchestra, and they've done it in a completely different way. I hadn't even thought of doing it like that, and it's really good. And is that right? Because it's different to what's been written. You can't think in those terms and pass value judgements to say well this is right! You may prefer it from your point of view and think this is more what the composer originally intended, but that changes. There's a section in one of my pieces where someone took a much steadier tempo and I thought that really works. The music's still there, all the notes and things, but they've interpreted it differently as to how I originally thought of it, and that changed the way I do it as well!'

What is most apparent when talking to teachers about the way they work with their students is, once again, the importance of imagination. To reiterate Runco (2008), imagination leads to original ideas, and original ideas are necessary for creativity as it is original ideas that form creative potential. A focus on creative potential in learning enables the teacher to move away from exclusive ideas of creative product – some can produce, some can't produce – and move to an inclusive approach that understands that everyone holds creative potential. Hargreaves et al. (2012: 3) agree that there are problems in associating creativity with just one specific way of making music and suggest that focusing on imagination is more useful as it 'encompasses a much broader range of concepts and behaviour' (3). I would suggest that imagination is the starting point of original ideas and therefore fundamental to developing creative potential.

In considering different definitions of creativity, using the examples from the teachers above, and addressing some of the tensions that arise, creativity is understood here as a collaborative and social process as much as an individual endeavour and when we perform creatively, we are balancing novelty with acceptability (Frith, 2012). Furthermore, what the teachers are doing is helping their students to use their imaginations to discover different possibilities, which is the essence of all definitions of creativity (Craft, 2012). It is through exploring possibilities that students are developing creative and critical thinking that is essential for advanced learning (Hallam and Bautista, 2012).

> Steve: 'They've got to have their own thoughts in everything they do, it's not just about music, this is just a small part of it. It's then they become creative in other things that they do and hopefully think for themselves. They can lead things because they've got the mind to be able to create things rather than having to have everything given to them.'

There is not a dichotomy between divergence and conformity, but we work within the parameters of style and context in order to communicate meaning to an audience. To do this, we draw on our imaginations and help to unlock the imaginations of our students so that they can find different possibilities. This is where creativity lies in instrumental teaching.

Using Imagination

When a teacher shifts the focus to developing imagination a whole range of teaching possibilities emerge. Students might use imagination to consider how the music will sound, what the music might mean, why the music is written as it is, what the potential of the music is, what the potential of themselves as musicians is, and so on. The key to this lies in giving the students activities that will develop their curiosity and, most importantly, that they will be successful in doing.

> *Tholly: 'Even just the word improvisation makes people tense up so I use keys that fit the fingers really well. I start with E pentatonic and then E minor and having my computer there I just have a few backing tracks in different keys and just set it going. Then I'll play 2 bars and then they will play 2 bars, they don't even realise what we are doing. And once they have wandered around up and down and got a bit familiar, we start building little sounds and repetitions.'*

> *Fiona: 'The great thing with the Gavottes and Minuets now is that we've got YouTube. I've got a playlist of all the pieces with YouTube, especially the ones that are old fashioned dances, with people on YouTube actually dancing those dances, with the wigs and the silk dresses and the high heels and you say, "oh, do you see why it wasn't that fast? Look what they are wearing. There's a bow and a courtesy at the end so that's why this sounds a bit formal."'*

Having said this, what is crucial is that teachers themselves can use their imagination in teaching. This means not always prescribing what the students should do and giving them both permission and the means to explore a different way of doing things. This will also help to build a trusting relationship that enables the student to find their musical freedom. Fundamentally, it is recognising that as a teacher you are constantly learning, and the beauty of teaching music is that you will always come across a student who sees things differently to you. As the teachers explain, the key to unlocking musical imaginations is asking questions rather than telling them the answers and putting them at the centre of learning.

> *Jon: 'You might be working on a piece and looking at it in depth and a student might well come up with a different way of doing it, a way of phrasing it, and you think actually that really works and so you ask, "why have you done that?"'*

> *Laura: 'If they have come back and said, "look I've played a low C" or "what is this note?", I'm quite happy for us to explore that for however long it takes. I never say to them, "yeah that's fine but let's do this now."'*

> *And if you've planned to do dotted rhythms with them, you can do dotted rhythms down there. I think it's important for them to feel that what they've done outside of the lesson is worth something. If they come back and say I've practised this piece or this rhythm hard, then we go with that don't we? It's equally important if they come back and say, "I've discovered a note", then we say, "it's this and this is how it feels" or "and you can do it with this fingering." You make it just as valid for them.'*

Both these examples show that the skill of the teacher is being able to respond flexibly and creatively.

> *Fiona: 'You've got to improvise your lesson. It's scary for some people. I think probably the most important thing is be prepared to abandon the lesson plan, be prepared to go with the flow, and don't just stick with the straight route all the time, you've got to go with it, you've got to be brave. But it's so hard in these days when people are told to write and submit lesson plans, but you've just got to be brave.'*

If the teacher teaches with a view that creativity is a special, mysterious quality of special people, they are one step away from saying that only special people can make music. Musical creativity means different things in different musical settings. Think about what it means to you and place your imagination at the centre of that. Combine this with an approach where you work with the student and acknowledge and respect their imagination and you will take your teaching to another level. Hargreaves et al. (2012) refer to Aaron Copland's view that 'it is the freely imaginative mind that is at the core of all vital music making and music listening'. I would add to this and say that the imaginative mind is at the core of all vital music teaching.

Acknowledgements

Thank you to my friends and colleagues from Cotswold Music Tutors, Steve Barnett (drum kit), Justin Lewis (trumpet and secondary class music), Tholly Mason (violin and composer), Laura Morris (French horn), and Jon Trim (violin, conductor and composer), and also Fiona Lau (piano) for their inspiration and generosity in sharing their views.

References

Burnard, P., Boyack, J. and Howell, G. (2017) Children Composing: Creating Communities of Musical Practice. In: *Teaching Music Creatively*, P. Burnard and R. Murphy, eds. 2nd edn. pp. 39-59.

Clarke, E. F. (2012) Creativity in Performance. In: D. Hargreaves., D. Miell and R. Macdonald., eds. *Musical Imaginations: Multidisciplinary Perspectives on Creativity, Performance, and Perception*, pp. 17-30.

Craft, A. (2012) Childhood in a Digital Age: Creative Challenges for Educational Futures. *London Review of Education*. 10(2), pp. 173-190.

Craft, A. (2001) An Analysis of Research and Literature on Creativity in Education. *Qualifications and Curriculum Authority*. 51(2), pp. 1-37.

Dietrich, A. (2007) Who's Afraid of a Cognitive Neuroscience of Creativity? Methods, Neurocognitive Mechanisms of Creativity: A Toolkit, 42(1), pp. 22-27.

Frith, S. (2012) Creativity as a Social Act. In: D. J. Hargreaves, D. Miell, and R. Macdonald, eds. *Musical Imaginations: Multidisciplinary Perspectives on Creativity, Performance and Perception*, Oxford: Oxford University Press, pp. 62-72.

Gooderson, M. and Henley, J. (2017) Professional Song-Writing: Creativity, Collaboration, and Tensions between Higher Education Song-Writing and Industry Practice. In: G. Dylan-Smith, M. Brennan, P. Kirkman, Z. Moir, and S. Rambarran, eds. *Ashgate Research Companion to Popular Music Education*. Farnham: Ashgate, pp. 257-271.

Hallam, S. and Bautista, A. (2012) Processes of Instrumental Learning: The Development of Musical Expertise. In: G. E. McPherson and G. F. Welch, eds. *The Oxford Handbook of Music Education*, New York: Oxford University Press, pp. 658-676.

Hanson, M. H. (2015) The Ideology of Creativity and Challenges of Participation. *Europe's Journal of Psychology*, 11(3), pp. 369-78. https://doi.org/10.5964/ejop.v11i3.1032.

Hargreaves, D. J., MacDonald. R. and Miell, D. (2012) Explaining Musical Imaginations: Creativity, Performance, and Perception. In: D. J. Hargreaves, D. Miell, and R. Macdonald, eds. *Musical Imaginations: Multidisciplinary Perspectives on Creativity, Performance, and Perception*. Oxford: Oxford Academic, pp. 1-14.

Harris, P. (2008) *Improve Your Teaching!: Teaching Beginners: A New Approach for Instrumental and Singing Teachers: The Companion Book to Improve Your Teaching!* London: Faber Music.

Henley, J. (2015) Music: Naturally Inclusive, Potentially Exclusive? In: M. Deppeler, T. Loreman, R. A. L. Smith, and L. Florian, eds. *Inclusive Pedagogy Across the Curriculum*. Bingley, UK: Emerald Publishing, pp. 161-186.

Henley, J. (2009). *The Learning Ensemble; Musical Learning through Participation*. PhD. Thesis Birmingham City University.

Hill, J. (2012) Imagining Creativity. In: D. J. Hargreaves, R. MacDonald and D. Miell, eds. *Musical Imaginations: Multidisciplinary Perspectives on Creativity, Performance, and Perception*, Oxford: Oxford University Press, pp. 87-109.

Humphreys, J. T. (2006) Toward a Reconstruction of 'Creativity' in Music Education. *British Journal of Music Education*, 23(3), pp. 351-361.

Ng, P. T. (2017) *Learning from Singapore: The Power of Paradoxes*. New York: Routledge.

Runco, Mark A. (2008) Creativity and Education. *New Horizons in Education*, 56(1), pp. 1-8.

Viladot, L., Hilton, C., Casals. A. Saunders J., Carrillo, C., Henley, J., González-Martín, C., Prat, M. and Welch, G. (2017) The Integration of Music and Mathematics Education in Catalonia and England: Perspectives on Theory and Practice. *Music Education Research*, 20(1), pp. 71-82.

Wilf, E. (2014) Semiotic Dimensions of Creativity. *Annual Review of Anthropology*, 43(1), pp. 397-412. https://doi.org/10.1146/annurev-anthro-102313-030020

Chapter 8 Commentary

Every child should have the opportunity to learn a musical instrument. It's a simple statement to make and something that many, or perhaps most, instrumental music teachers believe. But the reality is that for many children and young people there are significant barriers to taking up and continuing with an instrument. It is relatively rare to see opportunities for learning an instrument provided free as part of a mainstream education, but even where the financial barrier is reduced or removed altogether, there may remain physical or cognitive barriers. A further obstacle is often presented by the curriculum itself, with a frequently heavy emphasis on the norms and practices of western classical music, which can be alienating to many children and young people.

Gary Spruce argues in this chapter that by applying a social justice model to instrumental learning we can gain a better understanding of the barriers to instrumental music learning that many children and young people face. In such a model it is not enough just to address the financial and physical barriers to learning, but also the curriculum itself where children and young people 'perceive their needs not being met and the musical values and practices to which they are committed accorded little value'. To address this Spruce argues for curricula in which children and young people's 'voices might be heard and acted on and through which they might achieve agency over their music making and musical learning'.

The chapter considers the issue of inclusion and how instrumental music teaching can be offered in ways which meet the needs of every pupil. Although in education we commonly think of inclusion as something that applies in class and group contexts, we will see in this chapter that it is fundamental in all teaching contexts, from the classroom to the individual teaching studio. As we will discover here, it is not about offering each learner the same experience, but offering each the experience which is most relevant to their needs, aspirations and passions.

In the final section Gary Spruce considers the issues surrounding children and young people identified as being gifted or talented and invites us to consider a model developed by McPherson and Williamon which might help us identify learners with particular ability in areas of music making other than playing and performing.

The approach to inclusion outlined in this chapter is perhaps most clearly expressed in a quote included from Jellison (2012) who argues that self-determination and agency are best 'fostered in music environments where children feel safe and secure, and where they experience autonomy, demonstrate competence, and make decisions about music, music making, and other music activities in their lives'.

8 Inclusive Approaches to Instrumental Teaching and Learning: A Social Justice Perspective

Gary Spruce

Introduction

Inclusion in music education has been the focus of significant attention in recent years. It has been addressed from multiple perspectives by academic scholarship, research reports and policy documents. These perspectives include examining how young people with cognitive and physical disabilities and from deprived socio-economic groups experience barriers to music education and consequently to having their music education needs met (e.g. Ockleford, 2008; Philpott, et al., 2016; Incorporated Society of Musicians (ISM), 2019). Examples include a report from the United Kingdom's *Youth Music* which found that only 7% of disabled children and young people were making music in groups organised by the local music education hubs[1] (Youth Music, 2020). In 2014, the Associated Board of the Royal Schools of Music, one of the main providers of graded exams, noted that 'The cost of learning to play and of taking lessons is a major barrier …Regional provision is variable and the diverse ways in which learners progress are not necessarily well supported by the sector' (ABRSM, 2014). Similarly, reports from the Incorporated Society of Musicians (ISM, 2019 and 2022) have drawn attention to the impact of poverty on the music education chances and opportunities of those from the lowest socio-economic groupings. In 2017, only 3.5% of entrants to United Kingdom music conservatoires were from the most deprived socio-economic backgrounds, whereas almost 40% came from the highest socio-economic band (ISM, 2019). A follow up report in 2022 (ISM, 2022) revealed that funding for music departments in UK independent schools (those typically attended by young people from the most affluent socio-economic groups) was almost five times higher than for music departments in state schools. All these reports point to how young people experience significant numbers of barriers in gaining access to the structures and resources of music education.

Research and reports from a sociological and social science perspective have also identified how the very structures of music and music education can work against the inclusion of groups and individuals. These include research on how

---

1   Music Education Hubs are groups of locally based music education organisations in England working together to develop a coherent and 'joined up' approach to music education in their area.

the gendering of musical practices and instruments can have a detrimental impact on the musical and music education opportunities afforded to females participants (e.g., Green, 1997; Gathan, 2014). More recently, attention has been drawn to the marginalisation of the music of women and BAME composers in formal music education (e.g., Holder, 2022), including graded examination syllabuses. Related to this, over many years it has been argued that music education in many western countries has traditionally placed greatest value on the processes, practices and repertoire of classical music (Small, 1998; Bull, 2019) with music of other styles, traditions and cultures often being evaluated in terms of these processes and practices rather than on their own terms, and consequently found wanting (Green 2003; Spruce and Matthews, 2012). The dominance of classical music within many curricula and music education approaches has then led to the alienation of many young people from music education (Philpott and Kubilius, 2016) as they perceive their needs not being met and the musical values and practices to which they are committed accorded little value in formal music education structures.

Although many of the examples cited above are taken from a United Kingdom context, the issues that they raise are common to many contexts. Despite the commitment of the majority of music teachers and music education organisations to inclusive practices, many young people continue to experience significant barriers to music education and/or find that the music education they have access to does not meet their needs and aspirations. More especially, they perceive music education as placing limited value on their musical ways of working and the musical traditions and styles within which they have chosen to make music.

In the short space of this chapter it is not possible to address all the issues of inclusion identified above. What the chapter will seek to do, however, is to provide a framework for thinking about inclusion in music education – particularly from the perspective of instrumental teaching – that is rooted in inclusion as fundamental to the provision of socially just approaches to music education. This framework will draw on one of the key discourses of social justice, which Spruce (2017) describes as the relationship and balance between *distributive* paradigms of social justice (Rawls, 1971) and Nancy Fraser's (2005) 'relation model' of social justice. In distributive paradigms the primary focus is on the equitable distribution of music education's resources and opportunities. Conversely Fraser's 'relational model' has at its heart an individual's right to participatory parity[2], agency and dialogical engagement[3] through which their voices might be heard and acted on, and through which they might achieve

---

[2] Fraser's concept of participatory parity concerns the right of individuals to participate fully in the decision making and construction of values that impacts on their lives.
[3] Dialogical pedagogies are characterised by approaches to teaching which see knowledge as constructed through the interactions of the 'teacher', the 'learner' and 'knowledge'.

agency over their music making and musical learning. Whereas equitable access to, and distribution of, resources is an important aspect of a socially just approach to music education inclusion, it is not sufficient in itself. Rather it is necessary also to interrogate the extent to which music education's structures and the values embodied within them respect and embrace what young people bring to their music education and allow them space for the exercise of musical agency or have an exclusionary effect. A key characteristic of inclusive approaches to music education is that young people are enabled to develop a sense of agency in and through their musical learning as an important aspect of their development as musicians and musical learners. At the heart of this chapter is a belief that socially just approaches to music teaching enable young people to gain agency over both their music making and also their musical learning and provides spaces within which their voices might be heard.

The chapter will therefore seek to maintain a balance between these perspectives of distributive and relational social justice and identify synergies between them. It will proceed as follows: Drawing on categorisations provided by Philpott et al. (2016), it will identify some of the barriers to music education – and particularly instrumental learning – experienced by young people individually and in groups. Following from this the chapter will identify how flexible and differentiated approaches to instrumental teaching have the potential to overcome some of these barriers. These sections will be interspersed with brief snapshots of the way in which these differentiated approaches might create opportunities for agency and the facilitation of young people's voices as part of a move towards inclusion as participatory parity. The section 'Differentiation through Support' will develop further the notion of participatory parity and act as a bridge to a concluding section which discusses the implications of Fraser's participatory model of social justice for instrumental teaching and learning.

Activity 8.1

Think back to your own music education and development as a musician. What barriers did you encounter and how were these overcome? What actions did others (such as parents or teachers) take to help you? Were there any barriers that you were unable to overcome? If so why was this so and what impact have these had on your development as a musician?

What are the Barriers to Inclusion in Music Education Experienced by Young People?

In the introduction to this chapter, we identified a range of barriers encountered by many young people in gaining access to music education opportunities which meet their needs and enable them to make musical progress. Drawing on the principles of inclusion found in the English National Curriculum (2013), Philpott et al. (2016: 174), identify three categories of barriers:

1. Common Needs: Barriers to music education that all young people might encounter; for example gaining access to music education including learning to play an instrument.

2. Individual and Unique Needs: Barriers to music education and progression resulting from physical and cognitive disabilities or emotional and behavioural difficulties.

3. Exceptional and Shared Needs: Barriers to music education experienced as a result of social factors such as gender, ethnicity, religion, social class and social deprivation.

These three categories are examined below with particular attention given to their implications for learning a musical instrument and how these barriers might be addressed through providing opportunities for pupil agency and space for young people's voices to be heard. It is important to note that differentiation is equally important for teachers whose teaching is mainly with individual pupils as it is for those whose teaching primarily takes places with groups or classes of pupils.

Addressing 'common needs' through differentiated approaches to music teaching

Certain barriers to musical learning – e.g. those around access to instruments – *may* be beyond a teacher's immediate control. However, many barriers can be addressed through adapting teaching to ensure that all young people have the opportunity to make progress in learning an instrument and developing musically. In this section we consider how individual needs and 'common barriers' to inclusion can be addressed through teachers differentiating their teaching strategies, resources and assessment approaches.

Daubney defines differentiation as adaptations to teaching that are 'aimed at meeting the needs, interests and aspirations of *all* pupils and offering challenge *in all given music situations*' (2017: 61) (italics added). To adapt teaching approaches to meet the musical needs of all pupils is an important skill for classroom music teachers who typically will be required to teach large groups of children who often have widely differing musical experiences, attainments and needs. It is also an important consideration for instrumental teachers who, whilst primarily teaching pupils individually, will encounter pupils with different needs and musical aspirations. Therefore although they may, for example, be teaching the same music to more than one pupil (e.g. the music for a particular grade exam) they will need to differentiate their teaching approaches according to the needs of each pupil.

Whatever the contexts of their teaching, thinking about differentiation encourages teachers to consider how they might adapt their pedagogical approaches so that these have at their heart addressing the barriers to musical learning of each individual instrumental learner.

Daubney (2017) identities five types of differentiation:

1. Differentiation by task

Differentiation by task – particularly in the context of instrumental teaching – typically takes the form of asking for less technically demanding musical contributions of those pupils that are less technically advanced. This technical demand might be reduced through, for example, asking beginner string players to use open strings only or by the musical part itself being more or less technically demanding. This approach can work well if some or all of the following conditions are met:

- Where music making and learning is taking place in an ensemble/group context, young people feel they are making a valuable contribution to the musical performance as a whole.
- Young people's musical contribution is musically satisfying and provides a basis for extending their musical skills, knowledge and understanding.
- The task encourages them to 'think musically' and go beyond simply technical issues. For example: encourages them to consider phrasing and dynamics; think about what is appropriate to the musical style within which they performing; encourages them to listen carefully to how their contribution fits into the music as a whole.

Possibilities for musical agency

Improvisation activities have the potential to create space in which young people might develop both technically and in their musical thinking. Given a simple musical stimulus for their improvisation task, they can develop this in more technically and musically demanding ways, self-directing their own learning.

2. Differentiation by outcome

Differentiation by outcome is where all pupils are working on the same musical task but the outcomes will be different. An example of this might be where pupils work individually or in pairs to develop an improvisation or short composition based on the same stimulus. This might be a musical idea such as developing a riff into a more extended composition or improvisation or responding to a non-musical stimulus such as a picture. Differentiation by outcome can encourage young people's creativity by encouraging them to think about the potential different outcomes of a musical task and to work towards one or two of these. It is less effective where pupils, for example, are simply given the same music to perform and left to 'sink or swim'.

> **Possibilities for musical agency**
>
> Differentiation by outcome offers significant potential for creative agency as pupils use their instrument to work on their own responses to the given stimuli. On occasions they might also be given the opportunity to select their own stimuli.

3. Differentiation by content

Differentiation by content occurs where pupils are working on different content. In instrumental teaching, differentiation by content often occurs naturally through choice of repertoire. Content may also include some pupils working on musical activities that are not primarily performance based but are focused on composing or improvising, or perhaps evaluating different recorded or live performances of a piece they are studying themselves.

> **Possibilities for musical agency**
>
> Agency can be facilitated through opportunities for young people to select the music they will learn and to develop their own repertoire rather than being pre-determined by the teacher or the requirements of the examination syllabus. Improvising activities and critically evaluating the performances of others provides opportunities for creative agency and musical thinking whilst supporting the development of instrumental learning.

4. Differentiation by resource

Differentiation by resource occurs when young people work on the same or similar task but have differentiated access to resources. Daubney gives an example of this form of differentiation which has relevance to learning an instrument '...in order to help them work out how to play a short melodic phrase (e.g. a short video tutorial of how to play the bass line, some possible note names written on notation, a pictorial view of the shape of the melody they are trying to work out by ear'.) (Daubney, 2017: 61).

Possibilities for musical agency

Opportunities for agency lie in enabling pupils to select the resources that best support their instrumental learning. This is an aspect of metacognition (an awareness of how one learns best) that is explored below when discussing differentiation by support.

Activity 8.2

Consider one lesson that you teach and employ differentiation in four ways as described above. What do you find to be the advantages and disadvantages of each?

Differentiation by support: the bridge to agency

One of the most important forms of differentiation is achieved through differentiated support, and in one sense this can be seen as encompassing all the other forms of differentiation explored above, as illustrated in this figure from Dickinson and Wright (1993), cited in Philpott et al. (2016).

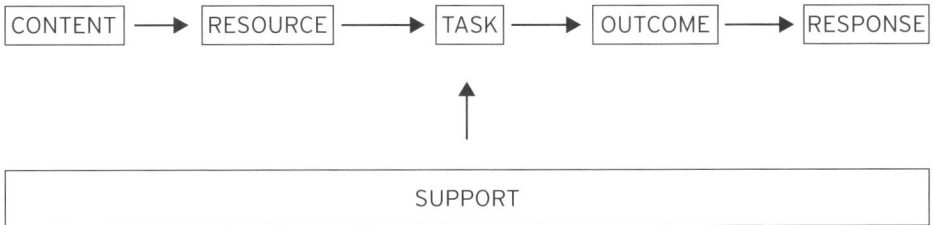

As Daubney notes, differentiated support often occurs naturally as teachers identify and provide support for young people as a lesson proceeds. Some of the most effective support can be through teachers drawing on their own music skills to model music outcomes and giving young people a sense of musical security through providing a musical framework for their music making (e.g. Burke, 2018); Daubney gives the example of teachers performing with their pupils in order to maintain a steady pulse. Teachers could also model a range of musical outcomes such as alternative ways of phrasing or subtle applications of dynamics. They might also demonstrate ways of overcoming particular technical or musical challenges that pupils are experiencing, using their own instrument to do so. For example, in a study of inclusive music pedagogies across four different countries an Australian teacher describes how they use their own skills to such ends '[I] show them and let them watch my hand or the voicing of the piano…That would make more sense to them. It's visual and aural' (Burnard et al., 2008: 118).

Differentiation by support is also the form of differentiation that perhaps best enables young people to develop their sense of agency as both musicians and musical learners.

Adopting a Vygotskian approach to differentiation by support

Vygotsky's concept of the 'Zone of Proximal Development' (ZPD) is a much cited theoretical framework for understanding the role of the teacher in relation to the pupil and what there is to be taught and learnt. Vygotsky describes the ZPD as being 'the distance between the actual developmental level as determined by independent problem-solving and the level of potential development as determined through problem-solving under adult guidance, or in collaboration with more capable peers' (Vygotsky, 1978: 86). It centres around the idea of the gap between what a young person can achieve unaided and that which they are capable of achieving with the support of a teacher or other more experienced person; what Vygotsky refers to as the 'more knowledgeable other'.

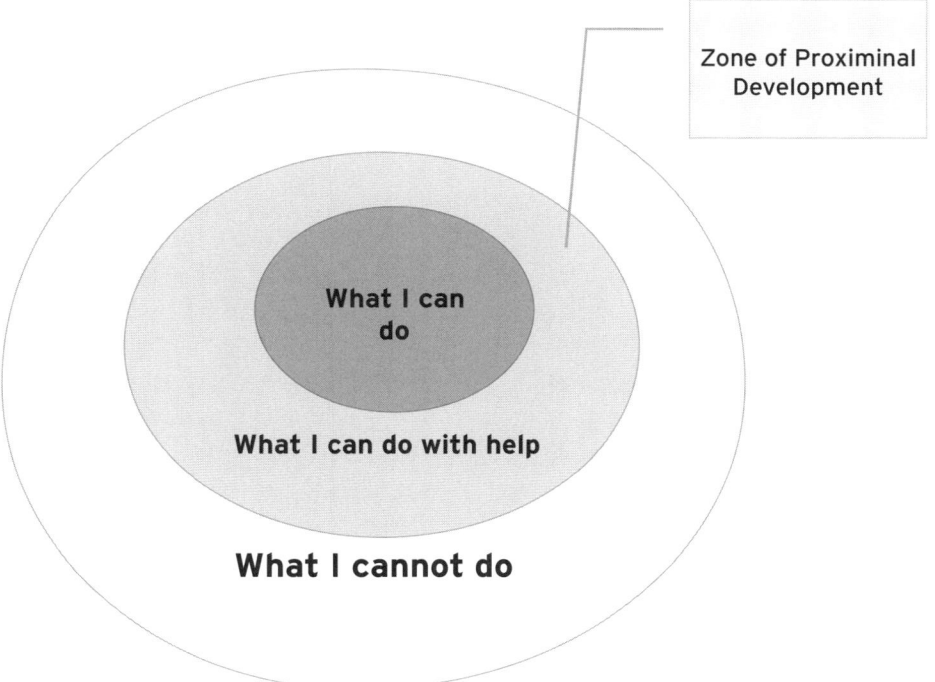

As Wells (1999) notes, the ZPD can be conceived of simply as a framework for determining the level at which teacher instruction is pitched, with the pupil having limited agency both in terms of the lesson content and the nature of the pedagogical support. However, Wells argues that the concept of the ZPD has much greater potential than this. He argues for a much richer conceptualisation of the ZPD which '… is created in the interaction between the student and the co-participants in an activity' and includes 'the available tools and the selected practices' and is dependent 'on the nature and quality of that interaction as much as on the upper limit of the learner's capability' (np). Wells is pointing here to the possibility of the ZPD underpinning a dialogical approach to pedagogy rather than instructional approach to teaching. A dialogical approach to music teaching argues for a perception of musical knowledge as emergent and co-constructed through interactions 'with real or imagined others' and where the voice of the pupil is heard and their potential for agency operationalised. As Wells points out, the dialogical interactions need not be only those that are spoken but can include 'the various modes of artistic expression, such as dance, drama and musical performance' (np).

Conceived in a such a way the ZPD offers a framework where young people might be supported in thinking carefully about what they can do, what they wish to be able to do, and the kinds of support that will help them attain the latter. It also encourages them to think about the processes of their own learning – metacognition. It gives them agency over their learning where their voice can be heard. It also invites teachers to think about who the more knowledgeable others might be. These may be the teacher themselves or another young person who has particular musical skills and knowledge. For example, Scott and Jellison (2007) note how peer support can be particularly useful in supporting those with exceptional shared needs, which is the focus of part of the next section.

In providing support, instrumental teachers will be aware of the benefits of creating space for pupils to manage their own learning (self-directed learning) as part of the journey towards musical agency and autonomy.

Activity 8.3

Apply the ZPD to one of your lessons in the context, perhaps, of a new piece your pupils are learning to play. Talk with your pupil about what they feel they can already do, what they want to achieve and the kind of help and support they need to achieve this. Ensure the conversation is wide ranging and not restricted to technical issues. Also think about who, other than you as a teacher, might be able to provide this support.

Exceptional Shared Needs: Possibilities for Agency

Exceptional shared needs can be categorised as follows:

- Those with communication difficulties.
- Those with cognitive limitations which cause them to experience difficulties with learning.
- Those with emotional and behavioural difficulties.
- Those with physical limitations (e.g. the use of only one arm or hand or a visual impairement).

Young people who are particularly gifted in music are also sometimes defined as having exceptional shared needs, and we discuss briefly the issues in providing for their needs at the end of this part of the chapter.

Hallam (1998), writing specifically about instrumental teaching and learning, identifies the challenges likely to be experienced by young people who have particular special needs and the teaching approaches that might support them.

Table 8.1 (Hallam, 1998: 66-67 adapted)

SEN	Challenges and support
Physical impairments	▶ Appropriate choice of instrument is important to maximise success ▶ Making changes to the way the instrument is set up e.g. to be played with the left hand ▶ Modifying the instrument so that it can be played with feet, mouth etc. ▶ Providing special stands or supports for an instrument
Hearing impairments	▶ Instruments are audible to some extent for most people with hearing impairments ▶ Use amplified headphones or induction loops
Blind and partially sighted	▶ Playing by ear (using recordings) ▶ Providing larger print music through magnification/photocopying or using technology ▶ Moving music closer ▶ Providing Braille music
Severe and profound learning difficulties	▶ Provide a safe and secure environment ▶ Praise the smallest achievement ▶ Provide open-ended learning opportunities ▶ Give clear instructions
Emotional and behavioural difficulties	▶ Provide opportunities for instant success ▶ Use familiar material when introducing a new activity ▶ Establish the new activity so that it becomes familiar ▶ Use the now familiar activity to introduce new music

Recognising and understanding the challenges experienced by young people with particular special educational needs and the approaches that are best likely help them address these challenges is important to inclusion in music education. However as Zimmerman (in Philpott et al., 2016) points out, what is also important is that we do not label a young person purely in terms of their needs and in doing so lose sight of their individual identity as a person and musician. Particular attitudes and disposition towards young people with such needs can result in their sense of self and individuality being erased.

Darrow (2015: 212), for example, notes that:

> *People without disabilities often spend more time thinking about a person's disability than the person with the disability. Most students with congenital disabilities are not mindful of their disabilities, and find them inconsequential to their happiness, or to their academic life. They are often only reminded of their disability when others make reference to it.*

The point that Darrow is making is a tendency to identify those with disabilities entirely in terms of that disability. This is typically reflected in language where the disability is foregrounded in the description of the young person, e.g. 'blind child' or a 'special needs pupil', rather than, perhaps, a child with a visual impairment or with special needs. In foregrounding the disability, other aspects of the young person's identity are erased or at the very least cast to the periphery of cognisance, and the focus becomes entirely on that disability and the extent to which it is perceived as acting as a barrier to their engagement with music education.

As Darrow goes on to say (citing Brown, 2002), whereas those with physical or cognitive disabilities share a 'common bond of experiences and resiliences' and are members of a 'disability culture' that has its own shared values, beliefs and artifacts, it is not the only culture to which they belong. They are 'also members of different nationalities, religions, colours, professional groups and so on' (Brown in Darrow, 2015: 207). Zimmerman notes that, 'Music will play an equally important part in the lives of those children who have SEN as in the lives of other children and they are just as likely to bring to the classroom [or other contexts of musical learning] a wealth of musical experiences which teachers need to recognise, value and build on' (2011: 55). Therefore, when considering how music education might meet the needs of young people with disabilities, it is necessary to recognise that the perhaps more obvious physical and cognitive barriers may not be the only barriers that these young people are experiencing. Those with disabilities will have musical interests and aspirations and experience challenges to learning and musical engagement similar to other young people who may not share their cognitive and physical disabilities, all of which contribute to their sense of identity and self. An important consideration is the extent then to which barriers to music education they experience are rooted in their disability or in other aspects of their identity, such as class or ethnicity. Zimmerman argues that it is the individual's needs that should be the focus of attention rather than assumptions about the needs that young people with a particular 'condition' might have. As she says, 'It is important ... that ... we teach the individual not the label' (Zimmerman, 2011: 54).

When considering adopting differentiating teaching approaches to meet the needs of young people with exceptional shared needs, Zimmerman argues that 'Although specific strategies might be required ... all that is often needed are minor changes to what teachers typically do in addressing the range of needs in their classroom' (2011: 55). Darrow offers a pedagogical approach to the inclusion of pupils with exceptional needs which similarly seeks not to emphasise difference but rather to accommodate their needs within flexible and *inclusive* pedagogical frameworks. She argues for a Universal Design for Learning (UDL) approach which is 'designed from inception to meet the needs of as many students as possible' (215). Jellison (2012: 70) and Darrow (2015) offer the following principles based on UDL for developing inclusive musical pedagogies. These can be summarised as follows:

- Provide multiple, flexible methods of *presentation* (give learners various ways to acquire information and knowledge).
- Provide multiple, flexible methods of *expression*... (offers alternative methods and approaches for learners to navigate a learning environment and express what they know).
- Provide multiple means of *engagement* (gives options to capture learners' interest, challenge appropriately, and motivate), (Darrow, 2015: 215).

Both Darrow and Jellison contend that such an approach has the potential to address the musical learning needs of all students, including those that are designated as having special educational needs, including exceptional ability or talent in music.

Activity 8.4

Plan a lesson for a pupil or group of pupils which draw on the three principles set out above. Describe in the table below how these principles are met and then evaluate its effectiveness.

UDL principle	Outline of working out in lesson
Provide multiple, flexible methods of *presentation*.	
Provide multiple, flexible methods of *expression*.	
Provide multiple means of *engagement*.	

Meeting the needs of the young people identified as gifted and talented in music

Included in the category of young people with exceptional needs are those who are identified as gifted and talented in music. In a survey of the literature and research on young people identified as gifted and talented, Abramo and Natale-Abramo (2020), drawing on Renzulli and Reis (2018), suggest that giftedness can be framed in terms of particular dispositions:

- Abilities within in a domain that are significantly above the average (e.g. music).

- An ability to think creatively, characterised by 'novel thinking ... combining ideas that commonly do not go together and devising unusual but interesting solutions to problems' (Abramo and Natale-Abramo, 2020: 40).

- Strong commitment to any task undertaken with a determination to see it through to completion.

These definitions or characteristics of young people who are gifted and talented moves our thinking away from traditional conceptions based perhaps on psychometric tests, to an understanding of gifted and talented that is multi-faceted, context specific and ongoing.

It is tempting to assume that if young people are gifted and talented then their engagement with educational settings will be relatively unproblematic. However, as Abramo et al. (2020) say, this is not always the case, and some young people who demonstrate gifted and talented dispositions may react against the constraints of educational settings or particular teaching approaches. This might be particularly so where these settings provide limited opportunities for them to demonstrate and develop what they know and can do and restrict their sense of agency; this might result from tasks being insufficiently challenging.

Abramo et al. (2020) also warn that whilst it is relatively easy to identify and support those young people who demonstrate musical giftedness in conventional ways and within the kinds of music-making often valorised within music education (e.g. high level performing skills within classical music, and particularly performing from notation), it is easy to miss those pupils who perhaps demonstrate their giftedness in other ways and within musical traditions with which the teacher is less familiar e.g. through, for example, learning by ear and improvising. McPherson and Williamon (2006) are alive to the dangers of defining giftedness and talent within the narrow parameters of performing and identify seven additional sub-domains of music within which giftedness might be demonstrated – improvising, composing, arranging, analysis, appraising, conducting and teaching' (249), noting that 'The point we wish to stress is that all too often children's ability to perform music from notation is taken as the defining skill, while the range of abilities needed to develop musically in the broader sense are often neglected' (250).

> **Activity 8.5**
>
> Thinking about your own pupils, how might giftedness and talent be demonstrated in the seven 'sub-domains' of music identified by McPherson and Williamon? Note your thinking and observations in a table such as the one below. Consider ways in which opportunities might be created for pupils who are gifted and talented to exercise agency over both their musical learning and decision making.
>
> | Domain | Notes and observations |
> |---|---|
> | Improvising | |
> | Composing | |
> | Arranging | |
> | Analysis | |
> | Appraising | |
> | Conducting | |
> | Teaching* | |
>
> *When thinking about teaching, perhaps consider this in terms of Vygostsky's idea of the 'more knowledgeable other' explored earlier in the chapter and the potential it provides for dialogical engagement.

Conclusion: The Pedagogies of Participatory Parity

In examining inclusive music classrooms and programmes, Jellison suggests that musical agency and self determination is 'fostered in music environments where children feel safe and secure, and where they experience autonomy, demonstrate competence, and make decisions about music, music making, and other music activities in their lives' (Jellison, 2012: 67). This chapter has argued that fundamental to realising this vision is an approach to inclusion in music education that focuses not just on the redistribution of resources and induction into the pre-existing structures of music education but which also embraces the voices of young people in a process of participatory parity through which they gain agency over their musical learning and music making. Throughout the chapter we have identified snapshots of how such agency and the facilitation of the student voice can be realised through differentiated pedagogical approaches.

At the beginning of this chapter we identified how socio-economic factors could both benefit and disadvantage different individuals and groups of young people in terms of their access to the resources and opportunities that music education can offer. We noted how gender and social class and other social groupings are also significant factors in determining the kinds of music education opportunities available to young people and the extent to which these opportunities affirm or negate the musical practices, skills and values young people bring to their music education, including their instrumental music lessons.

Music plays an important role in the formation of individual and group identity. The musical tastes, preferences and the music practices in which young people (particularly from the teenage years onwards) choose to engage are significant signifiers of the groups to which they consider they belong and are expressions of their individual and collective identity. These social and cultural groups include those around social class, gender, ethnicity and religion, with individuals likely to be members of more than one social group.

The extent to which these musical preferences and practices are reflected and valued within music education – including instrumental teaching – and the extent to which young people believe their voices are heard, is a significant factor in whether they experience inclusion or exclusion from the formal structures of music education. Where young people's voices are not heard they may experience what Fraser (2005) refers to as lack of 'participatory parity' and 'misrecognition'. Misrecognition is defined by Fraser as rooted in 'an institutionalized pattern of cultural value that constitutes some categories of social actors as normative and others as 'deficient' or 'inferior'. The latter are then constituted as 'less than full members of society and [prevented]...from participating as peers' (Fraser, 2000, cited in Spruce, 2017: 727).

Misrecognition acts as a powerful tool of exclusion in music education. One of the most common forms of misrecognition occurs through the privileging of the repertoire, practices and values of western classical music, where these are perceived as universal and/or as self-evidently superior to the practices and values of other musical styles and traditions. Here the patterns of 'cultural value' that are deficient are those which do not accord with the 'patterns' – the values and practices – of western art music. Spruce (2017) and Vaugeois (2007) both suggest that casting certain forms of musical practices as deficient leads to a salvationist approach to music education where its main focus becomes a process of inducting young people into a set of *fixed* musical norms associated with western classical music and into the educational structures which support these. Such approaches are frequently accompanied by a social justice, 'changing lives' rhetoric which seeks to position 'deficient' groups as in need of saving through the alchemic qualities seemingly possessed only by classical music. Redistributive approaches to social justice are then appropriated in pursuit of this, with funding prioritised for those organisations and approaches that focus primarily on western art music.

As we have noted, a primarily (re)distributive approach to inclusion and social justice typically fails to challenge the structures which lead to lack of participatory parity and can be the means by which young people are excluded from music education. The central argument of this chapter is that socially just approaches to inclusion in music education require structures and pedagogies that respond flexibly to young people's needs and aspirations. Also, that they provide spaces in which the voices of young people can be heard and then acted upon, and where the musical values, skills and practices that they bring to their musical learning are respected and valued. Central to such approaches are what Spruce (2015) describes as dialogical approaches to music education where, as noted earlier, musical knowledge is not fixed but emerges from musical interactions between 'pupil', 'teacher' and 'the music' within the unique spaces of each lesson. Here musical knowledge and understanding are not closed forms and predetermined but fluid and dynamic and responsive to young people's musical engagement and music making within the particular traditions and practices in which they participate. As Elliott eloquently puts it:

> *My knowing [musical knowledge] is in the actions of my artistic music making ... if I compose or arrange artistically – in relation to the relevant standards and traditions of a genre – then I have a working musical understanding of that practice...* (Elliott, 1995: 105).

Here inclusion and social justice are seen not as simply things that are 'done' to young people and which have an end point but rather are a continuing and dynamic process where young people's voices are placed at the centre of the pedagogies of music education and instrumental teaching.

References

Abramo, J. M. and Natale-Abramo, M. (2020) Reexamining "Gifed and Talented" in Music Education. *Music Educators Journal*, 106(3), pp. 38-46.

Associated Board of the Royal Schools of Music. (2014) *Making Music: Teaching, learning and playing in the UK*. London: ABRSM.

Bull, A. (2019) *Class, Control and Classical Music*. New York: Oxford University Press.

Burnard, P., Dillon S., Rusinek G. and Saether, E. (2008) Inclusive pedagogies in music education: a comparative study of music teachers' perspectives from four countries. *International Journal of Music Education*, 26(2), pp. 109-126.

Darrow, A-A. (2015) Ableism and Social Justice. In: C. Benedict, P. Schmidt, G. Spruce and P. Woodford, eds. *The Oxford Handbook of Social Justice in Music Education*. New York: Oxford University Press.

Daubney, A. (2017) *Teaching Primary Music*. London: Sage Publications.

Department for Education. (2013) *National Curriculum in Music : Music programmes of study*. London: Crown Copyright.

Dickinson, C. and Wright, J. (1993) *Differentiation: A Practical Handbookof Classroom Strategies*. Coventry: NCET.

Elliott, D. (1995) *Music Matters*. Oxford: Oxford University Press.

Fraser, N. (2000) Rethinking Recognition. *New Left Review*, 3. May-June.

Fraser, N. (2005) Reframing Social Justice in a Globalizing World. *New Left Review*, 36. November-December.

Gathan, Kelly (2014) *Gender Bias and Music Education*. Masters Thesis. University of Delware.

Green, L. (2003) Music Education, Cultural Capital and Social Group Identity. In: M. Clayton, T. Herbert and R. Middleton, eds. *The Cultural Study of Music*. London: Routledge.

Green, L. (1997) *Music, Gender, Education*. Cambridge: Cambridge University Press.

Hallam, S (1998) *Instrumental Teaching*. London: Heinemann.

Holder, N. (2022) *Moving towards decolonising music education*. Lecture, Birmingham City University, May 2022.

Incorporated Society of Musicians (2021) *Music: A subject in peril?* London: ISM.

Incorporated Society of Musicians and University of Sussex (2019) *Music Education: State of the Nation*. London: ISM.

Jellison, J. (2012) Inclusive Music Classrooms and Programs. In: G. McPherson and G. Welch, eds. *The Oxford Handbook of Music Education*, Vol 2. Oxford: Oxford University Press.

McPherson, G. E. and Williamon, A. (2006) Giftedness and Talent in G. E. McPherson, ed. *The Child as Musician*. Oxford: Oxford University Press.

National Foundation for Youth Music (2020) *The Sound of the Next Generation*. London: Youth Music.

Ockleford, A. (2008) *Music for Children and Young People with Complex Needs*. Oxford: Oxford University Press.

Philpott, C, Wright, R. with Evans, K. and Zimmerman, S. (2016) Addressing individual needs and equality of opportunity in music education. In: C. Cook, K. Evans, C. Philpott and G. Spruce, eds. *Learning to Teach Music in the Secondary School*. London: Routledge.

Philpott, C. with Kulbrick, J. (2015) Social Justice in the English Secondary Music Classroom. In: C. Benedict, P. Schmidt, G. Spruce and P. Woodford eds. *The Oxford Handbook of Social Justice in Music Education*. New York: Oxford University Press.

Rawls, J. (1971). *A Theory of Justice*. Harvard, MA: Harvard University Press.

Renzulli, J. S., & Reis, S. M. (2018). The three-ring conception of giftedness: A developmental approach for promoting creative productivity in young people. In S. I. Pfeiffer, E. Shaunessy-Dedrick, and M. Foley-Nicpon (eds.), *APA Handbook of Giftedness and Talent* (pp. 185-199). American Psychological Association.

Scott, L. and Jellison, J. A. (2007) Talking with Music Teachers about Inclusion: Perceptions, Opinions and Experiences. *Journal of Music Therapy*, 44(1), pp. 38-56.

Small, C. (1998) *Musicking: The Meanings of Performing and Listening*. Middletown, Connecticut: Wesleyan University Press.

Spruce, G. (2017) The Power of Discourse: Reclaiming Social Justice from and for Music Education. *Education*, 3-13 45(6), pp. 720-733.

Spruce, G. and Matthews, F. (2012) Musical ideologies, practices and pedagogies. In: C. Philpott and G. Spruce, eds. *Debates in Music Teaching*. London: Routledge.

Vaugeois, L. (2007) Social Justice and Music Education: Claiming the Space of Music Education as a Site of Postcolonial Contestation. *Action, Criticism, and Theory for Music Education*, 6(4), pp. 163-200.

Vygotsky, L. S. (1978) *Mind in society: The development of higher psychological processes*. Cambridge, MA: Harvard University Press.

Wells, G. (1999) Dialogic inquiry: Towards a sociocultural practice and theory of education. In: G. Wells, ed. *The Zone Of Proximal Development And Its Implications For Learning And Teaching*. New York: Cambridge University Press.

Zimmerman, S. (2011) Including those with special educational needs: "whole" class instrumental and vocal teaching. In: N. Beach, J. Evans, G. Spruce, eds. *Making Music in the Primary School*. London: Routledge.

Chapter 9 Commentary

Assessment in music is not, nor cannot ever be, a wholly neutral or objective act. It is a process that is inevitably imbued with personal and communal beliefs and values. These beliefs and values lie at the heart of our understanding of what music is, what constitutes good music and, in the context of instrumental teaching, how an effective performance is defined and evaluated.

In this chapter, Francesca Christmas unpicks how these values and beliefs are constructed and how they are so deeply embedded in teachers' thinking that they are taken as self-evident and consequently rarely questioned. She argues that in order for assessment to be fair and just teachers have a responsibility to interrogate how the values that they bring to assessment result both from their own musical enculturation and from the dominant musical values that underpin music education; these being most often those of western classical music. She argues that such interrogation requires teachers to engage in what Freire (1970) refers to as a 'conscientisation', a process where one comes to question those things which one has taken as self-evident and which have unconsciously impacted on the way one thinks and acts.

Her chapter is based on her own research study into the role of assessment in instrumental music undertaken in six countries and draws on conversations with instrumental teachers about their use of assessment. She begins by considering the tensions between assessment which has the primary purpose of supporting learning, and assessment which is concerned mainly with assessing what a pupil can do at a particular point in time. She then argues for the importance of locating musical assessment within the values and processes of the tradition of the music that is being learnt and performed. This leads on to an exploration of the importance of music teachers recognising how their musical life-stories play a vital role in constructing their musical values and beliefs and hence to how and what they assess in music. Finally, she argues for a dialogical approach to instrumental assessment as a shared process between teacher, learner and the musical style and tradition within which they are working.

9 Assessment, Values, Beliefs: Working Towards a 'Conscientised' Approach to Assessment in Instrumental Music Teaching

Francesca Christmas

'So... here she is about to play the C♯ and I can already feel my toes curling [laughs]... this position is not our best... did you see that? I asked her to stretch before she even played it because I could see her tense up... I think I've pushed this one a few times too many with her and perhaps she's overthinking now... so I ask her to stop [laughs]. I worry about parents seeing this, don't laugh... I get them to pretend to be jelly in their arms to shake out tension... she hates this [laughs] but listen... see? So much better in tune, right?... and look at her face... a cat who got the cream!'

Strings Teacher, UK

This chapter draws upon a research study conducted in six countries exploring the role of assessment in music instrumental education. Examples and quotes feature throughout the chapter from teachers across these territories, working in range of teaching contexts from one-to-one to small-group. In this transcript excerpt, a UK-based cello teacher is providing commentary on a video of her own lesson, taught the previous day. She is describing the actions and reactions of both herself and her pupil. The question she was asked in the interview: *What is happening in the lesson at this time which relates to the assessment of instrumental performance skills?*

Introduction

Whilst much of what goes on in the day-to-day practice of instrumental teachers might be described as assessment in one form or another, it is perhaps infrequently understood as such and perhaps even less frequently do we as instrumental teachers analyse and reflect on the factors at play in making those minute-to-minute assessments in the lesson, including the importance of our own musical and educational beliefs and values. This bringing to the fore of these beliefs and values is a process that in this chapter we will call conscientisation. The process of conscientisation as described by Freire (1970) involves critical self-reflection. Critical self-reflection enables us to become aware of our own value systems and beliefs and how these shape the assessment judgements we make and the implications of these judgements for our learners. The chapter will argue that a better understanding of these beliefs and values can result in assessment which is more relevant to and reflective of the musical ambitions and achievement of our pupils.

In tandem with conscientisation we will look at the pedagogical context within which assessment sits, and in doing so will argue that assessment is at its best when it is embedded within dialogical instrumental teaching pedagogies. Spruce (2012) suggests that dialogical pedagogies are those where musical knowledge and learning emerges from the interactions of the teacher, the learner, and the music. In such approaches, knowledge doesn't just flow from the teacher to the learner, but is developed jointly through discussion, interaction, questioning and feedback.

In order to support the process of conscientisation of assessment practices, this chapter will consider three key concepts:

- Tensions within the purposes of assessment – what are the purposes of assessment and more specifically is there a conflict between assessment which informs learning and assessment which is undertaken in order to gain a certificate or qualification?
- Genre-specific assessment – we cannot assume that assessment which is relevant for one type of music will be appropriate in another. The pedagogies and practices inherent within a musical style, genre, or tradition are not always transferable.
- Individual beliefs – the values and beliefs that we hold as teachers have an impact on our assessment practices.

We will examine these three concepts in the following sections.

1. Tensions Within the Purposes of Assessment

This section explores the tension between assessment for the purposes of learning and assessment as part of an exam or an end of year test. Understanding the differences between these and why and how they should feature in the processes of instrumental learning is unpicked here within the familiar framework of 'formative and summative' assessment.

Instrumental teachers as instinctive assessors

Fautley suggests that music teachers are 'highly skilled in the art of formative assessment' (i.e. assessment which occurs through the process of teaching in order to inform the learning) and that formative assessment is the 'mother-tongue of the professional music educator' (2007: 2). The full narrative from which the extract at the start of this chapter is taken is a fascinating example of this. The teacher can identify multiple occasions on which she assesses the pupil's playing and suggests interventions for improvement. There are complex processes at play: for example, the instance in which she identifies an intervention ('I asked her to stretch before she even played it...') and then, realising that it is having a negative effect, she re-evaluates and suggests a different, ameliorative activity. In the lesson 'conversation', when the pupil responds with discomfort, the teacher recognizes it and adapts her approach. The teacher can describe the minutiae of her pupil's body language, and what those signals represent in terms of frustration, compliance or feeling of achievement, and talks not only of the performative content of the lesson, but also of the emotional and inter-personal exchanges.

The full transcript of the lesson from which this excerpt is taken is 21 pages long, and there are 86 examples of the teacher's assessments within that time. The level of detailed analysis described above is only possible because the interactions within the lesson are purposeful and intentional, carefully designed to support and further the learning in the lesson. It is clear from the transcript that there are no serendipitous accidents of effective teaching, it is deliberate and informed, and the teacher is working consistently with her pupil towards the improvement of musical performance. It is also, inter alia, an example of the emergence of dialogical teaching, in which the learner is not merely passively receiving instruction but interacting with the teacher and the music itself, and in doing so shapes the course of the lesson.

Formative and summative assessment

In the *Report from the National Curriculum Task Group in the UK* (1987), summative assessment is described as 'Assessment of learning' (AoL) and formative assessment 'Assessment for learning' (AfL). This provides a useful insight into what the purposes of these two assessment approaches might be, and who they might be for. AoL is an appraisal of attainment at a point in time. A driving test would be an example of AoL, or a graded music exam, or an end of year exam in school or university. AfL is assessment that is designed to support and serve the pupil's learning and might manifest as a teacher observing a learner engaged in a task, and then feeding back to them on what could be developed to improve further; for example, the case study at the beginning of this chapter.

For instrumental teachers, these two types of assessment do not always exist harmoniously, and can in fact be conceived of as binary:

▶ Assessment as measurement, against units of accountability, measuring individuals against externally defined standards, and/or each other

vs

▶ Assessment as understanding the uniqueness of the individual learner, employing feedback as a means of furthering progress according to the individual needs and values of the learner

Table 9.1 below describes the differences between them:

Formative	Summative
Intended to inform learning	Intended to inform on attainment
Requirements informed by the learner	Requirements designed by the assessor
Builds a picture of progress over time	Provides a snapshot of attainment level at the time
Has the potential to promote agency of the learner	Locates authority within the assessor

2. Genre Specific Assessment: The Significance of Musical Styles and Genres

Instrumental teaching and learning take place in a range of pedagogical contexts, for a panoply of different purposes, and within a range of musical styles, genres and traditions. Enshrined within these genres and traditions are sets of pedagogical (and therefore assessment) practices and beliefs. This next section looks at how the assessment practices of western art music — arguably the dominant stylistic context for the majority of instrumental teaching and indeed music education more broadly (Spruce and Matthews, 2012) — have been exported to instrumental teaching and learning in other musical traditions, risking the imposition of inappropriate assessment processes.

In the 1980s, David Elliott undertook a small-scale study with a small number of musicians to investigate the reliability of judgements about musical performances (1987). Three judges (adjudicators) and six musicians with expertise in western art music were asked to rate six classical musical performances without any set criteria to refer to. In summary, there was significant consensus between the judges and musicians in many areas. Even when their rationales diverged, there was frequent agreement as to the overall standards of the performances they listened to.

This is perhaps unsurprising in a small study where the six performances were all of the western classical tradition, performed by 'classically trained' students on orchestral instruments and judged by experts in the style. But on further reflection, taking into consideration the deeply subjective and personal nature of musical performance appreciation, it is perhaps a more remarkable phenomenon. This consensus could be attributed to a phenomenon that is known as a community of practice (Lave and Wenger, 1991) where a community of people are drawn together with a common purpose of learning and endeavour within a domain of interest. There is a shared but tacit understanding within the community around the domain, often not explicitly expressed, but transmitted, osmosis-like amongst its participants. It could be argued that knowledge of a particular musical style or genre is sometimes acquired in this way and also that it is how, within these communities, participants learn communally and develop a sense of shared identity and endeavour (Waldron, 2009). Cultural and social values, pedagogical and procedural processes are tacitly learned and understood, which leads to a *sometimes unconscious* adherence to the protocols of the musical style.

It is seen here, in an interview with an examiner for a small, local music examination organisation in Germany (examining only in western classical music), when asked what marking criteria were used within the exams:

> *'Our stomachs! [laughs] We do not need it written down ... it is easy to know in the heart, in the gut when a child is good, bad or excellent ... that is the role of the expert'.*
> Examiner, Berlin

The examiner's response assumes that all 'experts' share the same set of standards, values and beliefs around the music they are assessing, and that all subjects of the assessment would share them too. This is indeed a likely outcome of any music learned through a community of practice but is also an example of how the dominance of western art music (its practices and institutions) has arguably resulted in tacitly understood and shared conceptualisations of standards in instrumental learning and an associated set of assessment practices. This unconscious adoption of a set of unexamined values and beliefs around a music genre so prolific and universal in the world of instrumental teaching poses the risk that they become indiscriminately adopted across styles and genres that are *not* western art music. Spruce (2001, 2017), Green (2002, 2008), and Bull (2019) have written about how the dominance of the processes and practices of western art music in music education has resulted in the 'othering' of musics not from that tradition, such that as Spruce says: '... even when the focus of attention is on music from other traditions, the values promoted by the pedagogical and assessment approaches tend to continue to assert the primacy of Western Art Music to the disadvantage of those whose musical enculturation and practices are embedded in 'other' musical traditions' (2017: 722).

The outcome is the development of 'folk standards' in instrumental learning and assessment – i.e. a set of standards that are not sufficiently and consciously theorised by those enacting them but achieve a dominant position and become normalised. It raises issues for assessment, as folk standards not only require all of the stakeholders (for example, the teachers, student, parent, school, employer and others) to share the same innate comprehension of the musical context and associated standards, but also risks ignoring the personal, individual values and beliefs of the learner or teacher who may not be sufficiently enculturated (or wish to be!) into the style or genre to participate fully. This reduces opportunities for learner and/or teacher agency, and the ability of the learner to assert their own objectives and outcomes for their learning.

What then is the significance of this for instrumental teachers? It is a caution to be aware of hegemonic values and practices which have become normalised in instrumental teaching and assessment. It asks teachers to deliberately consider the appropriateness of assessment approaches according to the individual learner in the lesson and is an exhortation against considering the design of any assessment activity as universal, able to transcend musical styles and genres and the pedagogical implications enshrined within them. For example, when rehearsing a piece of repertoire with a learner, whose idea of a 'good performance' is being developed? Is it that of the teacher, and, if so, how has that been informed? Is it a received sense of 'correct' according to a set of tacit folk standards, and are those standards appropriate to the genre of music in question? Perhaps most importantly, is it the learner's idea of 'good'? It is important to recognise that learners at every stage in ability of experience will hold a set of declared or undeclared musical values and beliefs which may not accord with those of their teacher, but which should be recognised and reflected in the activity of assessing.

Activity 9.1

In this section we have explored how the traditions of western classical music/art can serve to sustain and reinforce particular hegemonic musical values and processes. Jot down some ideas for how you might mediate the imposition of particular musical values when teaching non-western classical repertoire.

3. Individual Beliefs: The Importance of the Values and Beliefs of the Individual and How These Can be Recognised Through Dialogical Teaching Contexts

We outlined at the start of this chapter that dialogical pedagogies are those where musical knowledge and learning emerges from the interactions of the teacher, the learner and the music. Both the teacher and the learner will bring their own beliefs, values and personal histories to those interactions, and we propose in this next section that a better understanding of these is important in dialogical teaching approaches.

Teachers' own stories

Dewey (1933), reminds us that reflection is a challenging, rigorous, intellectual, and emotional activity that requires time and patience to do well and that objectively interrogating the building blocks of one's own value system is a complex act. However, there are many models of reflection as well as much literature on the subject of teacher reflection that instrumental teachers may draw on in order to 'become better acquainted with their own story' (Conle, 2000: 51).

For example, teachers might call on autoethnographic literature and methodologies to better understand their own values and beliefs. In Peshkin's 'Subjective I's' (1988) he analyses different aspects of his own beliefs, life experiences and identities to better understand his own subjective norms. There are examples of music educators drawing on this model, such as Savage's work (2007) where he identifies the 'Musically Conservative I'; 'The Technologically Enthusiastic I'; 'The Musically Radical I' and others, and then articulates the beliefs and experiences which characterise each of these in order to better understand the subjectivities he brings to his teaching and his research. Another example of a reflective model might be that of Kushner (2000), who writes of the importance of teachers understanding their own role and influence in the classroom through understanding their own life histories. Examples of these types of critical self-reflective work include personal narratives or stories in which teachers articulate their experiences first as learners and then teachers, and then reflect on the events within those stories which have bearing on their own identities as teachers and musicians. Whichever approach is taken, the most important outcome of it will be the conscientisation of the teacher's own habitus and understanding of the values and beliefs that they bring into the teaching space.

Learners' own stories – feedback in dialogical contexts

The other person in the teaching space is the learner, and each learner will also bring with them their own set of values and beliefs. In a constructivist approach the understanding of the learner's musical habitus is as important as the understanding of the teacher's own. This allows for interactions where teacher and learner are not only working together but are co-creating knowledge and understanding. This is dialogical teaching, a participatory format of feedback and questioning in which teachers and learners transform learning into a collaborative process through which knowledge is re-created together (rather than simply delivered from the teacher to learner).

A framework for dialogical teaching developed by Alexander (2017: 5) describes the principles as:

Collective – the teaching space is a site of joint enquiry.

Reciprocal – participants interact and listen, and share ideas.

Supportive – ideas are freely expressed without fear of embarrassment, and participants work together to reach common understandings.

Cumulative – participants build on each other's contributions.

Purposeful – interactions are structured towards goals and objectives.

Importantly for instrumental teachers, dialogical teaching goes beyond mere discussion as it is situated in the thoughts, language, aspirations, and conditions of both learner and teacher (Shor and Freire, 1987) and in the pedagogies and practices of the music explored.

Activity 9.2

Think about the five principles of dialogic teaching as proposed by Alexander. Draw up a table with a row for each principle and two columns. Thinking about some of your recent lessons, note down in the first column some examples of how your teaching has reflected Alexander's principles. During your lessons over the next few days, think about the things you have written down. Then return to the table and note down in the second column any new ideas you have come up with to further embed dialogical teaching in your work.

Through doing the activity above, you may have become aware that providentially, the opportunities for rich, dialogical interactions are already embedded into instrumental teaching and learning contexts. The limited number of participants in a one-to-one or small-group lesson enables these meaningful interactions. As already discussed earlier in this chapter, instrumental teachers are naturally inclined towards initiating these through feedback. Feedback tends to take the form of 'instant reinforcement that occurs within short teaching frames' (Parkes, 2010: 102). Within a behaviourist context, feedback might be a series of observations or directions from the teacher, designed to support learners towards achieving a set objective around the development of skills or knowledge. An example of this in instrumental teaching might be a teacher feeding back to a learner that they are not playing in time with an accompaniment with the expectation that the learner will adjust their performance accordingly. Within a constructivist context, feedback is more likely to be bi-directional and designed by the teacher to be 'problem-posing' (Shor and Freire, 1987) for learners to respond to and build upon, collaboratively constructing the learning.

It is important to understand the differences between feedback that is simple and transactional: 'You did not play the notes of the scale correctly', and that which is dialogic, informed by what a learner is currently doing, what they want to achieve, suggesting what they might do next. The latter facilitates agency for the learner; instead of merely receiving instruction, they are able to be part of a dialogue in which they have influence over what happens subsequently in their learning.

Conclusion

This chapter has explored three key concepts supporting conscientised assessment approaches, which are those of:

- The purposes of the assessment.
- The pedagogies and practices inherent within the musical style, genre, or tradition in which the learning is situated.
- The individual values and beliefs of teacher and learner.

However, within the research study that this chapter draws on, many teachers expressed that there are often significant barriers and feelings of disempowerment: e.g. the expectations of parents, and the measure of their success as teachers resting on the exam grades of their learners. For example, an extract from a focus group within the research study, in Singapore in 2018:

> 'It's great to go to training courses, but you have to realise that parents are the customer… and they see the exam board as the medic who writes the prescription. They then give it to the teacher who administers the medicine, and the expertise of the teacher is measured by how much better the student gets as a result – like, what mark they get in their exam.

> *And if the student doesn't do so well, then the teacher doesn't either. Our students' grades are the measure of our success...'*
> Piano teacher, Singapore

In addition, the scarcity of accessible music teacher development opportunities such as courses and workshops is a challenge for many instrumental teachers who would benefit from professional development opportunities that would support the processes of conscientisation. Shulman describes teachers as 'apprentices of observation' (2005: 57), suggesting that teachers tend to model their practice on that which they experienced as learners, and perhaps this is even more so the case for instrumental music teachers who do not always have a background of formal teacher training or education. The lack of professional support for instrumental teachers in many parts of the world means that it can be difficult to interrogate existing – and develop new – pedagogical approaches which might diverge from or contradict those that they may have experienced as learners.

For teachers – feeling these pressures, now at the end of this chapter – wondering how to develop their assessment practices, it is helpful to briefly refer back to some of the arguments explored; that instrumental teachers are naturally inclined towards formative assessment and feedback, that the teaching space of small group or one-to-one lessons lends itself usefully to dialogical interactions; and conclude by suggesting that the very act of engaging with this chapter in this book is in itself a positive step towards the self-reflection and criticality required for conscientisation. From this will then emerge the development of expertise in assessment practices which encourage music learners in self-reflection, self-direction, criticality, and responsibility for their learning (Tan, 2007).

From a teacher in Milan, Italy:

> *'This ... this music teaching .... is the greatest tradition, yes? The ultimate in aesthetic, the intellectual, the arts ... the beauty ... the teaching of the next generation of greatest musicians. My job is only to find the way that provides least barrier to the greatness of my learners ... to allow them to be fantastic ... and so I continue to learn and find new ways .... There is no correct way, no 'Abracadabra!' for assessment ... I continue to learn ....'*
> Singing teacher, Milan

References

Alexander, R. (2017) Developing dialogic teaching: Process, trial, outcomes.
In: *17th Biennial EARLI Conference, Tampere, Finland*. (Vol. 31).

Bull, A. (2019) *Class, Control, and Classical Music*. Oxford: Oxford University Press.

Conle, C. (2000) Narrative Inquiry: Research tool and medium for professional development.
European Journal of Teacher Education, 23(1), pp. 49-63.

Department of Education, Department and Science, London (England) (1987) *National Curriculum: Task Group on Assessment and Testing. A Report*. ERIC Clearinghouse, pp. 1-67.

Dewey, J. (1933) *How we think: A Restatement of the Relation of Reflective Thinking to the Educative Process*. Boston, MA: Heath and Co. Publishers.

Elliott, D. J. (1987) Assessing Musical Performance.
British Journal of Music Education, 4(02), pp. 157-184.

Fautley, M. (2007) Lost in Translation – The Changed Language of Assessment in Music Education, *Magazine of NAME*, pp. 2-4.

Freire, P. (1970) *Pedagogy of the oppressed*. New York: Herder and Herder.

Green, L. (2002) *How popular musicians learn: a way ahead for music education*. Aldershot, Hants; Burlington, VT: Ashgate.

Green, L. (2008) *Music, informal learning and the school: A new classroom pedagogy*.
London: Routledge.

Kushner, S. (2000) *Personalizing Evaluation*. London: SAGE.

Lave, J. and Wenger, E. (1991) *Situated learning: Legitimate peripheral participation*. Cambridge: Cambridge University Press.

Parkes, K. A. (2010) Performance assessment: Lessons from performers.
International Journal of Teaching and Learning in Higher Education, 22(1), pp. 98-106.

Peshkin, A. (1988) In search of subjectivity. One's own. *Educational Researcher*.
American Educational Research Association (AERA), 17(7), p. 17-21.

Savage, J. (2007) Reflecting through Peshkin's I's.
International Journal of Music Education, 25(3), pp. 193-203.

Shor, I. and Freire, P. (1987) What is the "dialogical method" of teaching?
Journal of Education, 169(3), pp. 11-31.

Shulman, L. S. (2005) Signature pedagogies in the professions. *Daedalus*.
MIT Press, 134(3), pp. 52-59.

Spruce, G. (2001) Music assessment and the hegemony of musical heritage.
In: C. Philpott and C. Plummeridge, eds. *Issues in Music Teaching*. London, UK: RoutledgeFalmer.

Spruce, G. (2017) The power of discourse: reclaiming social justice from and for music education.
Education, 3-13, 45(6), pp. 720-733.

Tan, K. (2007) Conceptions of self-assessment. In: D. Boud and N. Falchikov, eds.
Rethinking Assessment in Higher Education: Learning for the Longer Term. London: Routledge.

Waldron, J. (2009) Exploring a virtual music community of practice: Informal music learning on the Internet. *Journal of Music, Technology and Education*, 2 (2-3), pp. 97-112.

Chapter 10 Commentary

Many education systems around the world offer classroom music lessons as a part of the school curriculum. But very often instrumental teaching has little or no relationship to a student's experience of music in school and sometimes these operate as though the two were completely different subjects.

Children and young people experience music in a multitude of ways. A young learner might have private piano lessons, be a K-Pop fan, learn music in the school classroom, and have a guitar on which they occasionally work out some riffs. Often as instrumental teachers we can forget that our students can have complex musical lives beyond what they do with us. This is not to suggest that we should necessarily interfere in that broader musical life, but perhaps if we had a better understanding of the other places and ways in which our students learn music, we might be able to help them understand some of the relationships between them.

Adam Whittaker and Martin Fautley argue that closer working between instrumental teachers and classroom teachers could enrich learners' musical experiences. In their words: 'Instrumental musical learning has significant potential to make general music education utterly transformative'. The relationship between the two is complex, however, and perhaps not helped by a lack of clarity about what each is trying to achieve. The area of instrumental learning is rendered even more complex by the fact that so many learners learn instruments without the support of a teacher, utilising online videos, etc.

In order to demonstrate such collaborations in practice, the authors draw on two case studies: Whole Class Instrumental and Vocal Teaching (UK) and JustPlay, an initiative from Musical Futures which has gained significant popularity in Australia and the UK, with an increasing following in SE Asia. In including these case studies, they are not suggesting these programmes as a route that the reader will necessarily want to follow, but that there will be something in them which teachers may draw on in order to develop closer relationships with others who are involved in our students' musical development.

10 Instrumental Teaching as Part of a General Music Education

Adam Whittaker and Martin Fautley

Terminology in music education is as important as it is complex. Finding agreement on definitions and interpretations of terminology is always challenging given the diverse cultural, political, and social landscapes that shape understandings of what it is to be musical. The idea of a 'general music education' is no different. What does this mean? How is it different from other forms of music education? What are our aims? Indeed, to whom does the 'our' refer here? And how is this different from instrumental teaching? These questions are all pertinent to understanding the relationship between instrumental teaching and a general music education and draw attention to key debates in the field. In this chapter, we examine these issues using the English context as a case study. However, it is important to observe that the locational specificity of this setting should not detract in any way from the implications for teaching and learning wherever these are taking place. Conceptualisations of instrumental learning within general music education need to be considered and operationalised in a reflective fashion, wherever in the world they are occurring.

In England two key documents – the National Curriculum for Music (DfE, 2013) and the National Plan for Music Education (DfE and DCMS, 2011) – set out some key principles for music education as it takes place in schools and formal settings. The National Curriculum (NC) sets out statutory guidance for state schools, and establishes the general principles that children will have the opportunity to perform music, create with sound, and listen to a range of musics. This is an entitlement for all children in state-maintained schools, and places music as a key part of a broader curriculum offer nationally. It is a powerful policy document that guides governmental inspection frameworks, informs strategic decisions by school leaders, and legitimises the place of music as part of a 'broad and balanced' education (Hall, 2016).

The National Plan for Music Education (NPME) is a separate document which sets out aims and objectives for Music Education Hubs (MEHs), organisations tasked with supporting music-making in schools and being accountable to local constituents. MEH lead organisations offer a range of musical opportunities in different configurations, but many tend to be the ones offering instrumental tuition and ensemble opportunities for children in a locality. The NC and NPME are specific to England, but their fundamental principles are recognisable across international contexts, with musical education being identified as a key part of a child's education in statutory policy and guidance. In many jurisdictions children have an entitlement to music education, which may involve creating, composing, playing and listening, but this is far from universal. In some contexts, the USA being a notable example, definitions of music education are drawn less widely, focusing upon specific aspects of music rather than a broader musical education. Indeed, for some, musical education is entirely synonymous with learning to play a particular instrument.

Although these principles apply mostly to schools, and it is through schools that many children experience a formal music education, there are many organisations offering other experiences and pedagogical approaches which can form equally valuable parts of a general music education. It is useful to distinguish here between formal, informal, and non-formal provision of music education, as the differences between them can affect that which is learned. Wright and Kanellopoulos (2010: 72-73) outlined the main differences between them:

> *Formal learning may be described as that which occurs in a traditional pedagogic environment where clarity of goals and procedures are clearly defined in advance and where learning results in certification or assessment. Non-formal learning occurs outside traditional learning environments, is not the result of deliberation and does not normally result in certification.*

Lonie and Dickens (2016: 88) explain the differences between informal and non-formal like this:

> *Informal, everyday spaces often constitute opportunities for musical encounters, rehearsal and performance in the development of musical awareness, aptitude and expression. Such experiences can begin early on in life, within family, domestic and otherwise mundane settings. Sometimes, they occur through participation in non-formal, funded provision of musical opportunities in youth centres, clubs and halls, musical studios and so on.*

One of the main differences between formal and informal learning in music was clearly defined by Folkestad (2006: 141), when he noted that:

> *The informal learning situation is not sequenced beforehand; the activity steers the way of working/playing/composing, and the process proceeds by the interaction of the participants in the activity.*

These formal, informal, and non-formal provisions can be offered by specialist music organisations and ensembles or might form part of other intervention and social development programmes, for which music-making is an access point to establish trust and common ground. For example, interactions and partnerships between formal and non-formal sectors can yield positive results for some of the most vulnerable young people, using young people's own musicality as a starting point to build fruitful exchange (Kinsella et al., 2019). In this spirit, this chapter explores the relationships that instrumental teaching and learning has to wider musical learning and development across a range of settings.

> ### Activity 10.1
> What are the main ways in which children and young people access music learning in your setting/country? Are there curriculum documents which set out what kinds of musical learning children and young people should experience? Make a brief list of these experiences and then identify which of these your teaching supports.

General Music Education

Perspectives on what is (and is not) a general music education (GME) will vary depending upon local contexts, musical cultures, and how different types, styles and genres of music are given relative degrees of importance by local, regional and national contexts; for example, in some areas there is strong policy and practice leaning towards western classical and related musical forms, in other areas pop, rock and jazz are afforded equivalent status in curricula. By its very nature, a general music education should be governed by principles which intersect, overlap and become usefully entangled with other aspects of cultural experience and artistic engagement. This links closely with notions of both cultural literacy (Hirsch, 1988), where a person knows the key aspects of what are deemed as culturally appropriate norms in a society, and cultural capital (Bourdieu, 1979), where the background and taste of an individual are important. GME may not prescribe specific content, and, in some cases, does not need to have a specific outcome in mind (Howard, 2012). This means there is a distinction that can be drawn between instrument-specific musical learning and other aspects of musical development; indeed, John Paynter – a leading figure in English music education whose ideas influenced at least a generation of teachers in many countries around the world – drew attention to this when he distinguished between different aspects within music education, those of musical education and music in education:

> *Musical education ... could describe adequately the training essential for anyone who is to follow a musical career. But music in education suggests something much broader – the use of music in the general school curriculum in such a way that it can make a significant contribution to the education of all pupils* (Paynter, 1977/2008: 34).

Whilst these areas are related, and developments in each may go hand-in-hand, they are underpinned by different aims and objectives and, as such, constitute different conceptualisations of teaching and learning. Thinking through these is of the greatest importance in considering the complex interrelationships between instrumental learning and general music education.

A general music education refers to holistic musical experiences which support a learner to become a musical citizen. Christopher Small's notion of musicking has gained much traction in community music circles and holds relevance here too (see, for example, Small, 1988: 1–18). To summarise his argument, musicking focuses on the processes of music-making as intensely social activities, and advocates a move away from music being viewed as a fixed work embodying the score as object. In effect, musicking turns 'music' into an active verb rather than a static object; it is dynamic, ever-changing and, importantly, determined by the people involved. Musicking is a process and activity to which we all contribute. The potential of musicking as an underpinning philosophy for general music education is significant, as it opens up music to being a democratic and socially grounded process. This view is played out in a range of varied contexts. For example, in Singapore the syllabus for music learning contains this statement:

> *The syllabus is developed on the premise that all children are musical and have the innate ability to listen, sing, dance, play and express themselves musically. When learning experiences are tailored to develop children's musical abilities, the complete musicians inside them begin to emerge* (Ministry of Education (Singapore), 2016: 1).

In this sense, a general music education can be seen to focus upon the development of ways of musical knowing as embodied knowing (Spruce, 2016: 26), where knowing is not simply a matter of factual recall, instead enabling a person to become a musical citizen through engagement in and with music as experiential and explorative processes. Importantly, hierarchical relationships between teacher and learner may become blurred, with student and teacher working together on an equal footing. Knowledge could well be shared, and information transfer may take place, but this is not necessarily the primary objective. Although such engagement can certainly be supported and enriched by instrumental learning, a general music education should consider the value of musical education beyond skills and proficiency on a musical instrument. What it ought to do is focus on developing understandings of music in relation to the wider world. This transcends genre classifications, and invites all to question and challenge perceptions of musical value, opening up discourses of music for consideration. Interactions and sharing of values between instrumental teachers and general music educators can therefore offer a fruitful site for musical discovery that is of mutual benefit. Instrumental teaching, in our view, should not be seen as an entirely satellite activity, neither should its presence be viewed as a deficit implicit in generalist classroom music education. Instrumental musical learning has significant potential to make general music education utterly transformative.

> **Activity 10.2**
> What is the relationship between your teaching and that which takes place in the other settings where your students learn music, e.g. schools. To use the authors' words, is your teaching a satellite, is it making up for a deficit, or is it something else? In what ways do you think you could work differently with other agencies to make music education 'utterly transformative'?

Instrumental Teaching

In many national contexts, the idea of 'music education' has often been uncritically conflated with learning to play a musical instrument. Instrumental learning is undoubtedly an important part of musical training but, on its own, represents one approach towards musical learning and is not necessarily the totality of a general music education. In a discussion of music education in the USA, Howard (2012) notes:

> ...*music education is not conservatory training. It is not in the business of training music performers. It is in the business of enlightening the public about music's various facets and influences from many perspectives, including how artists think* (Howard, 2012: 259).

Policy statements from Government ministers around the globe frequently centre on music education in terms of every child having the opportunity to learn a musical instrument, and not, importantly, on the possibilities of developing other aspects of musicality and musical understanding. However, many of those working in the sector understand that the relationship is much more complex, and that although instrumental music teaching and general music education are not synonymous, they are complementary. What this means is that music education in any national or local context needs to be considered in terms of what, precisely, it is describing, and what its intended purposes are.

In formal settings, instrumental teaching has traditionally taken place on an individual or small group basis, with an instrument specialist. These lessons might take place in the school with a visiting specialist instrumental music teacher, or outside of school taught by a private music teacher. Understandably the focus of these sessions is usually on instrument-specific musical learning, which may, of course, contribute to broader musical progression and understanding, but is normally predicated on specific instrumental technique and accomplishment. Formal instrumental teaching is often focused towards performance examinations, normally in the graded music examinations format, including those offered by the Associated Board of the Royal Schools of Music (ABRSM) and Trinity College London which have international reach. This conceptualisation of music teaching and learning as being primarily concerned with learning to play an instrument can sit uneasily with classroom general music. It has the potential to lead to quite narrow conceptualisations of musical education as being only about instrumental proficiency. However, not all musical learning takes place in such a formal supervised environment; quite the contrary in fact, with many young people engaging in learning instruments through their own explorations and DIY approaches supported by YouTube videos and tutorials (Youth Music & Ipsos Mori, 2019). What this means is that there can be an over-simplistic bifurcation where music training is only considered to be what Folkestad (2006) described as being

> ...*based, either implicitly or explicitly, on the assumption that musical learning results from a sequenced, methodical exposure to music teaching within a formal setting* (Folkestadt, 2006: 135).

This immediately renders as 'other' any different ways in which instrumental learning takes place. Given the current pace of technological development, such modalities seem likely to continue to grow in the coming years, and will present new ways for young people to engage in and with musical learning. Although such activities take place frequently in unsupervised settings, for example in bedrooms and garages, and without direct involvement of a teacher, the value of these experiences and approaches in supporting broader musical development cannot be underestimated (Thorpe, 2018). Pedagogically, these are operationalised differently. Nevertheless, they can represent a significant part of the instrumental musical experiences a young person receives; even the teaching and learning paradigm is somewhat different from traditional conceptions of instrumental learning.

In both formal and non-formal settings, instrumental learning can take place as an activity separated, and sometimes distanced, from general music education. This may particularly be the case when the musical instrument is the medium through which musical learning takes place and, by association, this colours the musical experience. Whilst this has clear benefits for the development of specific technique, skills and understandings linked to a particular instrument, considering the interfaces of such an approach with other musical activities and music-making possibilities is integral to all-round musical development (Hallam and Rogers, 2016; Philpott, 2001). As Savage summarises, to disconnect a performance lesson from wider musical learning is highly problematic:

> *The concept of a performance lesson without listening, or a composition lesson without reviewing and evaluating is a misplaced one. First and foremost, teachers should ensure that the Key Processes of music education are taught in an integrated way* (Savage, 2011: 7).

Approaching tunes or songs which your pupils know well can be a great way to relate instrumental learning with a more general music education through adopting an integrated approach to music teaching. In the next activity we ask you to consider trying out one example of this type of integrated approach to learning.

Activity 10.3
Select a song that the pupils know well.

- Ask them to listen carefully to a recording of the song, noting the important and striking characteristics of the song and its performance.
- Ask them to write alternative words for the song and perform these.
- Now return to the original words and improvise using the initial melody.
- Support the pupils in improvising on the melody, directing them perhaps to vary the rhythms or pitch and dynamics.

The notion of key processes being taught in an integrated way is central to the approaches delineated in this chapter. Careful consideration of the integration of instrumental teaching and learning with general music education is important, especially as these two conceptualisations of music education may not always exist in the same pedagogic spaces. To explore this in more detail, and to instantiate how this can be operationalised on a practical level, we turn now to a discussion of the Whole Class Ensemble Teaching programme, which has been in operation in England for a number of years.

Activity 10.4
What is the balance in your lessons between performing, listening and composing/improvising? What is the potential for adopting a more integrated approach to musical learning in your teaching? If you already do this identify what works well and what works less well?

Instrumental musical learning in classrooms: whole class ensemble teaching

In the early 2000s, a model of teaching and learning music in groups of around 30 pupils was piloted in English schools. The Whole Class Ensemble Teaching (WCET) programme, first known as Wider Opportunities or First Access, had the aspiration to give all children who wanted to the opportunity to experience learning to play a musical instrument:

> By 2011 we believe that all primary school pupils who want to can have the opportunity to learn a musical instrument (DCSF, 2008: 1).

Although it is a relatively recent addition to the English music pedagogy landscape, WCET holds similarities with many forms of music education recognisable to a broad international audience, including those of band and orchestra in the USA, and the specialist music schools of Austria. Most commonly, WCET consists of a visiting instrumental music teacher teaching a whole-class lesson in a primary school. Lessons are most often taught in a single instrument format (i.e. a whole class of trumpets), but sometimes groups are taught in instrumental families (i.e. strings), or in instrumental groups with common key-based transpositions (i.e. B♭ instruments). There are also instances where WCET classes are taught in band modalities in intensive programmes[1], again, akin to approaches seen in many international education systems. What is significant about WCET programmes in England is that they are funded separately from National Curriculum music for provision in school; it is an instrumental learning programme designed to complement general music education in school.

Throughout this chapter we are concerned with instrumental music teaching and learning and its integration or otherwise with general music education. The WCET programme provides a useful instantiation of the interface between these two ways of working, as viewed through an English curricular lens. Many WCET programmes operate on the presumption that this will be the first time a child has learned to play a musical instrument and, as such, offers 'first access' (which was, indeed, one of the programmes original titles) to instrumental learning. Because of this, many music hubs use WCET as an introduction to instrumental learning, with this supporting a voyage of musical discovery that extends into the realms of playing music together, creating with sound through composition and improvisation, and listening to a range of musics, and either acting as, or supplementing, general musical education.

---

1 See, for example, the 'Band On The Run' scheme run by Bromley Youth Music Trust: https://youtu.be/831zyCZoPU8 (accessed 14th August 2019).

Key to outlining these opportunities in more detail is a consideration of the conceptualisation of this complex relationship. Through this we can begin to move towards a space recognising these important points of complementarity. Instrumental teaching has a lot to offer general music education, especially if some attention is given to its conceptualisation. We contend that instrumental teaching can be conceptualised in at least two ways, going beyond simple definitions of this as 'learning to play an instrument'. In recent research we posited that there are two subtly different yet inter-related ways in which instrumental musical learning in the classroom can be conceptualised. These are:

1. Music education *starts with* the instrument, but then broadens out to encompass wider music education aims.

2. Music education takes place *via* the instrument (Fautley et al., 2019).

Differences between the two hinge on the ways in which the musical instrument/s in question are being employed. In the first instance the use of the instrument is as a means to end, musical learning is the overall goal, and in order to effect this goal, musical instruments are employed, but the object is musical learning, rather than learning to play the instruments in question. These instruments can range from classroom and Orff instruments, through to orchestral, band, guitars and keyboards. In the second instance, where music education takes place via the instrument, the purpose of the teaching and learning is to learn to play the instrument in question, and all subsequent musical learning is derived from this standpoint.

Thinking about these conceptualisations is particularly important in relation to a general music education, and the musical experiences that a young musician will have through these. These can have a fundamental impact on the ways in which musical learning and progress are understood. This has a number of implications for the relationship between instrumental teaching and general music education.

In the following two activities we ask you to consider an example of the first approach (how musical instruments are used as the means to achieve wider musical aims).

Activity 10.5 'A whole orchestra in one instrument'

Ask your pupils to find ten different (but non-damaging!) ways of making a sound from their instrument. What sound can be created? How might they be combined together to make music?

As they are doing this and reflecting afterwards on the process they went through, what musical learning do you think took place?

A high quality WCET programme that interfaces with general music education is likely to employ a range of activities to support musical learning (Hallam, 2019), and will normally include

> ...*singing, listening, composing, improvising, performing, and learning about music generally. These various components of musical learning will be approached via the medium of the instrument* (Fautley et al., 2017: 173).

By conceptualising instrumental learning as a point starting from the instrument rather than being conducted entirely via the instrument, students are likely to experience a range of improvising and composing opportunities which draw on instrumental skills, but also extend beyond these, into listening to unfamiliar music, and building up a deeper understanding of music through instrumental experience. All of these opportunities are afforded through an extended engagement with instrumental learning, and open all sorts of possibilities to further enhance a general music education.

Such potential has already been recognised in the sector, and in some schools a WCET programme which would be described principally as 'instrumental teaching' is being operationalised to fulfil other musical objectives. It represents a much broader musical education for the young people involved and is, for various reasons, the main modality of music education in some schools. The implications for instrumental teachers and classroom generalists are significant, not least in the conceptualisations of practice and the need to develop skills in both instrumental teaching and classroom/group management. However, this provides an example of how instrumental teaching and learning can interact and fulfil more holistic music educational ambitions for the children involved, and that instrumental teacher expertise can be developed to support high quality learning experiences.

Issues arising from the WCET programme and general music education are discussed below, but first we use another programme, not confined to the English context alone in this case.

An example: JustPlay

The Musical Futures JustPlay training and resources (Musical Futures, 2017) are no doubt familiar to many music educators around the world. JustPlay consists of animated charts to enable a whole class of children to play along to songs using some instrumental basics. The programme is designed to support a range of rock/pop instruments, guided by a philosophy of focusing on playing instruments as a way of learning. JustPlay can enable non-instrumental specialists to bring aspects of instrumental teaching into their classrooms and large group settings, providing an instrument-focused experience for the young people involved.

> Recent research explored how this programme was being used as part of a classroom curriculum offer to support transitions from primary school into secondary educational phases (Fautley et al., 2018). This transitional moment appears to be a significant area of drop-off for engagement in formal music education for many young people, either through changes in interest or a reduced presence of music in secondary school contexts.
>
> By drawing upon songs and musical styles with which young people are familiar, this approach was shown to build interest in making music amongst many young people across primary and secondary phases. In a sense, by taking the musical interests of these young people as a starting point, and providing the chance to make music in a low-stakes group environment, instrumental skills and confidence are established. In these schools, teachers were using these resources as part of 'curriculum' music lessons, with distinctly different aims from conventional instrumental teaching. Thus, curriculum music, a key part of a general music education for all children in England, was interacting with and offering a space for instrumental learning to occur.

Discussion

The two programmes outlined above both show how instrumental music teaching approaches have been integrated with general music education in England. However, what they also do is raise questions as to what music education actually is, and what it can, and, importantly, what it should involve. Learning to play an instrument is clearly important in musical endeavour, with the programmes described above, WCET and JustPlay, showing how two different approaches can integrate instrumental learning within the classroom. What these two programmes demonstrate is that it is possible to build instrumental learning into the generalist music class. However, what they do not show is whether this is the only way in which music can be learned. What becomes apparent is that teachers' decisions to navigate the multiple possibilities offered by music education are tempered by their individual viewpoints, and what they feel is appropriate for them, in their school, with their children and young people. As Westerlund notes:

> *For music teachers, navigating between diverse philosophies may seem time-consuming and even frustrating as each writer tries to persuade us of the superiority of their version over others: should we educate devoted listeners through selected classics or transmit musical hands-on knowledge for amateurs to enjoy in their future lives, or should we simply feed the existing musical institutions, symphony orchestras and the ilk, with new practitioners?* (Westerlund, 2012: 9).

This is a task for each individual teacher to consider. At the end of this chapter, we offer some reflective activities to help with this process.

Summary

Instrumental teaching and learning clearly have a key role to play as part of a general music education. The interactions between these two different spheres of musical activity can present significant opportunities which are to the mutual benefit of both spheres of musical learning. Teachers should seek, where possible, to forge strong links between instrumental activity and other areas of a musical education, integrating this into teaching in a seamless way. As seen in the examples in this chapter, placing instrumental teaching in dialogue with general music education can help build connections between instrumental learning and other musical skills. Conceptualising instrumental learning as happening via the instrument provides a framework which draws in a more holistic view of musical experience. Thinking in this way will improve the musical experience for all children involved. This is surely a good thing!

Activity 10.6

Make a table in which you list the benefits and disadvantages of the two approaches outlined above. One being music education that 'starts with the instrument' i.e. the goal is a broad music education rather than the specific instrument, and the other being music education which is provided 'via the instrument', i.e. in which proficiency on the instrument is the primary goal. Considering your table, think about which of these approaches best reflects your current teaching and whether there are any aspects that you might consider changing.

Reflective questions

Earlier in the chapter we noted the importance of teachers developing their own personal philosophies of music teaching and the context of the pupils they teach and the settings in which this teaching takes place. The questions below are designed to support you in doing this and to consider the interrelationship between your teaching and the general aims of a music education.

1. Do my instrumental lessons focus more on instrument-specific learning than listening and composing? If so, why have I chosen this route? If not, why not?

2. Building on question 1, how does music education work in the context of these children and young people, in this school, with me as their teacher?

3. What aspects of general music education can I support through instrumental teaching?

4. Am I aware of the other musical activities/interests of my learners? If yes, how can I connect these to instrumental teaching? If not, how can I find this out?

5. How do I track musical progress? Is this based on instrument-specific technical proficiencies, or on broader musical outcomes?

6. Is my instrumental teaching curriculum governed by external factors, for example graded music examinations? How does this work in the context of my own knowledge of musical progress?

References

Bourdieu, P. (1979) *Distinction: a social critique of the judgement of taste* (R. Nice, Trans.). Cambridge (MA): Harvard University Press.

DCSF. (2008) *Guidance on the Music Standards Fund Grant*: 1.11.2008-2011. London: The Stationery Office.

Department for Education. (2013) *Music programmes of study: key stages 1 and 2 (National curriculum in England)* (DFE-00175-2013). London, Department for Education.

Department for Education, & Department for Culture, Media and Sport. (2011) *The Importance of Music: A National Plan for Music Education* (DFE-00086-2011). Available at: https://assets.publishing.service.gov.uk/government/uploads/system/uploads/attachment_data/file/180973/DFE-00086-2011.pdf

Fautley, M., Kinsella, V. and Whittaker, A. (2017) *Whole Class Ensemble Teaching Research Report*. Available at: https://www.musicmark.org.uk/marketplace/whole-class-ensemble-teaching-wcet-research-report-2017/

Fautley, M., Kinsella, V., Whittaker, A. and Nenadic, E. (2018) *Croydon 'JustPlay' Evaluation Report*. Available at: https://www.croydonmusicandarts.co.uk/primary

Fautley, M., Kinsella, V. and Whittaker, A. (2019) Models of teaching and learning identified in Whole Class Ensemble Tuition. *British Journal of Music Education*, 36(3), pp. 243-252.

Folkestad, G. (2006) Formal and informal learning situations or practices vs formal and informal ways of learning. *British Journal of Music Education*, 23(2), pp. 135-145.

Hall, J. (2016) *A broad and balanced curriculum: key findings from Ofsted*. Available at: http://www.insidegovernment.co.uk/uploads/2016/09/joannahall-1.pdf

Hallam, S. (2019) What contributes to successful whole-class Ensemble Tuition? *British Journal of Music Education*, 36(3), pp. 229-241.

Hallam, S. and Rogers, K. (2016) The impact of instrumental music learning on attainment at age 16: a pilot study. *British Journal of Music Education*, 33(3), pp. 247-261.

Henley, D. (2011) *Music Education in England*. London: Department for Education/Department for Culture, Media and Sport.

Hirsch, E. D. (1988) *Cultural Literacy: What Every American Needs to Know*. New York: Vintage Books.

Howard, V. A. (2012) Must Music Education Have an Aim? In: W. Bowman and A. L. Frega, eds. *The Oxford Handbook of Philosophy in Music Education*. New York: Oxford University Press, pp. 249-262.

Kinsella, V., Fautley, M. and Whittaker, A. (2019) *Exchanging Notes: Research Summary Report*. Available at: https://www.youthmusic.org.uk/file/4697/download?token=MhB_6n95

Lonie, D. and Dickens, L. (2016) Becoming musicians: Situating young people's experiences of musical learning between formal, informal and non-formal spheres. *Cultural Geographies*, 23(10), pp. 87-101.

Ministry of Education (Singapore) (2016) *MUSIC TEACHING AND LEARNING SYLLABUS: Primary & Lower Secondary*. Singapore: Ministry of Education.

Paynter, J. (1977/2008) The role of creativity in the school music curriculum.
In: J. Mills and J. Paynter, eds. *Thinking and making - selections from the writings of John Paynter on music in education*, Oxford: Oxford University Press, pp. 34-38.

Philpott, C. (2001) Equality of opportunity and instrumental tuition.
In: C. Philpott and C. Plummeridge, eds. *Issues in Music Teaching*. London and New York: Routledge Falmer, pp. 156-169.

Savage, J. (2011) The key concepts for musical teaching. In: J. Price and J. Savage, eds. *Teaching secondary music,* London: Sage, pp. 1-11.

Small, C. (1998) *Musicking: The Meanings of Performing and Listening*. Middletown, USA: Wesleyan University Press.

Spruce, G. (2016) Culture, society and musical learning. In: C. Cooke, K. Evans, C. Philpott and G. Spruce, eds. *Learning to Teach Music in the Secondary School: A Companion to School Experience*. 3rd edn. Abingdon: Routledge, pp. 17-31.

Thorpe, V. (2018) An activity theory analysis of the relationship between student identity and the assessment of group composing at school. *British Journal of Music Education*, 35(1), pp. 5-22.

Westerlund, H. (2012) What can a reflective teacher learn from philosophies of music education. In: C. Philpott and G. Spruce, eds. *Debates in music teaching*, Abingdon: Routledge, pp. 9-19.

Wright, R. and Kanellopoulos, P. (2010) Informal music learning, improvisation and teacher education. *British Journal of Music Education*, 27(1), pp. 71-87.

Youth Music, and Ipsos Mori (2019) *The Sound of the Next Generation: A Comprehensive Review of Children and Young People's Relationship with Music*. Available at: https://www.youthmusic.org.uk/sites/default/files/PDFs/The Sound of the Next Generation.pdf

Part Four: The Future of Instrumental Teaching and Learning

Chapter 11 Commentary

The Covid-19 pandemic and the associated isolation rules brought about major changes in the way that many instrumental teachers worked. Suddenly teachers, many of whom might not have considered themselves to be particularly technologically adept, were teaching their lessons remotely through Zoom, Teams, Facetime, etc.

Such a shift is a good example of how hard it is to read how technology will impact on instrumental learning in the future. The rate of change in the world of digital technologies is dizzyingly fast – to many of us it seems only a short time ago that a 33.6kbit/sec modem was cutting edge, and the idea of face-to-face conversation over the web was a pipe dream. But as we move through these new developments, and incorporate some of them into our teaching, it is helpful to have some basis for understanding their impact on musical teaching and learning.

Andrew King begins his chapter by helping to clarify some definitions of the various areas which fall under the broad heading of digital technologies. He then goes on to look at some of the ways digital technology can support instrumental teaching and learning. If we are going to depend more on digital technology, especially for remote learning, it is important that we consider how teaching pedagogies and learning outcomes might be impacted in digital environments. In this chapter he looks in detail at a well-documented digital learning project in the UK to help us understand what these impacts might be and what lessons we can learn for the future.

Andrew King ends this chapter by considering briefly what the future might bring in terms of digital technology in education. Perhaps in the not-so-distant future the idea of the teacher and student appearing as holograms in each other's houses is not too far-fetched!

11 Music and Technology: Approaches, Challenges and Potential in Instrumental Teaching

Andrew King

What can music technology offer instrumental teachers? Music technology has promised much, but not always delivered results in music teaching, particularly instrumental teaching. Some researchers have considered the broad philosophical implications of technology in education and the seductive nature of new technologies (e.g. Taylor, 2011), but its possibilities for music instrumental teaching remain to be widely understood. However, the challenges posed in 2020 during a global pandemic (Covid-19) brought into sharp focus the use of technology in instrumental teaching, since restrictions on travel and movement meant that provision in this domain relied almost exclusively upon online delivery.

This chapter will examine the current position of technology in relation to instrumental teaching by reviewing approaches to its use in one-to-one or small-group tuition for pupils learning acoustic, electronic or digital instruments. In so doing, it will identify and interrogate the challenges and potential of technology to enhance music learning and to meet the needs of a wide range of music learners. By way of example, it will draw upon some of the developments in the use of technology in instrumental teaching in the UK and beyond over the last ten years. It will also consider emerging developments in both technology and our understanding of its relevance to instrumental teaching.

The chapter is in four sections:

1. A broad, albeit brief explanation of uses of technology in music education.

2. A review of different approaches to using technology in instrumental teaching along with consideration of the functional, practical and behavioural issues arising from them.

3. Discussion of online communities and support networks about instrumental teaching.

4. Potential directions for using technology in instrumental teaching.

1. Uses of Technology in Music Education

Broadly speaking, there are two main uses of technology in music education: first, as a tool to support the production of music; and second, as a tool to support learning. With regard to the first, the production of music might include composition and/or performance activities. For example, MIDI keyboards and notation or sequencing software can be used to aid the composition of music. Technology can also be used to produce musical performances, such as through live coding (used in improvised computer music) or in the diffusion of a pre-recorded work within an auditorium. Additionally, recording technology (audio or audio-visual) can be used to capture music performance, and specialist software can enable musicians to develop their material; for instance, controllable looping software can be used to layer different sounds in performance through a loop station (this technique is often used by commercially successful artists, such as Ed Sheeran).

With regard to the second, Learning Technology (LT), sometimes referred to as Educational Technology (ET), describes technology used to support the general pedagogy of a particular subject area, whether in a Virtual Learning Environment (VLE) or other such framework. Communication in LT can be in a synchronous format, such as a live online lecture, or asynchronous format, such as in the use of online video tutorials. LT has been used widely to support education for a number of decades, but the ability to share large files and stream live content has only been made possible in recent years due to advances in technology. The use of video tutorials to support teaching and learning within or alongside face-to-face lessons has become increasingly commonplace within and outside of music education. The affordances of digital technology have also allowed for the creation of global communities and networks of music practice, such as to support both formal instrumental music tuition (Seddon and O'Neill, 2001), but also more informal music-making and sharing.

The development and increased affordability of digital music-making hardware and software tools, including Digital Audio Workstations (DAW), has led to a democratisation of music-making practices, giving composers, performers, producers, teachers and learners alike increased access to resources once found exclusively within the realm of the professional music industry. Even though this chapter is primarily concerned with the second use of music technology, that is, as a tool to support learning, it is acknowledged that technology for music production may inevitably influence or impact upon the learning resources used in the context of instrumental teaching.

Activity 11.1

Do you presently use technology in your own teaching? If so, describe the types of technology that you use and the benefits you feel it brings to your students' learning? Do you feel there is greater potential for using technology in your teaching? If so, what are the barriers to making greater use of it? Come back to these questions at the end of the chapter and see if there are ways in which those barriers might be overcome.

2. Uses of Technology in Instrumental Teaching

Instrumental lessons in the western music education tradition normally involve teachers providing one-to-one or small-group tuition on acoustic or electronic instruments in a face-to-face or in-person setting. LT, however, can be used to support such lessons, thus offering a 'blended' approach whereby online or technological resources are combined with in-person teaching. In some cases, however, there is evidence to suggest that instrumental teachers are not able to provide face-to-face lessons, such as for geographical or other reasons, and thus may rely solely on technology. There are therefore three current modes for instrumental teaching: in-person only (that is, face-to-face without any technology), blended (that is, face-to-face with some technology to support lessons), and online only (that is, delivered online with no face-to-face contact).

Instrumental teachers are likely to be motivated by different factors in pursuing one or more of the above approaches (the Covid-19 pandemic is one such factor) and it may be necessary for teachers to adapt their teaching mode depending on the needs of individual learners within the same or different settings. Teachers will find it helpful to consider their motivations for pursuing a particular mode, not least to realise whether it is triggered by a desire for innovation or to address the practicalities of a particular teaching situation — both laudable motives.

Activity 11.2

Make a table where you can list the potential advantages and disadvantages of the three modes of instrumental teaching outlined above. Do you think any of your current students would benefit from a different mode to the one they currently experience?

Many studies highlight the challenges and barriers to using technology in teaching, including the availability of technology, technical problems, and the need for professional support and training (e.g. Leong, 2017). These perceived challenges may indirectly impact upon instrumental teachers' preferences for pursuing one format over another. Interestingly, Jorgensen (2014) discussed the issue of 'technological mediation' between pupil and teacher within an online-only environment and described what a potential 'eSchool' of music might look like. Even though she suggested that a blended approach to teaching might be preferred, she argued that an eSchool could be highly inclusive, involving an online community and a virtual space for all instrumental learners, not just those wishing to pursue a career in music.

Some studies about instrumental teaching in online-only settings provide in-depth insight into the lived experiences of teachers and pupils working in this mode. For example, Kruse et al. (2013) conducted a small-scale enquiry into online lessons with one teacher–pupil pair operated through Skype. The tutor was a well-respected teacher, and the pupil was studying for a Masters degree, but online teaching was alien for both the pupil and the teacher alike. Kruse and colleagues described the 'synchronous reality' of the lessons according to feedback from the participants, once the initial excitement and anxiety of pursuing an online lesson had passed, the lessons were able to be taught and learning took place. Some of the challenges reported in the lessons (unsurprisingly) related to constant technological glitches that interrupted the flow of the lessons and the lack of finance to access more sophisticated platforms other than those freely available.

One important consideration for teachers in pursuing blended or online-only instrumental lessons concerns the functionality of technology. On the one hand, there is ongoing concern relating to the speed at which technology, both hardware and software, becomes out-dated. On the other, there are increased possibilities for using technology because high-speed internet access allows wider access to digital resources. One area of interest in LT for instrumental teachers concerns the possibilities for sharing scores in lessons. Duffy and Healey (2017) explored the idea of a shared digital score in their study of instrumental lessons. They recognised that face-to-face lessons with classical instrumentalists often revolved around discussion of the musical score. Their research involved participants in different locations collaborating through a computer screen where both an overall view of the pupil or teacher was possible as well as the shared score. The teacher or pupil could annotate the score which could be saved for practice at a later date.

Some of the barriers to online learning can be mediated through use of multiple cameras. King, Prior and Waddington-Jones (2019b) examined the effectiveness of a simple and affordable audio-visual mixer that allowed for multiple cameras or single views of the teacher and/or pupils. Their research revealed there was value in the use of multiple camera angles since this allowed teachers to display themselves and pupils in different viewpoints. In one-to-one lessons, teachers could switch between close-up and overall views of themselves and pupils with ease to demonstrate something, such as the fingering for a particular instrument. Likewise, the pupil could show the fingering or technique that they were trying to learn. Alternatively, the teacher could view three different perspectives within the same shot through the use of a split screen, if the monitor was large enough. For example, in Figure 1, the teacher is presented in two different views (one close-up to show fingering and one overall) with a third camera to show the musical score. In small group lessons, the teachers used the multiple camera angles in two different ways: the first using the two cameras to show the front and side views of all the pupils, and the second using one camera for each student (see Figure 2). Teachers generally preferred to have the cameras set up in the first way, that is to display the overall and side view of the pupils.

Figure 1: Split screen view to show overall view of teacher, close-up of teacher, and musical score.

Figure 2: Multiple camera set up for group instrumental lesson

It is of course possible to use zooming functions with sophisticated web cameras that enable teachers to pan in and out, but in this particular study, it was felt that panning would interrupt the flow of the lessons while a single switch on an audio-visual mixer would facilitate seamless switching across different camera angles. The results highlighted that instrumental teachers with different levels of technological experience demonstrated similar levels of use of the different camera angles. The use of multiple cameras angles can therefore offer different perspectives of students as well as close-up images when demonstrating or modelling, which is so vital for learning.

Arguably, one of the greatest technological challenges facing instrumental teachers working in an online mode is that of latency, or the delay caused by the speed at which information can travel across the internet. This means that there is a delay between information leaving the teacher's computer and arriving at the student's computer. If the communication were one-way this wouldn't matter. However where music performance is concerned it is not possible for a teacher and student to play together over an internet connection with each hearing what the other is playing, thus rendering duo playing or accompaniment impossible.

Figure 3: Latency between computers of pupil and teacher

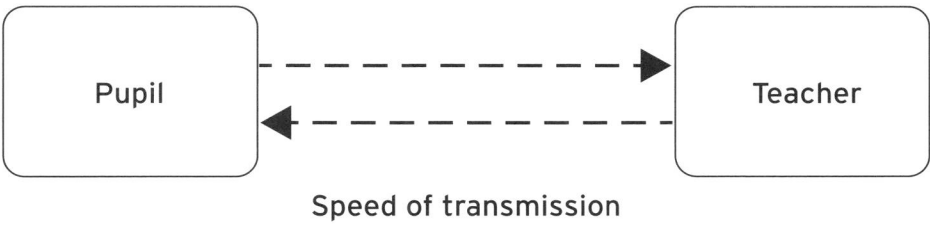

Speed of transmission

Technological latency means that some practical aspects of instrumental teaching, such as accompanying music pupils during lessons, are challenging (see Figure 3). Indeed, it is tricky for teachers and pupils to play together in online lessons because the length of the latency (normally measured in milliseconds) will result in asynchronicity. It should be noted that many of the examples of musicians playing together in online environments in discrete locations are in fact manipulated products that have involved musicians recording parts in isolation and then assembling files using a DAW to give the illusion of 'liveness'. The problem for instrumental teachers, then, is that 'liveness' is the reality.

There is latency in even the fastest of internet connections but technologies exist that reduce latency, such as *EverCast* and *ClearView Flex*, which offer so-called 'blink-of-any-eye' latency levels, but these are currently prohibitively expensive for many instrumental teachers, pupils and education providers. A project developed by the *Conservatoria di Musica Giuseppe Tartini* in Italy developed an approach called LoLa which is a low-level latency approach for the transmission of high-quality audio and video streaming designed for the purpose of musicians playing together over a network connection. At the moment, the software is freely available, but it requires specific hardware and a network connection that is not currently available from any commercial supplier (it is possible, however, that some academic and research networks will have this capability). The eradication of latency altogether in online streaming is beyond the capabilities of current technology and this may continue to be the case within existing infrastructures. Nevertheless, instrumental teachers have used creative ways to resolve the problems of latency in order to bring about synchronous performance in an online environment. For example, King, Prior and Waddington-Jones (2019a) found that the issue of accompanying could be resolved in some online lessons by having pre-prepared materials at the location of the pupil prior to the lesson.

The Online Orchestration Project (OOP, 2014-16) by Rofe looked at ways of controlling, rather than eradicating latency by locking it to musical tempo for groups of musicians collaborating online. Rofe and Reuben (2017) reported that a latency speed of 30 milliseconds or more is problematic in terms of performance in an online environment. This is the point at which it becomes noticeable to the instrumentalists or listeners. Latency can vary depending upon a number of factors and the first challenge for the OOP team was to stabilise the latency to make it consistent during a performance. The second challenge was to compose music that allowed for this level of latency in a group performance online by carefully mapping the tempo and harmony to allow for the levels of latency in the network. Although the OOP provided a complex solution to the problem, it did at least allow for group performances online across any distance without the requirement for prohibitively expensive hardware or software. A special issue of the *Journal of Music, Technology, and Education* covered in detail the approach used in the OOP, including the benefits of connecting remote communities together (Rofe, Murray and Parker, 2017), the experiences of those communities (Rofe, Gleehoed and Hodson, 2017), the design of the hardware and software (Prior et al., 2017), the evaluation of the different microphone techniques used in the project (Gleehoed, Prior and Rofe, 2017), and how to compose music in an environment that is latency-rich (Rofe and Gleehoed, 2017).

Music teachers have used a range of other creative ways of overcoming the latency issue to allow musicians to play together:

- Some teachers record accompaniments, etc., offline and send these to students in advance of lessons. When the student plays along with the local accompaniment and broadcasts the result to the teacher the impact of latency is no longer felt.

- Teachers have used drones and other slow-moving accompaniments which students can improvise over.

- Some have made judicious use of headphones so that the appearance of playing together can be maintained for some participants (e.g. if the teacher in the example above turns their headphones off the student is able to play with them – of course this has the disadvantage that the teacher cannot hear them).

The challenge of overcoming technological latency for instrumental teachers working in online-only (or even blended) formats lends itself to future endeavour.

Other practical problems have been reported in research about instrumental teaching that reflect indirect issues with using technology, specifically in online-only lessons. The Connect Resound project (King et al., 2019a; 2019b), which was a large-scale study about delivering online music lessons to pupils in rural communities in England, identified the following issues: problems with pupils assembling instruments; problems with tuning instruments; difficulties with overcoming technical problems with instruments; poor quality internet connections; and room space. Some of these were overcome with the support of teaching assistants or through advanced planning, such as by sending assembly instructions for an instrument to schools ahead of lessons. Tuning apps on mobile phones were also used by teaching assistants to help get pupils started at the beginning of lessons. The importance of having a dedicated, accessible and sizeable room to run the technology for online instrumental lessons was flagged up. The research revealed that interruptions during lessons occurred where rooms had multiple uses, while in small-sized rooms, it was not always possible to see all of the pupils on the cameras. Furthermore, it was necessary for rooms to be located away from other areas in the school because noise spillage was more acute in online delivery: attention to background noise was possibly more problematic in this format because of the nature of the acoustic cues. To mitigate these issues, King and colleagues suggested that a blended approach, that is combining online and face-to-face sessions, was preferable.

It is helpful to gain an understanding not only of the functional and practical aspects of using technology in instrumental teaching, but also its effects on the behaviours of teachers and pupils in lessons. As part of the Connect Resound project, King, Prior and Waddington-Jones (2019a) evaluated teachers' behaviours in online instrumental lessons (also see Hallam, 2006). Based on the model of teaching behaviours constructed by Simones et al. (2015) on face-to-face instrumental lessons, which included 'giving information', 'asking questions', 'giving feedback', 'modelling' and 'listening/observing', King and colleagues (2019a) applied the same categories in analysing online music. Interestingly, there was little difference in terms of the amount of time spent on many of the behavioural aspects between the two contexts: for example, in the online lessons, 29.14% of time was spent on 'teacher talk' (King et al., 2019a) compared to 31.5% in the face-to-face lessons (Simones et al., 2015). Interestingly, in the online study, this was not the perception of the teachers: tutors felt they were talking more than indicated by the data.

A related comparative study looked at the differences in learner behaviours between online and face-to-face instrumental lessons involving piano sight-reading skills. Pike and Shoemaker (2013) examined the effect of lesson delivery across two independent groups of learners using online-only and in-person teaching formats. The findings revealed that there was no significant difference between the two groups in terms of improvement, but it was noted that the pupils in the online group displayed more independence in terms of engagement. The researchers suggested that online-only lessons can be as effective as face-to-face lessons, while online delivery might encourage pupils to seek solutions themselves and thus take more ownership of their learning.

Even though there is evidence to suggest that online-only instrumental lessons can be highly effective – e.g. Cameron (2010) spent many years providing music lessons via video conference to remote areas of Scotland – researchers have pointed towards the possibilities of blended formats for instrumental teaching, whether using technology to support face-to-face sessions or via asynchronous delivery (Jorgensen, 2014; King, et al., 2019a; 2019b). Video is one key area that potentially provides a rich technological resource for instrumental teachers.

Since 2005, the rapid expansion of YouTube into a free online streaming service has allowed learners to access materials to develop instrumental practice. Kruse and Veblen (2012) examined forty instructional videos from YouTube that were representative of the type of materials available at that time in terms of their pedagogical and musical content. They selected instructional videos for learning folk-music instruments, specifically, banjo, fiddle, guitar and mandolin, and analysed the length of the videos, the amount of 'teacher talk', the gender, age and ethnicity of the tutors, the musical content and the teaching methods. They found that the content was aimed towards beginner musicians and that teachers focused on aural reinforcement, modelling and technique-based instruction as well as physiological prompts within the medium. Some diversity issues were highlighted (the majority of teachers were white, middle-aged and male) and they reported a surprising lack of opportunities for improvisation which is integral to the folk-music tradition.

These asynchronous approaches to instrumental teaching do not presume any formal dialogue between teacher and pupil and, as such, the teaching is effectively unregulated, unlike in synchronous online lessons where a rapport between teacher and pupil can develop. For beginner-level pupils setting out on a musical journey, this approach might be challenging, for without a frame of reference or understanding of how to learn a musical instrument, it would be necessary to navigate search results and make a decision about which video to select for support. The reviews on such sites may provide a reference point, but it would perhaps be better if this was framed within some sort of community of online practice with expert guidance, which is the focus of discussion in the next section of this chapter.

> **Activity 11.3**
>
> a) Research the available free online resources for learners of your instrument – you might start with YouTube and then perhaps look at individual providers. What are the factors that go to make a good online resource? Identify a resource that you feel might be useful in your teaching. Try it out and evaluate its effectiveness.
>
> b) Have a go at creating a resource for your students, perhaps making a video on your phone and posting it online. Talk to your students about how useful they found it and what advice they have for further resources.

3. Online Communities and Support Networks for Instrumental Teaching

The use of social media in building up online communities is well established and online communities can be viewed as important for learners to share ideas and support each other and can alleviate barriers to interaction and communication resulting from geographical distance. As such, an online community could, and does, form a vital support mechanism for instrumental learning for many types of music-making. Typically, online communities of practice centre upon either specific instruments (such as 'Banjo Hangout') or genres of music (such as Irish music). The opportunity to share knowledge with like-minded musicians or indeed gain access to expertise is something online communities are able to achieve with relatively inexpensive technology, compared with the challenges of travelling great distances to access such support.

In her extensive research about the Online Academy of Irish Music (OAIM), Waldron (2011; 2012; 2020) explores the workings of an online community of musicians and makes an important distinction between social media as tool and social network as online community (2020). She argues that the online environment provides opportunities to support music learning beyond learning an instrument, providing also opportunities for musicians to perform together. Likewise, Partti and Karlsen (2010) discuss societal and technological progress from the point of view of the music learner in relation to the experiences of an online Finnish music community called "Mikseri". They suggest that people's musical identities can be 'constructed and maintained in web-based reality' (369) and posit that online music sites may function as communities of practice.

In a recent survey by Ward (2019) on the OAIM, the transmission of tradition is scrutinised according to the role of technology. Ward draws attention to the notion of situated learning (Lave and Wenger, 1991) in the online community and argues that any group of musicians or learners coming together to share knowledge and interact is understood to have benefits for the participants.

Over 80% of the musicians in Ward's survey cited the internet as the principal source for their learning. This suggests that the traditional face-to-face practice of delivering lessons for traditional Irish instruments has changed over the past few decades through the development of the OAIM community. Of further interest in Ward's study is the discussion of the virtual classroom element. The OAIM introduced 'Audio Jam' (AJ) and 'Virtual Reality' (VR) sessions into the online community. The purpose of the AJ sessions is to enable learners to access a large database of traditional Irish Folk tunes so that they can download accompanying parts (and in some cases sheet music) and play along to them at home – this practice is similar to the approach of jazz musicians who play along with gramophone recordings (see Braun, 2002). In addition to the audio recordings, there are also a series of virtual sessions which offer 360-degree video recording of a public house in County Clare, Ireland. Participants use VR headsets, such as Google Cardboard, and are able to take part in a pre-recorded virtual jam session of traditional Irish Music. Whether these approaches offer a similar or complete experience of Irish music-making is a matter for debate and something discussed by Ward. However, in terms of increasing accessibility and promoting music-making within this tradition, there are clearly benefits to the development of an online community.

4. Potential Directions and Concluding Remarks

The use of technology in instrumental teaching, especially in blended and online formats, is likely to continue to develop as barriers in functionality and affordability are reduced and the potential benefits are promoted via synchronous online lessons and the development of online communities. Different types of virtual music-making environments have already emerged and are likely to continue to do so. For example, Williamon, Aufegger and Eiholzer (2014) developed a simulated environment to recreate the experience of a concert or an examination for music students. The simulator was designed to support performance preparation by teaching students how to manage anxieties in such conditions. Similarly, Grimshaw and Garner (2015) theorised musical sound within a framework of 'virtuality' where sound is object, event, wave and, therefore, phenomenon: imagine a virtual music practice room in which the pupil and teacher could co-exist, and acoustic cues are simulated from different environments. Kim, King, and Kamekawa (2015) also examined perceptual characteristics for virtual auditory online experiences.

The industry of immersive technologies is using terms such as virtual, augmented (AR) and mixed reality (MR) to describe environments that have become prevalent in recent developments. Increased access to technologies such as VR headsets could be beneficial in educational settings, including instrumental teaching, where learners are able to acquire experiences through different online worlds. An AR or MR scenario that places an instrumental learner in a natural environment with additional overlaid features could benefit musical training in numerous ways, such as by having the ability to view instantly video recordings of musical practice, or to provide access to teachers in remote locations, or to furnish musical accompaniment on demand for a range of different musical pieces. As such, projects such as Connect Resound (King et al., 2019a; 2019b) could potentially move into new developmental phases that examine the use of AR or MR immersive environments. The repurposing of VR and AR technology to provide technological solutions as well as new avenues for teaching and research may well be necessary.

This chapter has highlighted approaches, challenges and potentials for using technology in instrumental teaching, especially drawing upon research involving in-person, blended and online-only teaching in one-to-one and small-group lessons. Different aspects of the functionality of technology have been highlighted in online-only lessons, including the benefits of using multiple camera angles and the effectiveness of the 'synchronous reality', especially for pupils in remote communities without regular access to in-person lessons. We have discussed how the development of online communities and support networks have further increased opportunities for and access to music-making and instrumental learning, as exemplified by research about the OIAM. Challenges have been identified in online-only delivery, such as latency issues and practicalities, including mechanical and musical support for pupils (tuning and fixing instruments, providing musical accompaniment) and finding adequate room spaces in school settings.

There is a need to continue to integrate technology in instrumental teaching. However, support for both teachers and learners along with increased understanding of effective practices will need to be continually reviewed as ongoing developments in technology take place. The adaptability and agility of teachers and learners in this domain is therefore critical to the success of instrumental teaching and to ensuring that provision is more than just good enough.

References

Cameron, A. (2010) *Instrumental Music Lessons Delivered via Video Conference to Remote Schools in Scotland – (V & I Forum Pre-Conference)*. Paper presented at the Annual meeting of the ISME World Conference and Commission Seminars, China Conservatory of Music (CC) and Chinese National Convention Centre (CNCC), Beijing, China.
http://citation.allacademic.com/meta/p397831_index.html

Department for Education and Department for Culture, Media and Sport (2011) *The importance of Music: A national plan for Music Education*. London: Department for Culture, Media and Sport.

Duffy, S. and Healey, P. (2017) A new medium for remote music tuition. *The Journal of Music, Technology, Education*, 10(1), pp. 5–29.

Grimshaw, M. and Garner, T. (2015) *Sonic Virtuality: Sound as emergent perception*. New York: Oxford University Press.

Hallam, S. (2006) *Music Psychology in Education*. London: Institute of Education.

Jorgensen, E. R. (2014) Face-to-face and distance teaching and learning in higher education: Lessons from the preparation of professional musicians. *The Journal of Music, Technology, Education*, 7(2), pp. 181–197.

Kim, S., King, R. and Kamekawa, T. (2015) A cross-cultural comparison of salient perceptual characteristics of height channels for a virtual auditory environment. *Virtual Reality*, 19(3-4), pp. 149–160.

King, A., Prior, H. P. and Waddington-Jones, C. (2019a) Exploring teachers' and pupils' behaviour in online and face-to-face instrumental lessons. *Music Education Research*, 21(2), pp. 197–209.

King, A., Prior, H. P. and Waddington-Jones, C. (2019b) Connect Resound: Using online technology to deliver music education to remote communities. *The Journal of Music, Technology, Education*, 12(2), pp. 201–217.

Kruse, N. B., Harlos, S. C., Russell, M. and Michelle, L. (2013) Skype music lessons in the academy: Intersections of music education, applied music and technology. *The Journal of Music, Technology, Education*, 6(1), pp. 43–60.

Kruse, N. B. and Veblen, K. (2012) Music teaching and learning online; Considering YouTube instructional videos. In: *The Journal of Music, Technology, Education*, 5(1), pp. 78–87.

Lave, J. and Wenger, E. (1991) *Situated Learning: Legitimate Peripheral Participation*. Cambridge: Cambridge University Press.

Leong, S. (2017) Professional Development for Music Teachers. In: A. King, E. Himonides and A. Ruthmann, eds. *The Routledge Companion to Music, Technology, and Education*, New York: Routledge.

Partti, H., & Karlsen, S. (2010) Reconceptualising Musical Learning: New Media, Identity and Community in Music Education. *Music Education Research*, 12 (4), pp.369–382

Pike, P. and Shoemaker, K. (2013) The effect of distance learning on acquisition of piano sight reading skills. *The Journal of Music, Technology, Education*, 6(2), pp. 147–162.

Prior, D., Biscoe, I., Rofe, M. and Reuben, F. (2017) Designing a system for Online Orchestra: Computer Hardware and software. *The Journal of Music, Technology, Education*, 10(2-3), pp. 185–196.

Rofe, M. and Gleehoed, E. (2017) Composing for a latency rich environment, *The Journal of Music, Technology, Education*, 10(2-3), pp. 231-255.

Rofe, M., Gleehoed, E. and Hodson, L. (2017) Experiencing Online Orchestra: Communities, connections and music-making through telematic performance. *The Journal of Music, Technology, Education*, 10(2-3), pp. 257-275.

Rofe, M., Murray, S. and Parker, W. (2017) Online Orchestra: Connecting remote communities through music. *The Journal of Music, Technology, Education*, 10(2-3) pp. 147-165.

Rofe, M. and Reuben, F. (2017) Telematic performance and the challenge of latency. *The Journal of Music, Technology, Education*, 10(2-3), pp. 167-183.

Seddon, F. A. and O'Neill, S. A. (2001) An evaluation study of computer-based compositions by children with and without prior experience of formal instrumental music tuition. *Psychology of Music*, 29(1), pp. 4-19.

Simones, L. L., Schroeder, F., and Rodger, M. (2015) Categorizations of physical gesture in piano teaching: A preliminary enquiry. *Psychology of Music*, 43(1), pp. 103-121.

Taylor, T. D. (2001) *Strange Sounds: Music, Technology, and Culture*. New York: Routledge.

Waldron, J. (2011) Conceptual frameworks, theoretical models and the role of YouTube. *The Journal of Music, Technology, Education*, 4(2-3), pp. 189-200.

Waldron, J. (2013) User-generated content, YouTube and participatory culture on the web. *Music Education Research*, 15(3), pp. 257-274.

Ward, F. (2019) Technology and the transmission of tradition: An exploration of the virtual pedagogies in the Online Academy of Irish Music. *The Journal of Music, Technology, Education*, 12(1), pp. 5-23.

Williamon, A., Aufegger, L. and Eiholzer, H. (2014) Simulating and stimulating performance: introducing distributed simulation to enhance musical learning and performance. *Frontiers of Psychology*, 5(25). Available at: https://researchonline.rcm.ac.uk/id/eprint/14/1/fpsyg-05-00025.pdf

Chapter 12 Commentary

Do you see yourself as a musician or a teacher – or both? And if both, which of these identities do you favour or which do you feel predominates? The reality that Julie Ballantyne illustrates is that the role of a music teacher is complex and there are benefits to be gained from a rich understanding of these identities and how they go to make up who we are as musician teachers. In this chapter we will hear from a range of music teachers and where they see themselves in relation to this duality. As we will discover, music teachers who identify as musicians sometimes justify that identity through work they do outside the teaching context, and sometimes from their work within it. But Ballantyne offers us the opportunity to reflect on the musician tag by asking: 'in what way, and to what extent is the 'musician' identity helpful or harmful in my everyday practice as a music teacher?'.

Being an instrumental music teacher is a challenging role, and the research supports the common issues that teachers face with feelings of isolation, heavy workload, exam preparation, etc. But teachers also report high levels of job satisfaction and Ballantyne suggests that it may be the musician identity that helps teachers persevere through these difficulties. Ballantyne goes on to suggest that a re-examination of our own professional identities may help instrumental teachers to develop more complex and helpful ways of seeing ourselves and the work we do.

As we approach the end of this book a quote from Austin, Isbell and Russell (2012) seems to nicely capture not just the underlying message of this chapter but also that of this whole book. As quoted in the chapter they write that, 'the music profession needs teachers who are reflective thinkers and strong musicians, just as it needs musicians who are knowledgeable about the music they are performing and capable of drawing upon pedagogical principles to elevate their own performance or provide education in music to others'.

12 The Musician Teacher
Julie Ballantyne

Introduction

Are we 'musicians'? Or are we 'teachers'? Perhaps we are 'musician-teachers' or 'educators of musicians'? The multifarious labels that we assign ourselves and others, and the discussions we have with ourselves and others about our professional selves (and how they relate to our personal, or musical selves) reveal much. They tell us about the importance of knowing how we see ourselves in our jobs, and how we think others see us. These labels also reveal what we think is desirable in terms of what our identity should be. And perhaps where we feel we are not quite 'good enough'. The notion of 'professional identity' is one that has captured the imagination of teachers and musicians alike. The ways that we think of ourselves professionally influence every single aspect of our jobs – how we are perceived by ourselves and others influences the ways we interact with students, parents and colleagues. Our conceptualisation of ourselves in relation to the ideal 'professional' changes how we respond to challenges and disappointments, and therefore also how we are perceived by others. Our identity even impacts upon our job satisfaction and ultimately how successful we are likely to be and how long we will remain in the job. For this reason, mulling over our professional identities is an important step in gaining a foothold on who we are and finding a pathway to becoming the professional we had always hoped we could be. The intention here is to cover this very large topic in a way that hopefully demystifies the notion of professional identity and provides a way for instrumental music teachers to think about themselves in their roles in a productive and useful way.

The 'inner world' of an instrumental music teacher is the place where their notions of what music teaching should, and could be, is measured against the contextual challenges they face, the capacities of themselves as musicians and teachers and the abilities and motivations of their students. Other factors that contribute are the pressures of finances, the notion of what it means to be an 'artist/entrepreneur/educator' (among other 'roles'), and how they feel others are perceiving them. Writers such as Benedict (2009), Bowman (2010), Jorgensen (2010) and Roberts (1991; 2010) have set the foundation for a reconceptualisation of the role of music teacher identity and its relationship to the profession. Research into the identities of music teachers is burgeoning and producing a range of stories and accounts of what it means to be a music teacher. This chapter provides a perspective on music teachers' self-reported professional identities and concludes with recommendations for ways that studio music teachers can use consideration of professional identity to improve their practice, creating long and rewarding careers for themselves.

Defining Professional Identity

It is important, when discussing the notion of professional identity, to begin with a clear definition of the term. Broadly, it is acknowledged that professional identities are the ways teachers make sense of themselves within their professional lives. Beyond that, however, a clear definition of what constitutes professional identity is elusive. Beauchamp and Thomas, in their 2009 literature review, note several reasons for this elusiveness. Firstly, the notion of professional identity has been studied from the perspectives of education, psychology and anthropology with the various approaches taken by each discipline resulting in varied definitions. Secondly, professional identity has been treated as an analytical tool, an organising tool and as a resource that people use to define themselves. The final difficulty identified by Beauchamp and Thomas is the challenge of delineating between, for example, a 'discussion of emotion and identity...with discussion of the self and also with the discussion of the factors that enter into the shaping and the expression of identity' (2009: 176).

Rather than trying to define professional identity, which they acknowledge as difficult for similar reasons to those mentioned above, Beijaard, Meijer and Verloop (2004) recognise four features of professional identity. The first of these features is that professional identity is an ongoing process of discovery about who we are and who we want to become. Second, professional identity is shaped by the person and their context. Third, professional identity consists of sub-identities which ideally should harmonise. The final feature of professional identity is agency: teachers need to be active in the process of developing a professional identity, which in turn can assist them in explaining and justifying their position to others.

We know that 'professional identities' are interrelated with personal identities, social and cultural identities and norms, and professional roles and contexts. This is because teachers' professional identities influence, and are influenced by, self-perceptions of agency, self-efficacy, effectiveness and job satisfaction (Day and Kington, 2008; Skaalvik and Skaalvik, 2014). We also know that professional identities are the crux by which we can predict success, failure, satisfaction and longevity in a profession, and it is for this reason that exploring our own professional identities is a crucial step in ensuring a long and successful career.

What does it mean to be a musician?

Even the most successful and experienced (classroom) music teachers still consider being a (performing) musician to be central to their success as music teachers (Ballantyne and Grootenboer, 2012). The centrality of the discipline (music) to the identity of music teachers seems embedded in music teachers' psyche – an unquestioned 'fact' that colours all other conceptualisations of the self. Indeed, it was argued in previous work (Ballantyne and Grootenboer, 2012) that 'the privileged status of the musician identity ... reflects many assumptions that often go unquestioned in the music education profession' (378). The confidence (or self-efficacy) of experienced teachers as a performer seems related to how competent they consider themselves to be as music teachers. This appeared as an unquestioned truth evident in all the accounts in that particular piece of research. The perceived importance of the musician identity was also found in other research with both pre-service teachers and early-career teachers (Ballantyne, 2005; Ballantyne, Kerchner and Aróstegui, 2012; Ballantyne and Zhukov, 2017). Natale-Abramo (2014) conducted a study exploring the discourses underlying the construction of three instrumental teachers' identities. She found that the musician identity was not at the foremost of discussions. Rather, issues of social class, race, sexuality and the place of music in the curriculum were more prominent in influencing how teachers saw themselves. It is helpful for instrumental music teachers to think about how prominent the notion of 'musician' is in their conceptualisation of their role. To what extent does their perception of themselves as a 'musician' influence their engagement and enjoyment in their job, their sense of competence, their collaboration with others, and their vision of their role in the future?

Examples of teacher identities that align with those of performers/composers:

Simon:

> Yes, absolutely I think most of our staff see themselves as musicians and most of us have a professional life outside the school. So I'm a choral conductor as well as a pianist and organist; I run the music programme at my local church, which is a paid job; David, who is just walking past, plays in the State orchestra for example and in jazz groups, ... I've conducted festivals and workshops, that sort of thing, I've done the Mackay Choral Festival for 3 years ... so yes definitely I see myself as a musician.

Graham:

> I started as a musician ... my background was very similar to the bigger percentage of the kids with contemporary guitar and ear musician[ship] and singing ... I am a musician but compared to a violin player who studied at the conservatorium [I am a] different sort of musician, as I see it.

These teachers were all happy to label themselves as a 'musician', and could articulate how this was legitimated by their participation in music arenas located outside the classroom. It was also evident that these four participants also saw their musicianship as an essential prerequisite for their role as a music teacher, as exemplified below:

Peter:
> [I'm a] musician first ... the ability to teach is the ability to convey ideas ... you can't teach music unless you are first and foremost a music specialist ... I am a composer. I studied my music degree in piano. As a performer I also play jazz grooves. So I play jazz piano, I also play saxophone. But recently I've spent most of my time in composing.

John:
> I think excellent musicianship skills is what you need to have to be an effective music teacher ... we had the choral concert last Friday night and the kids were asking us, 'will you perform?' and so we [the music teachers] put something together and they were just so pleased to see that, yep, we are still practising musicians, we still get involved in it and I think that's something for them to look up to as well.

Examples of the view of self as a 'musician' largely to do with their musical work within the music classroom (their sub-identities):

Suzanne:
> It's about 50/50 and I also distinguish between my classroom teaching and my instrumental teaching as well so there's that whole other side of me in that respect also. When I'm in the classroom as a classroom teacher, I do think of myself more as a teacher than a musician, when I'm working with my instrumental kids or conducting I think of myself as 50 percent teacher, 50 percent musician.

Carmela:
> Okay do I see myself as a musician? That's a hard one now. I probably did 25 years ago when I started teaching but I don't think my skills are where they were then because of this gradual attrition when you're not constantly playing ... I see myself as a musician but not as a performer because teaching has kind of taken over more of my time and attention.

As seen in the quotations above, these teachers' identities as musicians are evident, but perhaps a little less certain than the participants whose identity was grounded in their musical activity outside of the classroom. Also, these teachers were more willing to finesse the conception of 'musician', and were able to appreciate the complexity of their musical identity.

An alternate conceptualisation of a musician:

Hilary:
> *So when I say musician ... a musician is anybody who feels and wants to get to others that feeling of the love of music so ... That's a musician ... so, yes, I'm a musician.*

Examples taken verbatim from Ballantyne and Grootenboer, 2012.

When considering their own professional identity, instrumental music teachers might consider the question – 'in what way, and to what extent is the 'musician' identity helpful or harmful in my everyday practice as a music teacher'? This question should invariably be followed by 'what should I do about it'? The critical consideration of the 'musician' within the professional identity may reveal much to individual teachers. It may indeed underlie the reconceptualisation of an individual's relationships with students, relationships with peers and the profession, and with music as a discipline.

Activity 12.1

Think about the musical activities you engage in during an average week. It might be listening to music, going to concerts, studying it, performing, composing or anything else. How do these activities impact on your view of yourself (your self-identity) as a teacher/musician? Are you happy with the balance – is there anything you would like to change?

What does it mean to be a teacher?

Often, when discussing their 'teacher' identity, music teachers tend to preference discussion of the relationship between teacher and student, and the particular opportunities afforded by teaching music (in developing said relationships) (Ballantyne and Zhukov, 2017; Natale-Abramo, 2014). But what might occur should teachers choose to examine in more detail the relationship between their job as a teacher and those aspects of the role that are common to all teachers (not just music teachers)? Some examples of identities that emphasise the 'teacher' component of music teachers' professional identities are seen in the interview transcripts below. These quotes demonstrate a perspective of 'music teaching' that preferences the 'teaching' of students (although the mention of 'music' is a definite feature).

Grant:
> I see myself as a teacher and a music teacher, but mainly as a teacher of students, again, with music as the tool [that] I use, but then again, if the deputy comes and says: 'can you teach maths?' I basically say no way, because that is not what I'm trained for, and they're not the tools I'm familiar with working with so ... I see music as a tool [to help develop] confidence, responsibility, work ethic, that sort of ... I get them enjoying something in their teenage years instead of being very negative.

Colleen:
> Someone said ... 'when someone on asks you what do you do, what do you say?' And I said that 'well honestly that I'm a teacher', and then they said, 'well, what do you teach?' and I said 'Music, English and SOSE'. It does come out in that order, not really intentionally, but I do see myself as a music teacher.

Kristen:
> I see myself as an educator first and foremost because I don't just teach music, I teach a whole heap of other things. I see myself as a behaviour manager because I am managing behaviour. I see myself as a curriculum designer because I'm constantly having to analyse curriculum and design it appropriately to fit my students' needs. I'm very involved with the local Council, so I help on a lot of their programs, and I am also on the Show Committee.

Susanne:
> *I see my professional identity as firstly how I conduct myself professionally and what I bring to the school as a music teacher or as a professional. It comes back to the way I present myself as a teacher. If I am not going to be very confident in what I present to the students, then I'm not going to get back what I'm looking for. If I have a strong professional identity when I am teaching, I'm probably going to get [more] back from the students.*

Examples selected from Ballantyne, 2005, and Ballantyne and Zhukov, 2017.

Where do these two notions intersect? What does it mean to be a music teacher?

Popper-Giveon and Shayshon (2017) argue that the conflict between discipline sub-identities and teacher identities is common among teachers of all teaching areas (from their study undertaken in Israel). Amongst research with music teachers, the established literature tells us that music teachers are often raised to think of themselves principally as musicians or performers and less so as teachers (Mills, 2006). Research by Austin, Isbell and Russell (2012) considered the occupational identities of students who were enrolled in a range of music-based programmes and would likely end up teaching music. These students were asked to provide estimations of the extent to which they were influenced by a range of role identities within the discipline of music. The authors argued that students arrive at the profession with a perception of what it means to be a music teacher that is based on experiences in school and university in which they make assumptions of, and identify with, particular aspects of professional roles. Yet Austin, Isbell and Russell (2012) found that there was merit in encouraging a less binary view of the profession. They wrote that 'the music profession needs teachers who are reflective thinkers and strong musicians, just as it needs musicians who are knowledgeable about the music they are performing and capable of drawing upon pedagogical principles to elevate their own performance or provide education in music to others' (81–82). By examining the place of one's own 'self within the culture' (Arnett, 2015: 63), new understandings can be fostered, which may facilitate teacher agency in moving towards inhabiting a productive or positive professional identity.

Activity 12.2
Jot down your initial thoughts in answer to the question 'what sort of music teacher am I ... ?' To what extent do you think of yourself as a 'musician' or as a 'teacher'?

The challenges of being a music teacher

As music teachers tend to define themselves mainly in reference to the discipline of music, it is prudent to consider the contextual issues that are specific to teaching music (Flores and Day, 2006). The idiosyncratic experiences of music teachers in schools and studio settings require adaptability and resilience (Gu and Day, 2007). Accordingly, much research has focused on the challenges that music teachers face – including problems around isolation, heavy workload, exhaustion, report writing, assessment, and difficult student behaviour. It is, however, tempting to rest here – focusing on the extreme challenges that music teachers face, and not providing an alternative story. And there is another narrative because music teachers that remain in the job report loving their work, finding it hugely rewarding.

For example, although there is evidence of teachers reporting stress and significant challenges associated with isolation, heavy workloads, and exhaustion, there is arguably a 'light at the end of the tunnel'. A careful analysis (Ballantyne and Zhukov, 2017) revealed that despite teachers still experiencing significant difficulties in their work, they were equally demonstrating signs of 'flourishing'. This evidence of 'flourishing' in the lives of teachers in the early stages of their careers allows the profession to map a new approach towards supporting and preparing teachers for the early years in the profession. It moves the narrative away from a 'deficit' approach where all is 'doom and gloom' to an approach which shows teachers ways to persevere for success. Key to this approach is the acknowledgement of the nature of the challenges involved in teaching music, and support and guidance (in a collaborative environment) to look for the ways to foster positive emotions, engagement, positive relationships, meaning and acknowledgement of achievements (Seligmann, 2011). The teachers in this study employed a wide range of professional and personal skills associated with a positive outlook on their lives and careers. They equally seemed to draw much of their positive outlook from the 'passion' that they found in and through music.

Evidence of the passion for music feeding the 'flourishing' found in accounts of early-career music teachers (selected from Ballantyne and Zhukov, 2017):

Joy:

> At the end of the day I teach music because that's what I love the most and I have so much fun playing music and playing in bands and orchestras. I guess I wanted to share that with other people, not just kids. We've got some adult members in our band, it doubles as a community band. It's just something that's really awesome and really fun!

John:
> In terms of context, in terms of the professional environment I'm in now, I think I'm doing really well and have all the skills which I need to get the job done and to be perceived in the community as getting the job done... for the first time in maybe five or so years we were able to enter our concert band into the WA Concert Band Festival ... It was like light and shade seeing their faces and being there ... the fact that we'd made it that far, even if it was in the novice division, it just felt like a really big win for us.

Coralie:
> I've successfully run the school choir and the band all term. Music is something I'm very confident about and it's obviously something that I really enjoy, so people can see that I'm very passionate about my job, I guess I put a lot of time into it, and people definitely can see that.

Robert:
> I feel like my music skills can always get better and are never good enough for where I want them to be. That's just always the way I've been, but for now I feel adequately prepared but [there's] plenty of work to improve.

Trudy:
> This school is happy with me and I've had some pretty good feedback from all the teachers I've spoken to at school. We went and did our first competition with my concert band and ended up coming first, which was just an amazing feeling! Yeah, it's the best job! I could not have chosen a better job. I'm loving it, it's great!

Anna:
> The goal for a teacher is to be inspiring to students and pushing them to do their best without being very overt about it. Inspiring in them the want to learn more and that thirst for knowledge and also the thirst for bettering themselves at their level ... A big part of what I try to do as a teacher is to make my students musically independent ... I think the main thing is I chose a discipline that I'm passionate about. I think being passionate about music has really assisted in making me a music teacher. I wouldn't be able to instil that passion in the students if I didn't have it myself.

Susanne:
> I'm definitely passionate and enthusiastic about what I do. I get excited when I see positive results, and when I'm able to see enjoyment that the students get out of it. I think what we do is rewarding because we get to tap into some other areas that other teachers may not get to.

> *I think it's important for music to have a positive profile within the school that I teach in. If the students are enjoying going and they're telling Mom and Dad, and Mom and Dad come to school and say, 'Well, music seems to be going really well'... It's a bit of thing that goes around in a circle.*

Eve:

> *I want the students to connect with me. I want to meet my students in 20 years' time and for them to say, 'You sowed the seed. There was a light bulb moment. It changed my life.' So, for me it's about the big outcomes and how they experience music in the big world.*

Joseph:

> *They kind of watched what I did, and they've seen what I did with my song-writing classes and composing stuff, and they said, 'Well, try this. Try that'. ... I felt validated as a professional teacher and musician.*

The predominance of 'music' in music teacher's accounts of their practice does not mean that the teachers are inhabiting a 'musician identity' to the exclusion of all other identities. As Austin, Isbell and Russell (2012) point out, the aim should be for those who teach to inhabit an 'integrated identity' which 'embraces the importance of being both a good musician (performer, conductor or composer) and a good teacher' (80). The reasons for this are that teachers' perceptions of what music is (what the critical tenets of music are, what it means to be proficient in music), their opinions of what constitutes 'good' pedagogy in music, their perceptions of themselves as teachers of music, and their perceptions of their abilities as music teachers and musicians, are all interrelated.

These accounts do, however, raise questions around what an integrated professional identity might look like for instrumental music teachers. Indeed, the passion for music as a discipline area and teaching area may provide these teachers with a reason to persevere through any difficulties that they are facing in their jobs. It may be that the extent to which music teachers view themselves through the idealised lens of 'musician first, teacher second' will impact on how they enact their teaching practice (for better or worse). This 'unconscious practice' reflects their identities, and also their preferences in terms of pedagogies employed, and their comfort extending themselves in terms of both approaches to teaching music, and genres with which they engage. It is proposed here that conceptualisation of music teacher identity as dynamic (moveable) and multi-faceted (not just on a continuum from 'musician' to 'teacher') might help music teachers.

Indeed, the contexts that teachers find themselves in may change the emphasis in terms of the ways that music teachers label themselves, and also in the ways that they enact their identities. Whilst the labelling may be a largely internal and deeply personal process, the enacting of identity is where professional action takes place. What is crucial to realise is that reflection on an enacted identity feeds information back to the individual about the accuracy of their label and this circular loop becomes the story of the individual's identity creation and development in relation to a particular context. Of course, each individual can have multiple identities, and these can be conceptualised and enacted in various ways, simultaneously.

Figure 12.1: A model of professional identity development

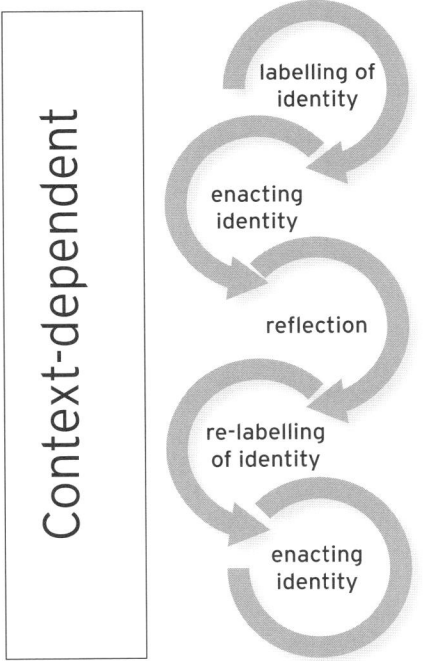

Critical reflection on professional identity throughout the career may enable instrumental music teachers to become aware of the possible impact of their identity on their ability to flourish. Clearer conceptualisation and harmonisation of the notion of musician-teacher professional identity may assist music teachers to improve as effective music teachers and enhance the rewards inherent in a music teaching career. Reflection on professional identity (in an ongoing process, in recognition of the context and possible sub-identities, and supporting teacher agency) is imperative to a teacher's efficacy, their commitment to the profession and their ability to cope with changes to their job.

How does the notion of dynamic, multi-faceted musician-teacher identity assist music teachers in developing their professional practice?

It is proposed that broadening the consideration of music teacher identity (within the ever-changing contexts that teachers operate within) may be helpful to music teachers. Examining 'music teacher identity' may be completed while at university, and also throughout the career. Coursework completed at university (including opportunities for real-world learning) plays a significant role in influencing music teachers' perceptions of their preparedness for the profession. The quality of music education students' preparation for the profession both informs their skills and knowledge and directly relates to the standard of their teaching in schools. Work with pre-service teachers forms part of the picture as the beliefs and values formed during study significantly shape teachers' lived experiences of work after graduation. Beijaard and Meijer (2017) propose a 'pedagogy of identity learning' to take place while music students are studying to be teachers. The suggested pedagogy incorporates pre-service teachers explicitly exploring and collaboratively negotiating their developing identities in a supportive environment. Thus, it could be argued that the model of professional identity development proposed in Figure 1 could be used as a framework for exploration of professional identity, even in the pre-service years.

> ### Activity 12.3
> How would you label your musician-teacher identity? Can you capture in two or three sentences the main characteristics of the musician-teacher you are or want to be? When you have done this, refer to your response from time to time during your working week and note down: activities which reflect well your identity label, activities which don't reflect your identity, and changes you would like to make to your identity label.

Identity work should not be relegated only to the pre-service experience, however. Particularly in the case of studio music teachers, who may (in many countries) not study to be teachers, the independent (and with mentor/collegial support) negotiation of identity may facilitate increased resilience across the career (Gu and Day, 2007). Indeed, a recent study by Ballantyne and Retell (2020) suggests that music teachers experience challenges to aspects of professional identity (including their self-efficacy, with concurrent experiences of praxis shock and burnout) throughout their careers. By responding to these challenges through an examination of the same concepts identified above (ownership, sense-making and agency), music teachers may be able to move towards the 'flourishing' career that they desire.

Music teachers (as all teachers) require engagement with mentors who possess well-developed professional identities themselves (Beijaard et al., 2004). Owing to the idiosyncrasies of teaching music (such as its relative isolation, public nature and the nature of behaviour management in an environment that can be noisy or have larger than average class size), some researchers emphasise the importance of mentoring by other music teachers. Our recent research (Ballantyne and Zhukov, 2017) found that discipline-specific mentoring was less critical than teachers finding themselves in a supportive environment where they could develop meaningful relationships with other teachers and students. And so, for studio music teachers, engaging with a community of other music teachers (whether online and/or in person) is a great way to engage in mentoring relationships and simultaneously develop a strong sense of professional identity.

As previously noted, 'professional identity' is not a fixed construct. It is fluid, and therefore as teachers' lives change (professionally, personally, and through experiences), so their identities change. Music teacher professional identity, therefore, needs to be continuously (re)considered in relation to broader issues, life challenges, stressors and conflicts. This consideration contextualises identity, enabling the exploration of how it as a construct (when reflected upon) can illuminate how teachers' perceptions of themselves shift over time.

Conclusion

Music teachers inhabit many professional identities. These identities shift and change, according to the context, the type of employment, their personal sense of musical efficacy, the idealised view of a musician versus the view of what being a teacher means at a particular point in time. This is consistent with research with pre-service music teachers who similarly found that there was fluidity in how they perceived themselves, depending on the situation in the classroom or ensemble and on the type of professional skills that the situation required of them (Ballantyne, Kerchner, Aróstegui, 2012).

Being explicitly aware of one's own identity, and how it is influencing all aspects of one's professional practice, seems crucial when teachers are aiming to maintain a long and rewarding engagement with teaching music. Teachers should consider engaging in an ongoing manner with both musician and teacher knowledge and skill development, to become increasingly expert musicians and teachers. They could be encouraged to inhabit and explore other identities, developing their skills as leaders, coaches, supporters (and many more). This enhanced confidence in practice as a multi-faceted musician-teacher will likely bolster the capacity of teacher-professionals to be resilient in the face of career challenges in the future. At the same time, self-reflection on identity can be slow, and sometimes a painful and confusing process.

And finally, the opportunities for social and professional connection in the online and real worlds are rich with opportunities to avoid isolation, and to develop networks in the profession. Maintaining strong relationships with others who have previously trodden the same path, and with those who are coming after, facilitates a community of music teachers who feel safe to struggle and learn alongside one another.

References

Arnett, J. (2015) Identity development from adolescence to emerging adulthood: What we know and (especially) don't know. In: K. McLean and M. Syed, eds.
The Oxford handbook of identity development. New York: Oxford University Press, pp. 53-64.

Austin, J. R., Isbell, D. S. and Russell, J. A. (2012) A multi-institution exploration of secondary socialization and occupational identity among undergraduate music majors.
Psychology of Music, 40(1), pp. 66-83. doi: 10.1177/0305735610381886

Ballantyne, J. (2005) Identities of music teachers: Implications for teacher education.
In: Maxine Cooper, ed. Teacher Education: Local and Global Proceedings of the 33rd Annual Australian Teacher Education Association Conference Brisbane, Australia: Australian Association of teacher Education, pp. 39-44. Available at: http://eprints.usq.edu.au/898/1/ballantyne_paper.pdf

Ballantyne, J. (2007) Crossing barriers between teacher preparation and teaching: Documenting praxis shock in early-career music teachers. *International Journal of Music Education*, 25(3), pp. 181-191. Available at: http://ijm.sagepub.com/

Ballantyne, J. and Grootenboer, P. (2012) Exploring relationships between teacher identities and disciplinarity. *International Journal of Music Education: Practice*, 30(4), pp. 368-381.

Ballantyne, J., Kerchner, J. and Aróstegui, J. (2012) Developing music teacher identities: An international multi-site study. *International Journal of Music Education*, 30(3), pp. 211-226.

Ballantyne, Julie and Retell, James (2020). Teaching careers: Exploring links between well-being, burnout, self-efficacy and praxis shock. *Frontiers in Psychology*, 10 (2255).
https://doi.org/10.3389/fpsyg.2019.02255

Ballantyne, J. and Zhukov, K. (2017) A good news story: Early-career music teachers' accounts of their "flourishing" professional identities. *Teaching and Teacher Education*, 68, pp. 241-251. doi:10.1016/j.tate.

Beauchamp, C. and Thomas, L. (2009) Understanding teacher identity: An overview of issues in the literature and implications for teacher education.
Cambridge Journal of Education, 39(2), pp. 175-189.

Beijaard, D. and Meijer, P. (2017) Developing the Personal and Professional in Making a Teacher Identity. In: D. J. Clandinin and J. Husu, eds.
The SAGE Handbook on Research in Teacher Education. London: SAGE.

Beijaard, D., Meijer, P. C. and Verloop, N. (2004) Reconsidering research on teachers' professional identity. *Teaching and Teacher Education*, 20(2), pp. 107-128. doi:10.1016/j.tate.2003.07.001

Benson, M. A. (2008) Effective mentoring for new music teachers.
Update: Applications of Research in Music Education, 26(2), pp. 42-49.

Bowman, W. (2010) No one true way: Music education without redemptive truth.
In: T. Regelski and J.T. Gates, eds. *Music Education for Changing Times*, Landscapes Vol 7: the Arts, Aesthetics, and Education. New York: Springer.

Blair, D. V. (2013) Chelsea's journey of becoming a teacher: A narrative of then and now.
Research Studies in Music Education, 35(1), pp. 36-47.

Conway, C. and Zerman, T. (2004) Perceptions of an instrumental music teacher regarding mentoring, induction, and the first year of teaching.
Research Studies in Music Education, 22, pp. 72-82. doi: 10.1177/1321103X040220011001

Day, C. and Gu, Q. (2007) Variations in the conditions for teachers' professional learning and development: Sustaining commitment and effectiveness over a career. *Oxford Review of Education*, 33(4), pp. 423-443.

Draves, T. J. (2019) Teaching Ambition Realized: Paul's Beginning Music Teacher Identity. *Journal of Music Teacher Education*, 29(1), pp. 41-55. https://doi.org/10.1177/1057083719844211

Flores, M. A. and Day, C. (2006) Contexts which shape and reshape new teachers' identities: A multi-perspective study. T*eaching and Teacher Education*, 22(2), pp. 219-232. doi:10.1016/j.tate.

Gu, Q. and Day, C. (2007) Teachers resilience: A necessary condition for effectiveness. *Teaching and Teacher Education*, 23, pp. 1302-1316.

Jorgenson, E. (2010) School music education and change, *Music Educators Journal*, 96(21), pp. 21-27.

Ketelaar, E., Beijaard, D., Brok, P. and Boshuizen, J. (2013) Teachers' implementation of the coaching role: do teachers' ownership, sensemaking, and agency make a difference? *European Journal of Psychology of Education*, 28(3), pp. 991-1006. https://doi.org/10.1007/s10212-012-0150-5

Kroger, J. (2015) Identity development through adulthood: The move toward "wholeness". In: K. McLean and M. Syed, eds. *The Oxford handbook of identity development*, New York: Oxford University Press, pp. 65-80.

Miksza, P. and Berg, M. H. (2013) Transition from student to teacher: Frameworks for understanding preservice music teacher development. *Journal of Music Teacher Education*, 23(1), pp. 10-26.

Mills, J. (2006) Performing and teaching: the beliefs and experience of music students as instrumental teachers. *Psychology of Music*, 34(3), pp.372-390. https://doi.org/10.1177/0305735606064843

Natale-Abramo, M. (2014) The Construction of Instrumental Music Teacher Identity. *Bulletin Of The Council For Research In Music Education*, 202, pp. 51-69.

Pierce, J. L. , Kostova, T. and Dirks, K. T. (2003) The state of psychological ownership: Integrating and extending a century of research. *Review of General Psychology*, 7, pp. 84-107.

Popper-Giveon, A. and Shayshon, B. (2017) Educator versus subject matter teacher: The conflict between two sub-identities in becoming a teacher. *Teachers and Teaching*, 23(5), pp. 532-548. doi:10.1080/13540602.2016.1218841

Roberts, B. (1991) Music Teacher Education as Identity Construction. *International Journal of Music Education*, 18, pp. 30-39.

Roberts, B. (2010) In search of identity: Prologue. *Action, Criticism and Theory for Music Education*, 9(2), pp. 1-10.

Seligman, M. (2011) *Flourish: A visionary new understanding of happiness and well-being*. New York: Free Press.

Wagoner, C. L. (2015) Measuring Music Teacher Identity: Self-Efficacy and Commitment Among Music Teachers. *Bulletin of the Council for Research in Music Education*, 205, pp. 27-49.

Welch, G., Purves, R. M., Hargreaves, D., Marshall, N. (2011) Early career challenges in secondary music teaching. *British Educational Research Journal*, 37(2), pp. 285-315. doi:10.1080/01411921003596903

Index

Page numbers in *italics* refer to Figures and Tables.

ability, musical (perceptions of), 76-77
Abramo, J. M., 144
Abril, C., 33
ABRSM (Associated Board of the Royal Schools of Music)
  examinations, 19, 20, 22-23, 24, 25
  report by, 131
action research, 47, 58
  see also research, contemporary
adaptations *see* differentiation and adaptations
Admiraal, W., 56
adolescence, 93
adult learners, 52-53
African music (inappropriate use of), 33-34
agency
  and differentiation, 137-140, *137*, 146
  and goal-setting, 109
  importance and principles of, 105-106, 132-133, 146
  and improvisation, 37-38, 135, 136
  and repertoire, 36, 136
  see also self-directed learning
Aitken, S., 23
Akbel, B. A., 54
Alexander, R., 159
Amp Up, 38-39
Anagnostopoulou, X., 55
anxiety and stress
  performance anxiety, 83, *85*, 192
  and self-efficacy, 103
aptitude, musical, 77-78
  see also giftedness; talent
Aróstegui, J., 209
assessment
  dominance of western art music values, 17-18, 155-156
  formative versus summative, 153-154, *154*
  grade examinations *see* grade examinations
  normalised 'folk standards' of, 155-157
  and student values and beliefs, 154, 157, 159-160
  and teacher values and beliefs, 151-152
'Audio Jam' sessions, 192
Aufegger, L., 52, 192
augmented reality (AR), 193
Austin, J. R., 196, 203, 206
Australia, 19, 21, 116, 164
Austria, 172
autoethnography, 158
autonomous learning *see* self-directed learning

Bailey, S., 93
Baker, D., 54
Baker, G., 18
Ballantyne, J., 199, 201, 203, 204-206, 208, 209
bands and orchestras, 29, 30, 31-32, 172
Bandura, A., 103-104
Banfield, S., 24
Barnett, S., 118, 122-123, 126, 128
barriers to inclusion
  disability, 131
  economic, 18, 22-23, 29, 131
  gender, 29, 30, 132
  misrecognition, 146-147
  'needs' categories of, 134
  repertoire, 17, 132, 147
  see also economic inequalities; gendered inequalities; inclusivity; racial inequalities
Barron, D. S., 50
Bauer, W., 52
Beauchamp, C., 198
behavioural difficulties, students with, *141*
Beijaard, D., 198, 208
Bentley, A., 78
Berklee PULSE (resource materials), 38, 39
bias
  productivity bias, 120
  unconscious bias, 77
Blackwell, J., 49
blended (face-to-face and online) teaching, 183, 184, 189, 190
  see also online lessons
Bloom, B., 80
Boyack, J., 122
Braille music, *141*
brass bands, 17, 19
Bull, A., 16, 156
Burnard, P., 122, 138

camera set-up, in online lessons, 185-186, *185*, *186*
Cameron, A., 190
Canada, 23-24, 33-34
canonical repertoire, 17, 20, 132, 147
Carey, G., 48, 59
challenges facing music teachers
  in general, 204
  technological challenges (online lessons), 184-188, *185*, *186*, *187*
Cheng, Z., 58
Clark, Larry (as Keiko Yamada), 34
Clarke, E. F., 117, 119

213

collaborative learning
    peer learning and support, 57, *61*, 140
    research on, 55-57
    student-teacher interactions in, 55-57, 58, *61*; see also dialogic teaching
colonialism see imperialism
colour-blindness, 33, 34
    see also racial inequalities
communities of practice
    for learners, 155-156
    for teachers, 209, 210
composition
    'creative genius' myth, 120
    and differentiation, 136
    in groups, 37, 40, 54
concert bands (North America), 29, 30
    see also Modern Band movement
conformity, versus creativity, 124, 126
Conle, C., 158
Connect Resound project, 188-189, 193
conscientisation, 150, 151, 158, 161
conservatoires, 18-19, 23-24, 56, 131
contextualising music
    diverse repertoires, 33-35, 73
    and emotional communication, 74
continuing participation
    and 'feeling musical,' 75
    possibilities for, *60*
    research on, 51-52, 101, 102, 175
Copland, Aaron, 128
correlational studies (as methodology), 46
    see also research, contemporary
Corrigall, K. A., 91
Craft, A., 116
creativity
    versus conformity, 124, 126
    'creative genius' myth, 120
    definitions and importance, 115-120, 124, 126
    and imagination, 126
    and mistake-making, 122-123
    and performance/interpretation, 119, 122-126
    and technique, 120-121
    see also composition; imagination; improvisation; playfulness in early music learning
Creech, A., 47, 56
Cremata, R., 38
Cresser, Dr, 21
Csikszentmihalyi, M., 106-107, *107*
cultural capital, 167
cultural literacy, 167
culturally relevant pedagogy, 35-36

Darrow, A-A., 142, 143
Daubney, A., 81, 83, 134-135, 137, 138
Daubney, G., 83
de Bruin, L. R., 56
delay (latency), in online lessons, 186-188, *187*
Denmark, 31-32
development, 90-93
    see also musical development
Dewey, J., 90, 95, 96, 158
dialogic teaching, 52, 58, 139, 147, 152, 158-160, 168
    see also student-centred learning; student-teacher relationship
Dickens, L., 166
Dickinson, C., 137, *137*
Dietrich, A., 124
differentiation and adaptations, 79, 134-140, *137*, *141*, 142-143
disabilities, students with, 50, 131, 140-143, *141*
distributive social justice model, 132, 147
diversification of repertoires, 25, 31, 33-34
Draves, T. J., 57
drumming ensembles, 33-34
duets (student-teacher), 121
Duffy, S., 184
Duke, M., 57
Dumlavwalla, D. T., 21

early musical development (infants and young children), 72-73, 90, 91, 94
early-career music teachers, 204-206
economic inequalities, 18, 22-23, 29, 131
    see also elitism
Edgar, S. N,, 58
Educational Technology (ET) see technology
Eiholzer, H., 192
Eisner, E. W., 85
elitism
    challenging elitism, 25
    and classical music training, 18
    and grade examinations, 16, 19, 22-23, 25
    and individual lessons, 14
    see also economic inequalities
Elliott, D., 31, 147, 155
embodied learning and expression, 53, *61*, 96
emotional and behavioural difficulties, students with, *141*
emotional connection and communication, 73-74
enculturation, and development, 90-91
epistemic beliefs of students (research on), 49, 56-57
epistemology (definition), 15
Erikson, E., 93

ethnographic studies (as methodology), 46
  see also research, contemporary
exceptional shared needs, teaching approaches for, 140-145, *141*
'expanded professionalism,' 50, 57-58
  see also teacher professional development
expectations and performance (Pygmalion effect), 77
extrinsic versus intrinsic motivation, 101-102

Fautley, M., 153, 174
feedback
  and flow state, 107, 109
  and motivation, 109
  video feedback, 55
'feeling musical,' by students, 75-76
financial prestige see elitism
Finland, 31, 191
flow state, 106-108, *107*, 109
fluency, musical, 74-75, 80, 86
Folkestad, G., 166, 170
Fonder, M., 30
football crowd, musicality, 71
formative assessment, 153-154, *154*, 159-160
Fraser, N., 132, 133, 146
Freire, P., 150, 151
Frith, S., 117, 119-120, 122

Gagné, F., 78
Gardner, H., 94
Garner, T., 192
Gaunt, H., 47, 56
gendered inequalities, 16, 17, 29, 30, 132
general music education (GME), 165-166, 167-168
  relationship/integration with instrumental teaching, 165, 168-177
Germany, 51
Ghanaian music (inappropriate use of), 33-34
Giddens, A., 105
giftedness, 78-79, 144-145
  see also talent
Gordon, E., 77, 94
grade examinations
  ABRSM, 19, 20, 22-23, 24, 25
  and creativity, 119, 124-125
  and elitism, 16, 19, 22-23, 25
  as focus of formal instrumental learning, 169
  and gendered inequalities, 16, 132
  and imperialism, 10, 16, 19, 20-25
  introduction and rapid uptake, 18-19
  and parental expectations, 160-161
  performance mistakes, 123, 125
  and racial inequalities, 16, 20-23
  syllabus diversification, 25

Trinity College of Music, 19, 21-22, 25
Grant, C., 48
'great canon' see canonical repertoire
Green, L., 28, 30, 36, 49, 54, 105, 109-110, 156
  see also Musical Futures
Grimshaw, M., 192
Grootenboer, P., 199, 201
Grove, Sir George, 22
Guildhall School of Music, 19

Hallam, S., 48, 56, 72, 76-77, 91, 94, 140, *141*
Hanson, E. M., 116
Hanson, J., 54-55
'Happy Birthday' song (fluency example), 74
Hargreaves, D. J., 83, 126, 128
Hartz, B., 52
Healey, P., 184
hearing impairments, students with, *141*
Hess, J., 33-34
Hill, J., 119, 124
home environment, and continuing participation, 51, 52
Howard, V. A., 169
Howell, G., 122

identity(ies), of students, 20, 30, 36, 141-142, 146
  see also values and beliefs, of students
identity(ies), of teachers
  personal, social and cultural, 198, 199
  professional see teacher professional identity(ies)
  see also values and beliefs, of teachers
imagination
  and creativity, 126
  importance to music teaching, 128
  storytelling, 73-74, *85*, 120-121
  teachers' imagination, 127
  unlocking, 115, 126, 127
  see also creativity; playfulness in early music learning
immersive technologies, 192-193
imperialism, 10, 15, 16
improvisation
  and agency, 37-38, 135, 136
  and differentiation, 136
  as integrated approach to learning, 171
  introducing students to, 127
  and music technology, 55, *61*, 182
  and musical fluency, 75
  and playing by ear, 54
  research on, 52, 54, 55, 56
  and technique, 120-121
  and whole class instruction, 37

Index

inclusivity
    and agency, 133
    differentiation, 79, 134-140, *137*, *141*, 142-143
    policies, 50
    research on, 50, 62
    social justice models, 130, 132-133, 147
    students with disabilities, 140-143, *141*
    Universal Design for Learning (UDL) approach, 143
    see also barriers to inclusion; inequalities
Incorporated Society of Musicians (ISM), 131
India, 21-22
inequalities
    economic, 18, 22-23, 29, 131
    gendered, 16, 17, 29, 30, 132
    racial, 16, 17, 20-23, 29, 30, 32-33
    see also inclusivity
infants, musical development, 72-73 90, 91
informal learning, 36-38, 166-167
    see also peer learning and support; student-centred learning
intervention studies (as methodology), 46
    see also research, contemporary
intrinsic versus extrinsic motivation, 101-102
Irish music community, 191-192
Isbell, D. S., 196, 203, 206

jazz instruction, 31, 32, 56
Jellison, J., 130, 143, 146
job satisfaction, 196, 197, 198
Johansson, K., 56
Johnson, E., 57
Jorgensen, E. R., 184
JustPlay resources, 37, 164, 174-175

Kamekawa, T., 192
Kanellopoulos, P., 38, 166
Karlsen, S., 191
Kearney, P., 52-53
Kerchner, J., 209
Kim, S., 192
King, A., 185, 187, 188-189, 193
King, R., 192
Kok, Roe-Min, 20, 24
Krupp-Schleußner, V., 51
Kruse, N. B., 184, 190
Kupers, E., 57
Kushner, S., 158

Ladson-Billings, G., 35
Laes, T., 50, 52, 62
Laird, S., 75
Lamont, A., 83, 90
latency (delay), in online lessons, 186-188, *187*

Lau, Fiona, 118, 120, 121, 124-125, 127, 128
learning difficulties, students with, 131, *141*, 142
learning styles and strategies (research on), 49
Learning Technology (LT) *see* technology
Lehmann-Wermser, A., 51
Lewis, Justin, 117, 119, 122, 128
literacy, musical, 95-96
    versus musical fluency, 74-75, 97-98
    see also notation
Little Kids Rock, 38-39
Long, M., 56
long term participation *see* continuing participation
Lonie, D., 166
López-Íñiguez, G., 56-57

Maas, A., 56
Maehr, M. L., 105
Malaysia, 20, 24
Mason, T., 118, 119, 123, 127, 128
master/apprentice model, 9-10, 18, 44, 47, 62, 100
McPhail, G. J., 58
McPherson, G., 92, 97, 101, 102
McPherson, G. E., 78, 144-145
McWilliam, E., 48
Meijer, P., 198, 208
mentoring (for teachers), 209
metacognition, 137, 140
Mexican music (inappropriate use of), 33
Miksza, P., 49
Milner, R., 32-33
misrecognition, 146-147
mistakes
    and creativity, 122-123
    in grade examinations, 123, 125
mixed reality (MR), 193
mixed-method research designs, 46
    see also research, contemporary
modelling, by teachers, *60*, 138, 186, 189, 190
Modern Band movement, 37-38, 39
    see also concert bands (North America)
Morris, L., 117, 120-121, 125, 127-128
Moscardini, L., 50
motivation
    and agency, 105-106, 109
    and feedback, 109
    and flow state, 106-108, *107*, 109
    and practice, 101-103
    and self-efficacy, 104, 109
Music Education Hubs (MEHs), 131, 165, 172
music hall songs, 19
music technology *see* technology
musical ability (perceptions of), 76-77
musical aptitude, 77-78

see also giftedness; talent
musical development
    culture-specific features, 90-91
    in infants and young children, 72-73, 90, 91, 94
    and musical training, 91
    reading skills, 74-75, 95-96
musical fluency, 74-75, 80, 86
Musical Futures, 37, 40, 58, 174-175
musical intelligence, 94
musical literacy, 95-96
    versus musical fluency, 74-75, 97-98
    see also notation
musicality
    aspects of, 72, 73-76, 81, *82*, 83, 144-145
    of football crowd, 71
    and general music education, 168
    nurturing, 73-76, 80-81, 83, 85-86
musicianship
    and playing by ear, 53-54, *60*
    possibilities for, *60-61*
    research on, 53-54
    simultaneous learning, 124
'musicking,' 168

Natale-Abramo, M., 144, 199
National Curriculum (NC) (England), 134, 165
    Report from the National Curriculum Task Group, 153
National Music Plan (England), 50
National Plan for Music Education (NPME) (England), 165
'needs' categories of barriers to inclusion, 134
'need-to-know' basis of teaching, 89-90
New York City, 38-39
Ng, P. T., 116
Nielsen, S. G., 49
non-formal learning, 166-167, 170
    see also informal learning
normalised standardisation, 15, 16-18, 25, 155-157
    see also standardised music education
North America, 16, 29, 31, 37-39, 166, 169, 172
Norway, 31-32
notation
    adaptations for visually impaired students, *141*
    avoiding over-reliance on, 74-75
    and interpretation, 122-124, 125-126
    reading skills development, 74-75, 95-96
'nourishment' provided by teachers, 75-76

observational studies (as methodology), 46
    see also research, contemporary

Online Academy of Irish Music (OAIM), 191-192
online communities and support networks, 191-192
online lessons
    blended teaching, 183, 184, 189, 190
    effectiveness, 189
    logistical issues, 188-189
    rationales for, 183
    research on, 184, 185-186, 188-190
    technological challenges and solutions, 184-188, *185*, *186*, *187*
Online Orchestration Project (OOP), 188
ontology (definition), 15
'opportunity gap' for students of colour, 32-33
    see also racial inequalities

Paris Conservatoire, 18
Parkes, K. A., 160
Parnutt, R., 72, 73
Parratt, Walter, 22
Partti, H., 191
passion for music, in teachers, 204-206
Paynter, J., 167
peer learning and support, 57, *61*, 140
    see also informal learning
perfection, 'myth' of, 122-123
performance anxiety, 83, *85*, 192
Perkins, R., 52
'personal construct' exercise, 81, *82*
Peshkin, A., 158
phenomenology (research methodology), 46, 58
    see also research, contemporary
Philpott, C., 133, 134
physical impairments, students with, 50, 131, *141*
Pike, P., 189
pitch perception, 90
playfulness in early music learning, 73-74, 80, 86, 96
    see also storytelling
playing by ear, 53-54, *60*, 75
Popper-Giveon, A., 203
popular music, pedagogies for, 39
popular music ensembles (Nordic countries), 31-32
popular musicians, instrumental development of, 28, 30
Pozo, J. I., 56-57
practice
    and motivation, 101-103
    research on, 48-50, 53, 55, 94-95
    and self-regulation, 49-50, 55, 95
    video use, 55, *85*
    and zone of proximal development, 94-95, 102-103

217

praxial music education, 31
Prince, V., 76-77
Prior, H. P., 185, 187, 189
productivity bias, 120
professional development of teachers *see* teacher professional development
professional identity of teachers *see* teacher professional identity(ies)
psychological flexibility, 83-84, *85*
Pygmalion effect, 77

qualitative research methodologies, 46-47
  see also research, contemporary
quantitative research methodologies, 46
  see also research, contemporary

racial inequalities, 16, 17, 20-23, 29, 30, 32-33
Rawls, J., 132
reading skills development, 74-75, 95-96
  see also musical literacy
reflective practice (of teachers)
  action research, 47, 58
  and adaptation, 76
  on beliefs and values, 151-152, 158
  on professional identity, 207-208, *207*, 209
  questions for, 176-177
  see also teacher professional development
Reid, A., 57
Reis, S. M, 144
relational social justice model, 132-133
Renzulli, J. A., 144
repertoires
  as barrier to inclusion, 17, 132, 147
  canonical, 17, 20, 132, 147
  diversification, 25, 31, 33-34
  gendered inequalities, 132
  student selection of, 36, 136; *see also* student-centred learning
  vernacular, 17
research, contemporary
  adult learners, 52-53
  collaborative learning, 55-57
  continuing participation, 51-52, 101, 102, 175
  early-career music teachers, 204-206
  emotion and music, 73
  improvisation, 52, 54, 55, 56
  inclusivity, 50, 62
  jazz instruction, 56
  methodologies, 46-47
  music technology use, 54-55, 57
  musicianship, 53-54
  online communities and support networks, 191-192
  online lessons, 184, 185-186, 188-190
  practice and self-regulation, 48-50, 53, 55
  self-directed learning, 48, 52
  teacher professional development, 57-58, 209
  teacher professional identity(ies), 199-203
  and transformational learning (overview), 47-48, 62
  YouTube videos, 190
Retell, J., 208
Reuben, F., 188
Reynolds, H. R., 33
risk-taking, 122
Ritchie, L., 52-53
Rofe, M., 188
Rosenthal effect, 77
Roseth, N. E., 49
Rostvall, A., 105
Round the Village ('problem piece'), 89, 97
Rowe, V., 55
Royal College of Music, 18
Ruddock, E., 75
Rumiantsev, T. W., 56
Runco, M. A., 115, 117, 120, 126
Russell, J. A., 196, 203, 206

salvationism, 25, 147
Savage, J., 158, 170
Scandinavia, 31-32, 116
Schellenberg, E. G., 91
school bands and orchestras, 29, 30, 31-32, 172
score-sharing, in online lessons, 184, *185*
Scotland, 50
Scott, L. and Jellison, J. A , 140
self-determination theory, 105
self-development, 'personal construct' exercise, 81, *82*
self-directed learning
  possibilities for, *60*
  research on, 48, 52
  see also agency; YouTube videos
self-efficacy, 103-104
  social comparison exercise, 83-84, *85*
self-regulation
  in middle childhood, 92
  and practice, 49-50, 55, 95
  research on, 48-50, 55
sexism *see* gendered inequalities
Shayshon, B., 203
Shoemaker, K., 189
Shulman, L. S., 161
sight-singing, teaching, 19
Simones, L. L., 47, 48, 189
simultaneous learning, 124
Singapore, 116, 168

singing before playing, 53, *60*, 75
singing movements, 17, 19
Slattery, P., 35
Small, C., 168
social comparison, 83-84, *85*, 92-93
social justice models, 130, 132-133, 147
South Africa, 22-23
Southcott, J., 58
Spruce, G., 132, 147, 152, 156
standardised music education
    grade examinations *see* grade examinations
    and imperialism, 10, 16
    normalised standardisation, 15, 16-18, 25, 155-157
Statham, Heathcote D., 21-22
StGeorge, J., 51
storytelling, 73-74, *85*, 120-121
    see also playfulness in early music learning
stress and anxiety
    performance anxiety, 83, *85*, 192
    and self-efficacy, 103
student-centred learning, 28, 30, 40
    and creativity, 127-128
    Modern Band movement, 37-38, 39
    Musical Futures, 37, 40, 58, 174-175
    repertoire selection, 36, 136
    see also agency; informal learning
student-teacher relationship
    in adolescence, 93
    dialogic engagement, 52, 58, 139, 147, 152, 158-160, 168
    differentiated support, 137-138, *137*
    in middle childhood years, 92-93
    power and agency, 105-106, 138, 139-140
    research on, 56, 58
summative assessment, 153-156, *154*
    see also grade examinations
Swanwick, K., 74, 75, 105
Sweden, 31-32, 116

talent, 78-81, *82*, 144-145
Tan, L., 49
Tanglewood Symposium and Declaration, 30, 31
Taylor, Franklin, 22
Taylor, P., 48
TCL *see* Trinity College of Music
teacher professional development
    'expanded professionalism,' 50, 57-58
    identity work, *207*, 208-210
    mentoring, 209
    possibilities for, *61*
    research on, 57-58, 209
    scarcity of, 161
    see also reflective practice (of teachers)

teacher professional identity(ies)
    conceptualisations and importance of, 197-198, 208, 209
    as dynamic and context-dependent, 206-207, *207*, 209
    exploration in pre-service teachers, 208
    'musician/performer' identity, 199-201, 203, 206
    relationship with personal, social and cultural identities, 198, 199
    'teacher' identity, 202-203, 206
teacher-student relationship *see* student-teacher relationship
technique teaching, creative activities for, 120-121
technology
    'Audio Jam' sessions, 192
    definitions and overview, 182
    immersive technologies, 192-193
    and improvisation, 55, *61*, 182
    for music production, 182
    online communities and support networks, 191-192
    online lessons *see* online lessons
    and peer learning, 57
    for students with hearing/visual impairments, *141*
    video tutorials, 54-55, 57, 109-110, 170, 182, 190
    videoing practices, 55, *85*
    YouTube videos, 54-55, 109-110, 127, 170, 190
testing musical aptitude, 77-78
Thomas, L., 198
tonic sol-fa choirs, 19
Toronto Conservatory of Music, 23-24
transformational learning
    possibilities for, *60-61*
    principles of, 47-48, 59
    and research (overview), 47-48, 62
Trehub, S., 72
Triantafyllaki, A., 55
Trim, J., 118, 125-126, 127, 128
Trinity College of Music, 19
    grade examinations, 19, 21-22, 25

unconscious bias, 77
United States *see* North America
Universal Design for Learning (UDL) approach, 143

values and beliefs, of students
    and assessment, 154, 157, 159-160
    and dialogic teaching, 154, 159-160
    and inclusivity, 132, 146-147
    see also identity(ies), of students

values and beliefs, of teachers
    and assessment judgements, 151-152
    and professional identity, 208
    self-reflection, 158
Varvarigou,M., 54
Vaugeois, L., 147
Veblen, K., 190
Verloop, N., 198
vernacular repertoire, sidelining of, 17
video
    recording practices, 55, *85*
    tutorials, 54-55, 57, 109-110, 170, 182, 190
    see also technology
virtual reality (VR), 192-193
visual impairments, students with, *141*
vocal music, grassroots, 17, 19
Vygotsky, L. S., 91, 94, 102, 138

Waddington-Jones, C., 185, 187, 189
Waldron, J., 191
Wall, M. P., 54
Ward, F., 191-192
Wells, G., 139
West, C., 38
West, T., 105
Westerlund, H., 50, 62, 105, 175
Whole Class Ensemble Teaching (WCET)
    programme, 172-174
whole class instruction, 37, 172-175
Williamon, A., 52, 144-145, 192
Wilson, A., 50
Wish, David, 38
Wright, J., 137, *137*
Wright, R., 38, 166
Wright, W., 20

Yamada, Keiko (Larry Clark), 34
Youth Music (charity), 131
YouTube videos, 54-55, 109-110, 127, 170, 190
    see also video

Zhukov, K., 204-206, 209
Zimmerman, S., 141, 142-143
zone of proximal development (ZPD), 94-95,
    102-103, 138-140, *139*